P9-AZX-130

Asia's
Wealth Club

NICHOLAS BREALEY
PUBLISHING

L O N D O N

ALLEN
&
UNWIN

Asia's Wealth Club

Who's really who in business –
the top 100 billionaires in Asia

Geoff Hiscock

First published in Great Britain, the United States and Asia by
Nicholas Brealey Publishing Limited in 1997

36 John Street
London
WC1N 2AT, UK
Tel: +44 (0)171 430 0224
Fax: +44 (0)171 404 8311

17470 Sonoma Highway
Sonoma
California 95476, USA
Tel: (707) 939 7570
Fax: (707) 938 3515

http://www.nbrealey-books.com
Reprinted 1997 (with corrections)

Text © Geoff Hiscock 1997
Portrait illustrations by Eric Löbbecke © Nicholas Brealey Publishing Limited 1997
The right of Geoff Hiscock to be identified as the author of this work has been asserted in
accordance with the Copyright, Designs and Patents Act 1988.

UK ISBN 1-85788-162-1
British Library Cataloguing in Publication Data
A catalogue record for this book is available from the British Library.

Library of Congress Cataloging-in-Publication Data
Hiscock, Geoff
    Asia's wealth club : a who's who of business and billionaires /
Geoff Hiscock.
    p.   cm.
    Includes bibliographical references and index.
    ISBN 1-85788-162-1 (hc)
    1. Billionaires--Asia--Biography. 2. Businesspeople--Asia-
-Biography. 3. Upper class families--Asia--Biography. I. Title.
HC411.5.A2H57   1997
305.5'234'09225
[B]--DC21   97-9103
                                                      CIP

Jointly published in Australia with Allen & Unwin
9 Atchison Street, St Leonards NSW 2065
Australia
Tel: (612) 9901 4088 Fax: (612) 9906 2218
http://www.allen-unwin.com.au

National Library of Australia Cataloguing-in-Publication Data
ISBN 1 86448 402 0
338.709225
A catalogue record for this book is available on request.

All rights reserved. No part of this publication may be reproduced, stored in a retrieval
system, or transmitted, in any form or by any means, electronic, mechanical, photocopy-
ing, recording and/or otherwise without the prior written permission of the publishers.
This book may not be lent, resold, hired out or otherwise disposed of by way of trade in
any form, binding or cover other than that in which it is published, without the prior
consent of the publishers.

Printed in the UK by Biddles Ltd.

Contents

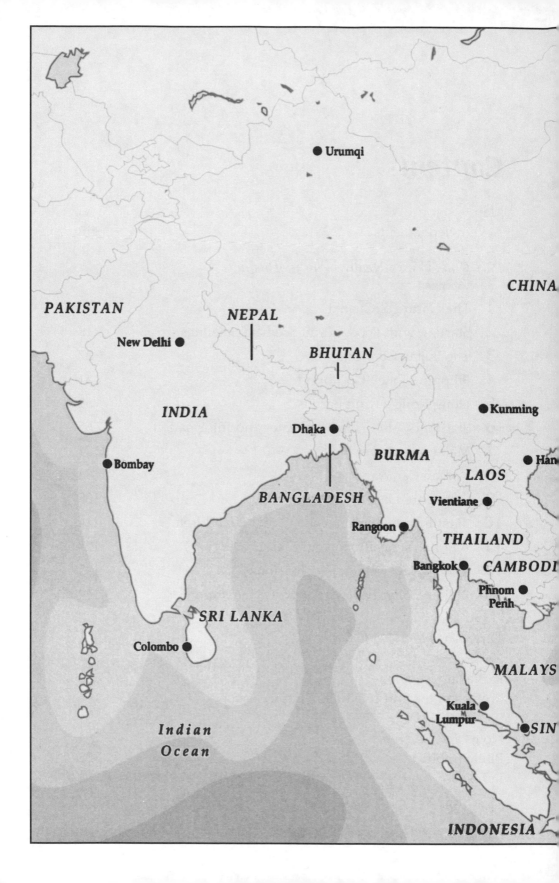

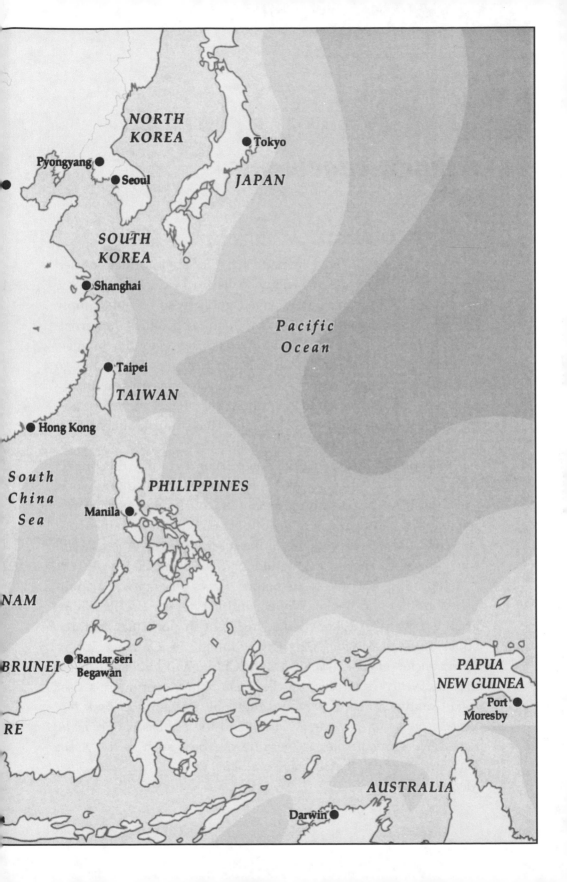

Acknowledgements

A great many people have helped me gather the information used in this book. They are too many to list individually and some would not wish to be acknowledged publicly, so I would simply like to express my sincere thanks to many colleagues in journalism and business throughout the Asia-Pacific region for nuggets of information, advice and assistance. In particular, my thanks go to David Smith, formerly of News Ltd in Sydney, for convincing me to be part of *The Australian Business Asia* project and rekindling my interest in the business of writing. That in turn launched me on the path to writing *Asia's Wealth Club*. Special thanks to Nicholas Brealey for seeing the potential and guiding this project through, and to Sally Lansdell Yeung for her skilful editing work. I also wish to express my appreciation to *The Australian* newspaper for providing me with the opportunity to carry on the work started at *Business Asia*. Some of the information in *Asia's Wealth Club* draws on articles I first wrote for *The Australian*.

In addition, a work of this nature draws on many other published articles and books. While a full list appears in the bibliography, I want to acknowledge my debt in particular to three books: *Business Maharajas*, by Gita Piramal, *The Overseas Chinese Entrepreneurs in East Asia*, by David Ch'ng, and *Overseas Chinese Business Networks in Asia*, by the Australian Government's East Asia Analytical Unit. Among regional magazines, *Asia Inc*, *Asiamoney*, *Asian Business*, *Asiaweek* and the *Far Eastern Economic Review* were invaluable, as were newspapers such as the *Asian Wall Street Journal*, the *Nihon Keizai Shimbun* and the *South China Morning Post*.

Part I

Who's Really Who in Business

1

The Nature of Guanxi

To get rich is glorious.

The late Chinese paramount leader Deng Xiaoping

I T IS LOY KRATHONG; THE NIGHT WHEN THAILAND'S PEOPLE LAUNCH thousands of tiny boats made from banana palm leaves into the country's myriad rivers and *klongs* (canals) as a way of honouring the water's life-giving properties. In each boat burns a candle, surrounded by flowers, money and food offerings.

But this year, the Chao Phrya river is in flood. With each high tide, brown water gently sloshes into old storehouses, temple grounds, villas, ordinary homes and the lush gardens of the high-rise hotels that front the river as it courses through the heart of Bangkok.

For this one perfect night, nobody seems to mind the misery and the destruction that the floods have wrought in Bangkok and the central plains of Thailand. The breeze comes gently off the river, obliterating memories of the industrial pollution and the traffic chaos that lie in wait outside this magic zone of peace by the river.

With the moon full and high, the water softly pours over the jetty and into the hotel grounds, kept from further intrusion only by a small wall of sandbags.

The hotel gardens are lit like a carnival. On the stage, the floor-show begins – love-songs, good-humoured beauty pageants, and exquisite dancers from Thailand's cultural wellspring, the north-east.

The hotel, the Shangri-la, is among the most luxurious in the city, its riverside setting the most desirable. It is where the rich and famous come to party on Thailand's most festive night. The food, the dancing, the decor, the magnificent Loy Krathong boats bobbing in the pool, all signify that culture and wealth occasionally do co-exist.

The man who owns this hotel is Robert Kuok Hock Nien [28], the Malaysian Chinese tycoon once known as Asia's 'sugar king' and now recognized everywhere as the brains behind the biggest and best business deals in Asia, across a range of interests that encompass real estate, commodities, franchises, media, tourism and construction. This is Robert Kuok's world, and the world of a hundred others like him. Welcome to Asia's Wealth Club.

Anyone can aspire to join the wealth club. Membership numbers, in theory, are unlimited, and by some estimates there are already more than 100,000 US$ millionaires in Asia today. But for the moment, let us say that the membership bar is set at a minimum net worth of US$1 billion – and US$2 billion in the case of Japan, to acknowledge the realities of 'purchasing-power parity', i.e. that a dollar buys a lot less in Tokyo than it does in, say, Bombay or Bangkok. That means that about 100 billionaires in Asia qualify. Between them, they have a total net worth of around US$300 billion and control businesses with annual revenues many times greater.

One hundred is an arbitrary number in an Asian business world that encompasses hundreds of thousands of entrepreneurs. But, even so, simply knowing some of the names of the key billionaires and groups is a starting point for understanding business in the region. When members of the wealth club are mentioned in the first part of this book, their position in the ranking is indicated by a number in square brackets.

The success and personalities of some of these people will emerge in the pages that follow, as we look at how 100 of Asia's wealthiest billionaires came by their money, and how they propose to keep their fortunes intact for the next generation.

Many of these families have seen the real fruits of generational labour start to emerge only in the last two decades, coinciding with China's huge economic push forward and the modernization of South-East Asia.

One such family is Hong Kong's Walter Kwok and his brothers, Thomas and Raymond [2]. Depending on the state of the Hong Kong stock market, the Kwok brothers have a family fortune of around US$13.5 billion, give or take a few hundred million. That is what ensures them a place at the top table.

In the case of the Kwoks, their wealth flows from the family flagship, the Hong Kong property-development giant Sun Hung Kai Properties. With a market capitalization of US$29 billion, it is Hong Kong's largest listed company and has been a stellar performer in the past decade.

It helps that their late father, Kwok Tak-sing, had the foresight to go into property acquisition in a big way after Hong Kong's 1972 stock-market crash. But the Kwok brothers have carried on the vision with such skill that their company is very much top of the pile, along with Hong Kong development companies like Cheung Kong and Henderson Land.

A good number of Asia's billionaires can be found, predictably enough, in Asia's richest country, where even half a decade of recession has been unable to destroy the oldest and biggest fortunes of names like Tsutsumi, Mori, Iwasaki and Otsuka.

Railroad tycoon Yoshiaki Tsutsumi [3] heads the Japanese list with a net worth of about US$11.5 billion, largely through his controlling stake in the Seibu Railway group (market capitalization US$20 billion), plus a string of amusement parks and the Seibu Lions professional baseball team.

Japan's second-placed Mori brothers [8], who built their US$6.5 billion fortune on a string of Tokyo property-development deals started by their late father, Yasukichi Mori, looked offshore to China in the mid-1990s. Their China trophy building will be a 460-metre skyscraper in Shanghai's fast-moving Pudong Development Zone, the booming new focus for the city's expansion

The Top 100 Billionaires
(Rank, Name, Country, Net Worth in $US)

1   **The Sultan of Brunei** and family, Brunei   30.0
2   **Walter, Thomas and Raymond KWOK**, Sun Hung
    Kai Properties, Hong Kong   13.5
3   **Yoshiaki TSUTSUMI** and family, Seibu Railway, Japan   11.5
4   **LEE Shau-kee**, Henderson Land, Hong Kong   11.0
5   **TSAI Wan-lin** and family, Lin-Yuan Group, Taiwan   8.5
6   **LI Ka-shing** and family, Cheung Kong,
    Hutchison Whampoa, Hong Kong   8.0
7   **Rachman Halim** and the **WONOWIDJOJO** family,
    Gudang Garam, Indonesia   7.7
8   **Minoru and Akira MORI**, Mori Group, Japan   6.5
9   **SUHARTO** family, Indonesia   6.3
10 **CHUNG Ju Yung** and family, Hyundai Group, Korea   6.2
11 **WANG Yung-ching** and family, Formosa Plastics
    Group, Taiwan   6.0
12 **DHANIN Chearavanont** and family, Charoen
    Pokphand Group, Thailand   5.5
13 **LIM Goh Tong**, Genting Bhd, Malaysia   5.2
14 **Eugene WU Tung-chin**, Shin Kong Group, Taiwan   5.0
15 **Yasuo TAKEI** and family, Takefuji Corp, Japan   5.0
16 **Masayoshi SON**, Softbank Corp, Japan   4.7
17 **SHIN Kyuk-ho** (Takeo Shigemitsu), Lotte Group, Korea 4.5
18 **LIEM Sioe Liong** (Sudono Salim), Salim Group, Indonesia 4.5
19 **Vincent TAN Chee Yioun**, Berjaya Group, Malaysia   4.5
20 **LEE Kun Hee** and family, Samsung Group, Korea   4.0
21 **Michael D. KADOORIE** and family, China Light &
    Power, Hongkong and Shanghai Hotels, Hong Kong   4.0
22 **KWEK Leng Beng** and family, City Developments and
    Hong Leong Group, Singapore   4.0
23 **QUEK Leng Chan** and family, Hong Leong Group,
    Malaysia   4.0

24	**Masatoshi ITO** and family, Ito-Yokado Group, Japan	3.8
25	**Eka Tjipta WIDJAJA (OEI Ek Tjhong)** and family, Sinar Mas Group, Indonesia	3.7
26	**Peter WOO Kwong-ching** and the **Pao** family, Wheelock & Co, Hong Kong	3.7
27	**NG Teng-fong** and family, Far East Organisation and Sino Land, Singapore & Hong Kong	3.5
28	**Robert KUOK Hock Nien**, Kerry Group, Malaysia	3.5
29	**Fukuzo IWASAKI** and family, Iwasaki Sangyo, Japan	3.5
30	**CHATRI Sophonpanich** and family, Bangkok Bank, Thailand	3.0
31	**Masahito OTSUKA** and family, Otsuka Pharmaceutical, Japan	3.0
32	**TAN Yu**, Fuga Internationale Group, Philippines	3.0
33	**KOO Cha-kyung** and family, LG Group, Korea	2.9
34	**Don Jaime Zobel de AYALA** and family, Ayala Corp, Philippines	2.8
35	**George TY** and family, Metrobank, Philippines	2.8
36	**TIONG Hiew King**, Rimbunan Hijau Group, Malaysia	2.5
37	**CHENG Yu-tung**, New World Development, Hong Kong	2.5
38	**Henry (Ying-tung) FOK**, STDM/Shun Tak, Hong Kong	2.5
39	**HSU Yu-ziang**, Far Eastern Group, Taiwan	2.4
40	**Dr THAKSIN Shinawatra**, Shinawatra Group, Thailand	2.4
41	**Manuel VILLAR**, C&P Homes, Philippines	2.4
42	**Stanley HO**, Shun Tak Holdings and STDM, Macau/ Hong Kong	2.3
43	**BANYONG Lamsam** and family, Thai Farmers Bank, Thailand	2.3
44	**Dr CHAIJUDH Karnasuta** and family, Italian-Thai Development, Thailand	2.3
45	**PUTERA Sampoerna** and family, Hanjaya Mandala Sampoerna, Indonesia	2.3
46	**Francis YEOH Sock Ping**, YTL Corp, Malaysia	2.2
47	**KHOO Teck Puat**, Malayan Banking Corp, Singapore	2.2
48	**CHANG Yung-fa**, Evergreen Group, Taiwan	2.1
49	**PRAJOGO Pangestu**, Barito Pacific, Indonesia	2.0
50	**Kumaramangalam BIRLA** and family, Birla Group, India	2.0

51	**KIM Woo-choong**, Daewoo Group, Korea	1.9
52	**Henry SY**, SM Prime Holdings, Philippines	1.9
53	**CHEY Jong-hyon** and family, Sunkyong Group, Korea	1.9
54	**TEH Hong Piow**, Public Bank, Malaysia	1.8
55	**LEE Seng Wee**, Oversea-Chinese Banking Corp, Singapore	1.8
56	**Djuhar SUTANTO**, share of Salim Group, Indonesia	1.8
57	**PIYA Bhirombakdi** and family, Boon Rawd Brewery, Thailand	1.7
58	**Lucio TAN**, Philippine Airlines, Fortune Tobacco, Philippines	1.7
59	**HALIM Saad**, Renong Group, Malaysia	1.7
60	**YAW Teck Seng** and family, Samling Corp, Malaysia	1.6
61	**BOONCHAI Bencharongkul** and family, United Communication, Thailand	1.6
62	**ADISAI Bodharamik**, Jasmine International, Thailand	1.6
63	**Andrew GOTIANUN Sr** and family, Filinvest Group, Philippines	1.5
64	**WEE Cho Yaw**, United Overseas Bank, Singapore	1.5
65	**KOO Chen-fu** and family, Koos Group, Taiwan	1.5
66	**PRACHAI Leophairatana** and family, Thai Petrochemical Industries, Thailand	1.5
67	**T. Ananda KRISHNAN**, Binariang Group, Malaysia	1.4
68	**KRIT Ratanarak** and family, Siam City Cement, Bank of Ayudhya, Thailand	1.4
69	**Eugenio (Geny) LOPEZ Jr**, Benpres Holdings, Philippines	1.4
70	**RASHID Hussain**, Rashid Hussain, Malaysia	1.4
71	**LEE Hon Chiu**, Hysan Development, Hong Kong	1.4
72	**ANANT Asavabhokin**, Land & House, Thailand	1.4
73	**CHEN Yu-hau**, Tuntex Group, Taiwan	1.4
74	**KIM Suk-won** and family, Ssangyong Group, Korea	1.3
75	**HUANG Shi-hui**, Chinfon Group, Taiwan	1.3
76	**Sjamsul NURSALIM** (Liem Tek Siong) and family, Gajah Tunggal Group, Indonesia	1.3
77	**Dhirubhai AMBANI** and family, Reliance Industries Ltd, India	1.2

78	**Gordon WU Ying-sheung**, Hopewell Holdings, Hong Kong	1.2
79	**TAJUDIN Ramli**, TRI and Malaysia Airlines, Malaysia	1.2
80	**Mohamad Bob HASAN**, Indonesian Wood Panel Association (Apkindo), Indonesia	1.2
81	**LO Ying Shek**, Great Eagle Holdings, Hong Kong	1.1
82	**MONGKOL Kanjanapas** and family, Bangkok Land, Thailand	1.1
83	**UDANE Tejapaibul** and family, Bangkok Metropolitan Bank, Thailand	1.0
84	**Ratan N. TATA**, Tata Group, India	1.0
85	**John GOKONGWEI**, JG Summit, Philippines	1.0
86	**Alfonso T. YUCHENGCO**, House of Investments, Philippines	1.0
87	**Sukanto TANOTO** and family, Raja Garuda Mas Group and Asia Pacific Resources International, Indonesia	1.1
88	**R. Budi HARTONO** and family, Djarum Group, Indonesia	1.0
89	**Mochtar RIADY** and family, Lippo Group, Indonesia	1.0
90	**KHOO Kay Peng**, MUI, Malaysia	1.0
91	**Eduardo COJUANGCO Jr** and family, UCP Bank, San Miguel Corp, Philippines	1.0
92	**Andres SORIANO III**, San Miguel Corp, Philippines	1.0
93	**William SOERYADJAYA** and family, Astra Group, Indonesia	1.0
94	**Hashim DJOJOHADIKUSUMO**, Semen Cibinong, Indonesia	1.0
95	**William CHENG Teng-jem**, Lion Group, Malaysia	1.0
96	**Sir Run Run SHAW**, TVB Holdings, Hong Kong	1.0
97	Estate of **YAHAYA Ahmad**,* DRB-Hicom Group, Malaysia	1.0
98	**ONG Beng Seng**, Kuo International, Singapore	1.0
99	**Mu'min Ali GUNAWAN** and family, Panin Group, Indonesia	1.0
100	**TUNG Chee-hwa** and family, Orient Overseas International Line, Hong Kong	1.0

*Yahaya Ahmad and his wife died in a helicopter crash in Malaysia in March 1997. Their four children are their heirs.

on the eastern banks of the Huangpu river. When it is completed by 2000, the building, to be known as the World Financial Centre, will be Asia's tallest.

But many of Japan's billionaires are simply new players who struck it rich during the 'bubble' economy of the 1980s and had the luck or the wit to survive the subsequent crash. Aside from some thought-provoking links to the Japanese *yakuza* gangs, they are a lacklustre bunch compared with their co-members of the billionaires club elsewhere.

The real interest lies with the majority of Asia's super-rich business people who are of Chinese origin. The focus is not necessarily on a 'red capitalist' like China's vice-president Rong Yiren, of China International Trust and Investment Corp (CITIC) fame, or even his wealthy and powerful Hong-Kong-based son, Larry Yung, of CITIC Pacific, but on the ethnic Chinese billionaires – mostly from the Guangdong and Fujian provinces of southern China – who left their homeland to carve out twentieth-century fortunes for themselves in agribusiness, shipping, real estate, manufacturing, franchises, food, timber and other commodities.

These seriously rich Chinese are part of the overseas Chinese networks, whose linkages through clan, guild, village and dialect constitute an economic force of such magnitude that only the United States and Japan generate a larger gross domestic product.

The networks include such Thai-based billionaires as Dhanin Chearavanont [12] of the Charoen Pokphand Group, Chatri Sophonpanich [30] of Bangkok Bank, and the computer king, Thaksin Shinawatra [40], who took a break from business to serve as Thailand's Deputy Prime Minister from 1994–96.

The Indonesian big names include the country's richest man, Uncle Liem (Liem Sioe Liong [18] of the Salim Group, also known as Sudono Salim), Eka Tjipta Widjaja [25] of the Sinar Mas Group, and the *kretek* (clove) cigarette kings, the Wonowidjojo family led by Rachman Halim [7].

From Malaysia, along with Robert Kuok – who is now more a property player than a commodity trader – the biggest names are ethnic Chinese like gambling guru Lim Goh Tong [13] of Genting,

Vincent Tan [19] of the Berjaya Group, and the Quek family [23], who, with their cousins the Kweks in Singapore, run the diversified Hong Leong group. Key names in the Philippines include banker George Ty [35], the shopping mall rivals Henry Sy [52] and John Gokongwei [84], and the politically indestructible beer and tobacco magnate, Lucio Tan [58].

In Hong Kong, besides the fabulously wealthy Kwok brothers and Lee Shau-kee [4], the list includes their various rivals cum partners such as the Hong Kong 'Superman' himself, Li Ka-shing [6] of Cheung Kong and Hutchison Whampoa, Cheng Yu-tung [37] of New World, Macau casino king Stanley Ho [42], and the sometimes embattled 'Mr Infrastructure' of Asia, Gordon Wu Ying-sheung [78] of Hopewell Holdings.

In Taiwan, the Tsai family [5] has built a fortune estimated at US$8.5 billion through the Lin-Yuan group that embraces Cathay Life Insurance and a construction operation, while the crusty industrialist Wang Yung-ching [11] and his children (net worth US$6 billion) run the mighty Formosa Plastics–Nan Ya Plastics empire that has expanded from petrochemicals into computers and financial services.

But while the Japanese and ethnic Chinese between them may dominate most of Asia's economies, the wealth club is not exclusively theirs. Koreans like Shin Kyuk-ho [17] of Lotte, Chung Ju-yung [10] of Hyundai and Lee Kun Hee [20] of Samsung are part of the billionaires' parade, along with noble names like Ayala [34], Lopez [69] and Soriano [92] of the Philippines, and India's Birla [50], Tata [83] and Ambani [77] families. Indeed, after adjusting for purchasing-power parity, India, with its vast potential for economic growth, may well claim to have many more than its current handful of billionaires before the decade is out.

While these super-rich scattered across Asia are busy with their networks, they are all shaded by the reputedly more than US$30 billion wealth of the world's richest royal, the Sultan of Brunei [1]. His is a special case, however, where family and national economic interests constantly overlap.

The Sultan's love of polo and his spending habits are the stuff of legend. When one of the younger members of the Brunei royal family enjoyed a birthday in April 1996, the Sultan secretly flew rock star Tina Turner and her band into the Brunei capital, Bandar Seri Begawan, for a surprise concert at the birthday party. He followed that up with a Michael Jackson concert to mark his own fiftieth birthday in July 1996.

Such displays of wealth aside, one thing is clear: with Asia's growth likely to be the dominating economic event of the early twenty-first century, the borderless networks that increasingly link the top billionaires are certain to control more and more of the world's riches.

Business success in Asia is not just about making money – important though that may be. Throughout the different economies of Asia, from the free-wheeling capitalism of Hong Kong to the market socialism of Vietnam and the technocrats of Singapore, the wheels of commerce run on power, prestige, influence, favours given and received, family fortune and what the Chinese call *guanxi*, or connections. With the right *guanxi*, sometimes anything is possible; without it, even the simplest business deals can come unstuck for unfathomable reasons.

Naturally, *guanxi* is not the sole property of the mainland Chinese and their overseas compatriots, although their influence daily becomes ever more pervasive. The Japanese, the Koreans, the Indians and the members of the ASEAN (Association of South East Asian Nations) bloc each have their own special connections when it comes to doing business. Ultimately, however, their business styles can be distilled to an essence of trust and credibility: who vouches for whom.

It is networking on a grand scale. A Singaporean Chinese trader, for example, may have family connections in Taiwan, Hong Kong, Guangdong, Fujian or Vietnam that remove the need for traditional banking services when it comes to shifting funds across borders.

Broadly speaking, there are six major economic groups in Asia that thrive on networking:

➤ the Japanese, with their *keiretsu* company connections
➤ the Koreans, with their *chaebol* conglomerates
➤ the mainland Chinese, with their party and military links
➤ the ethnic or overseas Chinese, with their stored wealth, and extended family, dialect and guild connections
➤ the emerging *pribumi* and *bumiputera* (indigenous) business leaders of Indonesia and Malaysia, with their political connections
➤ the Indians, with their family dynasties.

While Japan still dominates at the corporate level, the business of making serious money ebbs and flows through unlisted family groups, who essentially are Chinese – even those with Indonesian, Thai or Filipino names. Only India challenges the ethnic Chinese for family empires. But where there are an estimated 57 million ethnic Chinese abroad, the Indian diaspora numbers 18 million at the most.

Billionaires-to-be

So far, Asia's most successful wealth-makers have followed a consistent pattern. From the basics of food and shelter, they move gradually up the value-adding chain to embrace sectors such as real estate, construction, manufacturing, banking, telecommunications and transport.

But will this approach still work in the twenty-first century, when most of the new jobs and the new physical infrastructure that will exist in Asia in 2010 have yet to be thought of, let alone created or built? The uncertainty ahead means there is more than a good chance that many of the billionaires (or will inflation require them to be trillionaires?) who will stride the Asian business stage in 2010 have yet to begin their path to fortune. Their products and services may not yet exist; or they may be just taking shape – swapped with a friend, perhaps, as a scribbled design pushed across a coffee table, or an idea conveyed across the Internet to a potential partner in a different hemisphere.

If we were to hazard a guess about the industries which those billionaires-to-be might enter, we could start with the fundamental fact that information will be everywhere. That will make it cheap in some circumstances, but control of the quality and packaging of information (such as entertainment, news and education) is likely to remain strategically valuable. This suggests that there will be money in information technology, telecommunications (such as go-anywhere cellular phones), computer software, silicon chips, new home hardware arising from the convergence of computers, video and television (like NetTV), and the technology to handle electronic cash and encrypt commercial transactions.

As futurist and *Megatrends Asia* author John Naisbitt observed in 1996: 'Because of technology, information is as free as the air. We are moving towards a world where every call is local.'[1]

But while globalization ensures that information will be plentiful and cheap, good water and clean air may be scarce and expensive. At least US$1.5 trillion has to be spent on Asian infrastructure in the decade 1996–2005, with water and sanitation high on the list of needs. Delivering potable water and breathable air to the inhabitants of Asian megacities like Bangkok, Jakarta, Shanghai, Bombay and Manila may well be the making of some twenty-first-century fortunes. This will involve more than just physical infrastructure; it is likely to require new membrane materials and filtration processes, innovative recycling programmes and anti-pollution measures that are driven by commercial opportunity rather than government directives. The design and engineering of new industrial estates, for example, will include recycling, power-saving and pollution-control measures – not because governments require them, but because investors see the commercial benefits that flow from this approach. Massive 'money-in-muck' opportunities will arise in retro-fitting factories to clean their air and water discharges.

Even in gridlocked cities where air quality is poor, Asian consumers will still want cars to call their own. The Asian automotive market has yet to peak; by 2005 it is likely to be the biggest in the world, prompting even more attention from US and European makers like GM, Ford, Mercedes-Benz and BMW. Aggressive Korean makers such as Hyundai, Daewoo, Ssangyong, Kia and Samsung will compete head on with the well-entrenched Japanese brands, while Malaysia's Proton and homegrown Indian, Chinese and Indonesian makers will look for lower-cost niches. That means fortunes are still to be made in silicon chips as electronics takes an ever-growing share of vehicle manufacturing costs.

The need for programmable chips to run computer-controlled engines, airbag sensors, satellite-linked global positioning systems, automatic tollway collection and route plotting, mean that the billions being spent now on wafer-fabrication plants in Europe and the United States by tycoons like Lee Kun Hee of Samsung and Wang Yung-ching of FPG will be just the first of many waves.

Apart from semiconductors, another big automotive growth area will be in exotic materials – lightweight steels, ceramics and high-strength compounds, designed to keep car bodies smooth and weight down in the push for greater fuel efficiency.

Congested roads in many parts of Asia will make driving for pleasure hardly worthwhile, but rising incomes combined with information on new sights and experiences will conspire to make tourism (especially luxury travel) another potential money-maker. That means more hotels, restaurants and tour services, bigger airports to cater for 1000-seat jumbo aircraft, theme parks, shopping centres, brand names, eco-tourism niches and maybe credit-card-sized electronic devices to put the question 'How much is that?' in 20 different tongues.

Cruising through South-East Asian waters on a luxury floating casino, with the choice of venturing onshore every day for some local atmosphere or staying onboard to sample the duty-free delights of the shopping centre, may well be the holiday of choice for Asia's well-heeled early in the twenty-first century.

Even with reclamation schemes along the lines of those now planned in Macau and Hong Kong, the generally finite nature of land means that the choicest spots in Asia will be formidably

The Asian equation: population, GDP and growth

Country	Population 1995 (m)	GDP 1995 US$bn	Per capita GDP 1995 US$	Real GDP average growth 1990–95 %	Forecast average growth 1990–2000 %
South Korea	44.9	456	10,155	7.5	7.4
Taiwan	21.2	261	12,288	6.6	6.1
Hong Kong	6.2	144	23,213	5.5	3.7
Singapore	3.0	84	27,992	8.5	7.5
Malaysia	20.1	81	4,049	8.7	8.2
Philippines	68.4	74	1,083	2.3	5.8
Thailand	60.2	160	2,663	8.1	7.8
Indonesia	196.6	202	1,026	7.1	7.8
China	1210	624	516	11.3	9.2
India	938	326	347	4.1	5.4
Japan	125.6	5114	40,715	1.3	2.3

Source: EIU Country Forecasting Service

expensive. But the scarcity/price equation will be no deterrent; just as consumers want their own cars, so they will want their own houses, apartments and holiday villas. That should allow another wave of property developers to embark on the classic route to land-based wealth: sniff the wind for a coming boom, then landbank like crazy.

Along with water and shelter, that other basic of life, food, will be relatively plentiful. Even with increased consumption of grain and meat in heavily populated markets like China and India, new production techniques and high-yielding crops will keep food on Asian tables. Rather than struggle for food self-sufficiency, countries like Japan and Korea will choose to exploit their comparative advantage in high-technology goods and services, and buy most of their food from the best, most efficient producers with the most competitive prices.

This is the benign view of Asia's future: peaceful, cooperative economic progress, with tension confined to managing the growth of large cities and ensuring that pollution doesn't drift across a neighbour's boundary.

The alternative view of Asia's future is much more fluid and chaotic, and focuses on the one inescapable fact on which all forecasters agree: China will occupy centre stage in the twenty-first century. Its commercial, cultural and security relations with Japan and the United States will condition the economic health of Asia. As a key survey in 1996 noted, even with a 'highly uncertain' long-term outlook for China–Japan political relations, the two countries' trade relationship will be transformed during the next 20 years.[2]

In *Asia's Global Powers*, the Australian Government's East Asia Analytical Unit said it was reasonable to assume that China–Japan trade will become as important to the world in 2015 as US–Japan trade is today. China–Japan trade is now the world's fourth largest bilateral relationship behind US–Canada, US–Japan and France–Germany.

It is likely that the state of the relationship between Beijing and Tokyo will determine from which business sectors the next wave of billionaires will emerge. That is the other constant: whatever the political or economic climate, new entrepreneurs will pop out somewhere to take advantage of the situation.

John Naisbitt believes that most of those new billionaires will be members of the most important business network now in existence: the 57 million ethnic Chinese living outside China. He sees their capital, connections (*guanxi*) and entrepreneurial spirit as redefining the business world to the point where China and the ethnic Chinese are now the driving force in Asia's growth. He believes that Japan, on the other hand, despite its great accumulated economic wealth, has peaked and is now on a long, downward path.[3]

Australian business forecaster Phil Ruthven, executive chairman of IBIS Business Information, does not share the bullish views of China which envisage its uninterrupted run to regional economic dominance.

'Nobody has ever picked up 1.2 billion people and taken them forward. In that sense, China is a very big challenge – there is no precedent. The United States had a population of only 80 million when it started its drive to the top. I think China eventually should prevail, but it won't be smooth and it will take some time to become a dominant economic power,' he said in 1996.[4]

Ruthven said that the six key eastern provinces of China would have incomes of five to ten times those of the other provinces, and this would lead to polarization between the rich and the poor. 'In the United States, the Civil War was the outcome, with the North winning because of its industrial might. China will have the equivalent, but hopefully without the guns and sticks. With modern communications, China should have the facilities to overcome these income differentials,' he commented.

Another note of pessimism about Asia deals with the challenge of globalization. Can some Asian business practices – for example, the networking style of the Chinese entrepreneurs – co-exist with the regulated, rule-driven approach of western business? Can new Asian entrepreneurs promote their own brand names globally to the point where they have the same recognition as Toyota, Sony, Acer, Samsung and San Miguel?

Professor Gordon Redding of the University of Hong Kong, author of the 1990 work *The Spirit of Chinese Capitalism*, believes that this is unlikely. He claims that the concept of developing an international brand name conflicts with the traditional Chinese family business, dominated by one person and reliant on *guanxi*. The network of friendships with suppliers, customers and financiers is not easily transferred. Since the Chinese tend not to trust people they do not know well, they are reluctant to embark on global marketing.[5]

US management guru Michael Porter (Harvard professor and author of *The Competitive Advantage of Nations*) is another who believes that the conglomerates beloved of Asian family businesses will not handle globalization well. A focus on adding value, rather than diversity, will determine future success, he believes.[6] And soon, hot competition will be everywhere, with no more protected markets at home.

Porter's warning is that Asian business giants must change to meet globalization. But older billionaire players like Robert Kuok, Li Ka-shing, Liem Sioe Liong, Wang Yung-ching and Ng Teng Fong might well answer that they have already honed their business skills in tough markets beyond their own backyards.

The challenge really is for the younger generation of Asian entrepreneurs, some of whom are already part of Asia's Wealth Club.

2

Starting with Food – from Seeds to Satellites

The rise of East Asia, and of China, will not bring the Dark Ages ...
China will impart fresh energy and vigour to the West.

Singapore's Senior Minister Lee Kuan Yew, Beijing, 4 September 1996[1]

XICHANG SPACE BASE, SICHUAN PROVINCE, CHINA, JANUARY 1995:
45 seconds after liftoff, a Chinese Long March 2E rocket
explodes, scattering debris and expensive payload over the coun-
tryside. Two thousand kilometres away in Hong Kong, there is a
collective grimace from the members of the APT satellite consortium as their new Apstar-2 communications satellite sitting atop
the rocket is vaporized. All told, the bill for the failed launch and
payload runs to US$300 million.

Among the owners to bear the pain of that loss is Thailand's
Dhanin Chearavanont [12], one of the five most important ethnic
Chinese businessmen in Asia. Dhanin is chairman and chief exec-
utive of the Charoen Pokphand Group of Thailand, Asia's largest
agro-industrial conglomerate and a shareholder in Apstar with
Singapore Telecom and the Chinese government.

Dhanin, like his four ethnic Chinese colleagues at the top of the
influence tree – Liem Sioe Liong [18] in Indonesia, Robert Kuok
[28] in Malaysia, Li Ka-shing [6] in Hong Kong and Alfonso

Yuchengco [85] in the Philippines – is also a billionaire of truly momentous proportions (estimated net worth US$5.5 billion) and proof that humble origins are no barrier to Asia's wealth club in the 1990s.

Indeed, the path to fabulous wealth in Asia has a consistent ring about it; there is a pattern that can be traced. It starts with the most basic necessities of life – food and shelter – and over time moves into sectors like real estate, construction, manufacturing, banking, telecommunications and airlines. So many of the biggest family fortunes in Asia have been built on food: names like Kuok in Malaysia, Tan in the Philippines, Liem in Indonesia, Kwek in Singapore and, biggest of them all, the Chearavanont family in Thailand. Many of these families do business together; they speak the same Chinese dialects, share the same banking facilities, know the same movers and shakers in every major Asian capital, and have a common vision about the future of Asian business.

Dhanin and the other members of the Chearavanont clan have built up a 250-company empire with 1996 revenue of US$7.5 billion, with operations in more than 20 countries and 80,000 employees.[2] Starting with vegetable seeds, the family has moved on to fertilizers, pesticides, stockfeed, chickens, eggs, pork and new consumer foods like frozen chicken and shrimps, and more recently to manufacturing, real estate, distribution, petrochemicals and the glamour industry of the 1990s, telecommunications. Food is still the biggest earner; virtually on its own, for example, the CP Group (as Charoen Pokphand is known) has built up an aquaculture business that has created revenue of US$1.5 billion a year just in breeding black tiger prawns.

While the failure of Apstar-2 in 1995 may have been a major setback to the CP Group's regional plans, it was far from a fatal blow: Apstar-1 had been launched successfully six months earlier in July 1994, and Apstar-1A went aloft safely in July 1996. A third satellite, Apstar-2R, is due for launch in mid-1997, using a Long March 3B rocket. That the Chearavanont family was able to make the transition from seeds to satellites in the space of 75 years is indicative of the entrepreneurial spirit that pervades Asia's business milieu. It is but one of many families who have made their way into Asia's wealth club.

The Chearavanont story starts 2000km to the east of the Xichang space base, at Shantou, the old 'treaty port' on the south China coast once known as Swatow. Shantou was one of the first six ports forced open to trade by the British during the nineteenth-century Opium Wars with China, when opium was the solace to the Chinese population that gin was to the British. Despite an imperial ban on the drug in 1729 and the burning of more than 20,000 chests of opium by Commissioner Lin Tse-hsu at Canton (now the city of Guangzhou) in 1839 that touched off the first war, the British merchants forced the opium trade to continue. India was the source and the Chinese treaty ports were the destination, with an average 12 tonnes of opium being shipped into the country for every day of Queen Victoria's reign.[3]

From Shantou and other ports of Guangdong province, thousands of Teochiu-speaking Chinese *huaqiao* or sojourners made their way to the South Seas – or, more properly, the cities of South-East Asia – in the nineteenth and early twentieth centuries. In 1921, two such sojourners, brothers Chia Ek-chor and Chia Seow-whooy, arrived from Shantou in Bangkok. They were among 600,000 Chinese then living in Thailand – almost all of them in the capital, specifically in the narrow streets and alleys of Chinatown, not far from Bangkok's main railway station. Teochiu, the dialect of northern Guangdong province, was Bangkok's language of commerce, particularly in the rice trade. Even today, rice is controlled by the Teochiu traders. In a small store in Chinatown, the brothers set up a vegetable seeds operation, trading as Chia Tai Seeds Company, and began to weave the magic tale of Charoen Pokphand, which means 'commodity development' in Thai.

Standing in front of a display of Thailand's finest fruit, vegetables and seeds at an up-country fair late in 1995, the president of Chia Tai Co, Mr Manu Chiaravanond (a cousin to CP Group leader Dhanin Chearavanont) waved a hand expansively and summed up the CP story: 'This is how it all started – with the seeds.'

Today, Chia Tai operates from Songsawad Road in the heart of Bangkok's commercial district, and is still described by the CP Group leadership as 'our first-born business'. In the 1920s, the Chia brothers expanded from seeds into supplying farmers with fertilizer and plant pesticides. From the outset, the brothers used their Chinese connections, importing seeds from China and shipping back pigs, eggs and agricultural produce. Gradually, they built up what became Thailand's largest supplier of vegetable seeds. While China remained the primary focus, Chia Tai also had outlets in Singapore, Kuala Lumpur, Hong Kong and Taipei. The family ran its main operation from Shantou, finally consolidating back to Bangkok when the Communists came to power in China in 1949. Ironically, the CP Group, under Dhanin's leadership, has become the single largest investor in China, with more than 90 projects valued at more than US$2 billion.[4]

Dhanin, born in Bangkok in April 1939, was the youngest of four sons of Chia Ek-Chor, but emerged in the late 1970s as the group's leader. After high school studies in China and college in Hong Kong, he became general manager of the CP Group in 1963 and served in that slot until 1979. Although Ek-chor's eldest son Jaran (also known as Janin) was behind the group's initial step towards vertical integration – a decision to set up its first chicken feedmill in Thailand in 1953 – it was Dhanin who introduced contract farming in the 1970s, the radical innovation that propelled the group into the big league of Thai commerce.

What was crucial to Dhanin's success was access to money. It came from the Chinese connection – specifically Chin Sophonpanich, co-founder of Bangkok Bank in 1945 and the man who, until his death in 1988, was regarded as the most important ethnic Chinese business figure anywhere in the world.

Like Dhanin's father and uncle, Chin Sophonpanich claimed a Shantou background. Although he was actually born in Bangkok's floating market in 1910, Chin went to Shantou at the age of five and stayed there until he was 17.

When he returned to Thailand he followed the normal Teochiu route: he became a rice trader, then ran a smallgoods store. But the

Second World War brought new opportunities; Thai and Chinese businesses needed money from a bank that would look favourably on local entrepreneurs. They also wanted a mechanism that would allow them to remit money back to their families in Shantou. Chin saw the need and, with some Chinese associates, helped found the Bangkok Bank.[5]

Today, the bank is the biggest and most profitable in South-East Asia, with impeccable financial credentials and a 1996 profit figure of US$800 million. Its 22 offshore branches predictably include one in Shantou. But back in its early days, when Chin Sophonpanich saw the need to be close to the Thai military power brokers, the bank was known more for its association with figures thought to be involved in running heroin from the Golden Triangle to markets in Hong Kong and the United States. According to US author Sterling Seagrave, Chin was sometimes referred to as banker to the Asian drug trade.[6]

Chin left Thailand for Hong Kong in 1957, but returned in the 1960s. The Sophonpanich family still holds about a one-third share of the bank today, with Chin's second son, Chatri, 62, as executive chairman, and Chatri's eldest son Chartsiri (Tony) named president in December 1994 and being groomed for the top role.

With the crucial backing of Chin and the Bangkok Bank in the early 1970s, Dhanin was able to extend credit to farmers to allow them to buy seeds, fertilizer and pesticides. He also guaranteed to buy their vegetable produce. Later, he expanded this to include the raw materials and technology to raise chickens and shrimps – the foods that were to become the staple of his agribusiness empire and the choice of a whole new generation of fast-food consumers in Thailand.

By 1979, Dhanin was CP Group president. He became chairman and CEO in 1989 and set the course for the group's massive expansion into China, using the *guanxi* (connections) that bubbled forth from his Shantou family history. Dhanin's three elder brothers continue to play key roles in the group's global operations. Two, Janin and Montri, are honorary chairmen. The youngest of his elder brothers, Sumet Jiaravanon (one of several alternative English spellings of the family name), is vice-chairman and heads the CP Group's Hong Kong operations. He spends most of his time developing joint ventures in China and looking after the group's extensive interests there in feedmills, motorcycle production, retailing, petrochemicals and property development. Sumet and Dhanin control Orient Telecoms, which has a stake in the CP Group's US$7 billion listed telecommunications arm, Telecom-Asia. In this joint venture with the US company Nynex Corp, TelecomAsia is adding 2.6 million fixed telephone lines to Bangkok's stressed telephone system in a 25-year operating concession that will start feeding big dollars into CP's revenue stream from 1997 onwards.

Dhanin, a friendly, open man in his late fifties whose hobby is homing pigeons, is immensely proud of the CP Group's achievements. They are the result, he says, of more than 70 years of determination, creativity and hard work. And, he could add, access to credit at a crucial time in the company's growth.

Dhanin is also a modernist and internationalist. In a departure from the earlier practice of Chinese businessmen keen to keep everything in the family, Dhanin has shown a willingness to embrace technology, spend money on research and development, and bring in foreign partners with special expertise. He worked with US company Arbor Acres Farm to bring a new breed of broiler chicken into Thailand in 1970 and later formed a joint venture with a US seed producer that led to major productivity gains for the agribusiness side of CP.

Research has paid dividends for the group. With corn the major ingredient in animal feed, CP unveiled its agricultural masterstroke in 1995 – a hybrid corn variety known as CP-DK999 that produces a high yield but shortens planting time from 115 days to just 90 days.

'It is our duty and responsibility to aim to develop technology, so as to promote the agro-industry business in Thailand, placing it on the world stage,' Dhanin says.

Along with more than 70 feedmills in virtually every province of China, joint ventures in other lines have always been a part of Dhanin's diversification activities. CP's partners in China include Honda in motorcycles, Heineken in beer production, the National Oil Company of China and the Petroleum Authority of Thailand (PTT) in petroleum, and Siemens in a proposed wafer-fabrication plant in Shanghai.

More than a decade ago, in 1985, CP set up the Ek Chor China Motorcycle Company (named after Dhanin's father), licensing the necessary technology from Honda in a joint venture in which CP holds 70 per cent. It produces 300,000 motorcycles a year from its two plants, with production expected to rise significantly when a new plant in Shanghai is fully operational in 1997.

A new business line is petroleum and energy, where CP has set up PetroAsia International to explore joint ventures in Thailand, China and Vietnam, and PetroAsia Thailand, which aims to build a network of 300 retail service stations in Thailand. Fortuitously, every station will offer fast food, featuring the CP Group's franchises, such as 7-Eleven, Chester's Grill and InterSuki.

Dhanin's continued embrace of the family philosophy of vertical integration has paid off; the group controls around 60 per cent of the Thai seed-distribution market, while in animal raising its emphasis on chicken, shrimps and fish-farming has effectively redefined Thai eating habits. Where once there were just rice and vegetables, now there are chicken, eggs, pigs, freshwater prawns and fish varieties. 'Think ocean' is Dhanin's slogan for this part of the CP operation.

Dhanin, married with three sons (all in the family business, all educated in the United States) and two daughters, still exudes a down-to-earth simplicity. His role models are similarly frugal types: Hong Kong industrialist, property developer and fellow billionaire 'Superman' Li Ka-shing; and the founder of Wal-Mart Stores, American businessman the late Sam Walton. Work hard, think hard, gain experience is the Dhanin philosophy. He might add, and make some powerful friends. Dhanin is a strong supporter of the Thai royal family, has been close to virtually every Thai administration of the 1980s and 1990s, and is an adviser to the Chinese government.

And then, of course, there is the Bangkok Bank connection. The two Thai corporate giants share a toney address: CP's head-quarters is the CP Tower at 313 Silom Road, while just down the street at 333 Silom is the 32-storey Bangkok Bank building known as *pla buek*, or giant catfish – a reference to the bank's size. That size as the biggest fish in the river still holds true today, although the bank no longer dominates the financial landscape as absolute-ly as it did in the 1960s, 1970s and 1980s. In 1996, Bangkok Bank earned the largest profit yet of any listed Thai company, with income of US$800 million, up 4.7 per cent on its 1995 figures. Revenue was more than US$4.2 billion, while market capitaliza-tion in early 1997 stood at US$7.6 billion. The bank says that about 10 per cent of its profit comes from overseas business, such as its branch in Shantou, the Teochiu stronghold which has been the birthplace of so many of South-East Asia's successful business families.[7]

As well as lending money to local Sino-Thai entrepreneurs like the Chearavanont family, Bangkok Bank counts among its valued customers such names as Liem Sioe Liong's Salim Group in Indonesia, and Robert Kuok's various entities in Malaysia, Hong Kong and elsewhere. Liem and Kuok were friends of the late Chin Sophonpanich and, like the Chearavanonts, made their first mark in food.

3

The Fujian Connection

The argument about whether Shanghai will 'take over' from Hong Kong will be redundant by the middle of the 21st century. An economy the size of China's will support at least a dozen major financial centres.

Bank of East Asia chief executive David Li, 1996[1]

FROM THE ROOF OF SHANGHAI'S PEACE HOTEL OVERLOOKING THE Bund, a massive panorama of commerce in action unfolds. Directly across the muddy Huangpu river, churned by the propellers of barges, cargo ships and triple-deck passenger ferries bound for the Yangtse river, stands Shanghai's new symbol of twenty-first-century magnificence: the Oriental Pearl communications and television tower. At the base of the 450-metre tower, opposite the Peace Hotel, is Pudong Park, the starting point for the frenetic scramble of building activity that is creating a whole new financial centre and industrial zone in Shanghai: the Pudong New Area.

Shanghai, the 'head of the dragon', is a city redolent of the modern history of China. This was the great commercial and financial centre of the 1920s and 1930s, when foreign banks and merchant houses lined The Bund, when the Green Gang syndicate ran crime in the city and nationalist leader Chiang Kai-Shek was on the rise. This was where the Communist Party of China was founded in 1921: a few hundred metres southwest of The Bund is the site of the party's first national congress. Here too stand the former residences of the father of modern China, Dr Sun Yat-Sen, and Mao Ze-dong's long-term ally Zhou En-Lai. And to the north-west in Zhabei district is Shanghai railway station, where troops from both political camps rolled out to meet the common Japanese enemy in the 1930s.

There is a special link between Shanghai and one of Asia's best-connected ethnic Chinese billionaires – the man they call the 'sugar king': Robert Kuok [28] of Malaysia. It is in Shanghai that Kuok (estimated net worth US$3.5 billion) is making his biggest China property play, with a stake in the US$1 billion Kerry Everbright City. His partner in the deal includes another of the great Chinese billionaires: Hong Kong's Li Ka-shing [6], known simply in his home city as 'Superman'.

Kuok has traded in sugar, rice, flour, palm oil, timber and other commodities for half a century. In more recent years he has diversified into residential and commercial property, hotels, media investments, retailing, shipping, building materials, financial services and even fine Alhambra and Tabacalera cigars for his chain of luxury Shangri-la hotels.

But food and drink remain a constant in the Kuok scheme of things. His latest venture in the Philippines is in instant noodles. In China he has invested US$100 million in Coca-Cola bottling plants, and similar amounts in vegetable oil plants and a flour and feed mill. When he set up a 50–50 joint venture with Australian sugar and building materials group CSR in 1995, one of the specific new business areas was low-cost refined sugar, to meet the needs of Asia's rapidly growing market for soft drinks and confectionery. He bought a strategic 9 per cent stake in Australia's Coca-Cola Amatil for about US$500 million in August 1996, the better to draw some synergy from his own group's activities and CCA's beverage franchises in Indonesia and Eastern Europe.[2]

While Kuok's business plans are spread throughout China, his real ancestral roots actually lie several hundred kilometres south of Shanghai in Fujian province, from whence his parents emigrated to Malaysia in 1911. Kuok, although born in Malaysia,

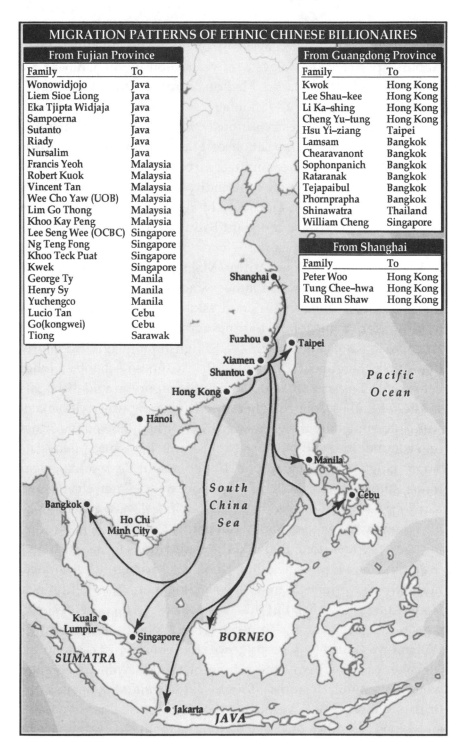

MIGRATION PATTERNS OF ETHNIC CHINESE BILLIONAIRES

From Fujian Province

Family	To
Wonowidjojo	Java
Liem Sioe Liong	Java
Eka Tjipta Widjaja	Java
Sampoerna	Java
Sutanto	Java
Riady	Java
Nursalim	Java
Francis Yeoh	Malaysia
Robert Kuok	Malaysia
Vincent Tan	Malaysia
Wee Cho Yaw (UOB)	Malaysia
Lim Go Thong	Malaysia
Khoo Kay Peng	Malaysia
Lee Seng Wee (OCBC)	Singapore
Ng Teng Fong	Singapore
Khoo Teck Puat	Singapore
Kwek	Singapore
George Ty	Manila
Henry Sy	Manila
Yuchengco	Manila
Lucio Tan	Cebu
Go(kongwei)	Cebu
Tiong	Sarawak

From Guangdong Province

Family	To
Kwok	Hong Kong
Lee Shau-kee	Hong Kong
Li Ka-shing	Hong Kong
Cheng Yu-tung	Hong Kong
Hsu Yi-ziang	Taipei
Lamsam	Bangkok
Chearavanont	Bangkok
Sophonpanich	Bangkok
Rataranak	Bangkok
Tejapaibul	Bangkok
Phornprapha	Bangkok
Shinawatra	Thailand
William Cheng	Singapore

From Shanghai

Family	To
Peter Woo	Hong Kong
Tung Chee-hwa	Hong Kong
Run Run Shaw	Hong Kong

Shanghai

Fuzhou
Xiamen
Shantou
Taipei

Hong Kong

Hanoi

Pacific Ocean

Manila

Cebu

South China Sea

Bangkok

Ho Chi Minh City

Kuala Lumpur

SUMATRA

Singapore

BORNEO

Jakarta

JAVA

is a Fuzhou Hokkien, a sub-dialect group whose members settled in large numbers in Malaysia early in the twentieth century. About 5 per cent of Malaysia's five million ethnic Chinese are Fuzhou, and other large Fuzhou communities live in the Philippines, Singapore and Indonesia.

Kuok takes his ancestry seriously. He is a high-level member of the International Association of Fuzhous and serves on the international executive committee, a role he shares with his frequent business partner in commodity and property deals, the Sino-Indonesian tycoon Liem Sioe Liong *[18]*.[3] Liem, also known as Sudono Salim, heads the giant Salim Group and, like Kuok's ancestors, hails from Fujian province.

Kuok was born in Johor Bahru, Malaysia, in October 1923, the youngest of three sons. His father, who died in 1948, arrived in Malaysia from China in 1911 and established himself as a commodity trader in Johor Bahru, across the causeway from Singapore. Kuok studied first at English-language schools in Johor and then spent 18 months in a Chinese school in Johor before enrolling at Raffles College in Singapore in mid-1941. His studies at Raffles College (where Lee Kuan Yew was a classmate) were interrupted by the war. After the war he followed his father into commodities and in later years became known as Malaysia's 'sugar king', controlling around 10 per cent of the world's sugar trade. Although his first company, Rickwood (later changed to Kuok Pte Ltd), was formed in Singapore in 1947 as a general trading company,[4] it was his Malaysian entity, Kuok Brothers, dealing in sugar, rice and flour, that laid the foundations for his fortune.

For much of his business life, Kuok has had high-level connections with governments in Malaysia, Singapore, the Philippines, Hong Kong and China. But this was not always the case. Tragedy struck the Kuok family in 1952 when Robert's elder brother William was killed by security forces in a communist camp in the Malayan jungle. This was the time of the Malayan Emergency, when communist terrorists fought a guerrilla war against the British. William Kuok was just one of 10,000 casualties in a nasty and bloody conflict that reached right to the very top of the

Malayan administration.

In October 1951, the British High Commissioner, Sir Henry Gurney, was shot and killed when terrorists ambushed his car on a mountain road about 100km north of Kuala Lumpur. Sir Henry and his wife were on their way to the mountain resort of Fraser's Hill when terrorists sprayed their vehicle and a police escort car with automatic fire. Sir Henry stepped from his car and was immediately cut down.[5] The incident prompted a harsh crackdown and wider powers for his successor, General Sir Gerald Templer, to 'resettle' the inhabitants of villages suspected of supporting the terrorists. By the time the 12-year Emergency ended in 1960 when support for the communist leader Ching Peng petered out, more than 10,000 soldiers, police, civilians (mainly rubber plantation workers and poor villagers) were dead, missing or wounded. At its height, the Emergency involved 40,000 Commonwealth troops, 60,000 police, 250,000 Home Guards and 3000 communist terrorists. At a time of great suspicion on all sides, the Kuok family left Malaysia for London.

When Robert Kuok returned from London in 1957 he set up Malaysia's first sugar refinery in a joint venture with the Federal Land Development Authority. Perlis Plantations, established in 1968, provided home-grown sugar cane in the 1970s, along with raw sugar from Thailand, Indonesia, Cuba and Australia. In addition to his plunge into the global sugar trade, Kuok was active in rice and wheat, and also plywood manufacturing. His shipping interests included Pacific Carriers in Singapore, one of the largest dry-bulk shipping lines in Asia, and Kerry Shipping in Hong Kong. He also helped establish the Malaysian International Shipping Corporation in 1971. His 30-per-cent-held joint venture with Cie Commercial Sucres et Denrées in France, known as Sucden Kerry International, was the world's largest sugar trader.[6]

Kuok was involved in several joint ventures with the Malaysian government before 1970 and became a founding director of Bank Bumiputera Malaysia, which extended credit to *bumiputeras* or ethnic Malays. By the 1970s, he saw that opportunities lay elsewhere in Asia and so in 1974 he established Kerry Trading

Co in Hong Kong. Over the next 20 years this was to develop into the Kerry Group, with extensive interests in property, hotels, financial services, shipping and media. Kuok, who has five children, moved to Hong Kong with his sons Beau Kuok (Kuok Khoon Chen) and Kuok Khoon Ean to concentrate on China, Hong Kong and other parts of Asia, leaving his eldest brother Philip to run the Malaysian and Singapore operations. Kuok's daughter Sue is married to one of Malaysia's highest-flying financiers, Rashid Hussain [70]. A cousin, Chye Kuok, helps with the family interests in Hong Kong and the Philippines.

Essentially, the Kuok Group of companies is active in commodity trading, property investments and development, hotels and hotel management, sugar and oil-palm plantations, beverages, shipping, financial services, retailing and general investments. The group's activities are mainly in Malaysia, Singapore, Hong Kong, Thailand, Philippines, China and Canada.

In May 1996, Kuok's Hong-Kong-listed hotel company, Shangri-la Asia Ltd (40 per cent held by Kerry Holdings), bought 13 hotels now under construction in China from the parent Kerry Group in a US$320 million deal that helped pave the way for the long-mooted float of Kerry Properties. It was the second time that Shangri-la had bought hotels from the Kerry Group. In January 1995 it paid US$540 million for six hotels in the Philippines, Fiji and Indonesia.[7]

Then in July 1996, Kuok put about 20 of his China and Hong Kong properties into Kerry Properties and floated 15 per cent of it on the Hong Kong stock exchange. When the sale of 150 million shares closed on 26 July, the price was HK$17.50 – at the low end of the price range, but still enough to raise US$320 million after expenses. The move valued the newly listed company at US$2.27 billion.[8]

The Kerry Properties float was seen as part of an overall restructuring of the Kuok empire, designed to make it easier to raise funds on international capital markets and prepare the way for his sons to take over the businesses. They are already active in Shangri-la Asia.

Kuok is an adviser to China on Hong Kong, he holds an 18 per cent stake in CITIC Pacific, the Hong Kong arm of the China International Trust and Investment Corporation, and his son Beau Kuok is a member of the Better Hong Kong Foundation, set up in late 1995 to bolster investor confidence in Hong Kong in the lead-up to the British territory's return to Chinese sovereignty in July 1997.[9] In a move seen as highly symbolic, in 1995 Kuok and CITIC bought the site of the former British naval base, HMS Tamar, in central Hong Kong to redevelop it as office space.

Property, mainly in the shape of five-star hotels, has been at the forefront of Kuok's massive push into China, with three hotels in Beijing alone. His extensive stable of Shangri-la Hotels includes Bangkok, Beijing, Fiji, Jakarta, Hong Kong (Kowloon and Central), Kuala Lumpur, Manila (Makati and Edsa), Mactan, Penang, Shanghai, Singapore and Vancouver. In China, Shangri-la Asia has thirteen hotels (nine of which are the luxury Shangri-la brand and four the cheaper Traders brand) either completed or due to be completed between 1998 and 2002. They include hotels in Shanghai, Harbin, Shenyang, Behai, Wuhan and Xian. Shangri-la Asia, which aims to build China's largest luxury hotel, also owns office space in the China World Trade Centre in Beijing and the Shanghai Centre in Shanghai, and the China World Hotel and Traders Hotel, both in Beijing.

Kuok sees Shanghai as pivotal to his China focus. While much of the building activity in the city is taking place on the eastern side of the Huangpu River in the new Pudong development area (where Japan's Mori brothers aim to build the world's tallest sky-scraper by 2000), for the moment Kuok is convinced that the real commercial action remains on the western side of the river. Nanjing Road, the main thoroughfare down to The Bund, still bustles with the vigour of 13 million people day and night. A short journey across murky Suzhou Creek – labelled 'that choking silthole' in a frank turn of phrase by Shanghai's mayor in 1995[10] – towards the city's elevated ring road brings the traveller to Zhabei district and the main railway station. This is the site of one of the city's largest property developments: the US$1 billion Shanghai

Kerry Everbright City that brings Kuok together with some of the biggest investors in China.

A construction hardhat perched on his head and a beribboned spade in his hands, a smiling Kuok joined Shanghai vice-mayor Xia Keqiang in November 1995 for the traditional 'topping out' of the first part of the development, a 50,000 square metre shopping complex. Joining the party were executives from Japanese retailer Jusco, who signed up as the anchor tenants for more than half the space.

The four-block Kerry Everbright City will revitalize the Shanghai station area. By the time it is completed in 2000, it will include a five-star hotel, two 38-storey towers for apartments and commercial office space, and several mixed-use buildings. Along with Li Ka-shing's Cheung Kong (Holdings), Kuok's partners in the mammoth project include the government-backed China Everbright group. The first stage, a five-floor shopping mall, opened in September 1996. Besides Everbright City, Kuok's Kerry Group has five other property projects in Shanghai.

Kuok likes to do business with people he knows best. And one who falls well and truly into that category is Liem Sioe Liong (also known in Indonesia as Sudono Salim), the Fujian-born tycoon who controls Indonesia's largest conglomerate, the Salim Group. Liem, born in 1917, is the dominant ethnic Chinese business figure in Indonesia, where he is known simply as 'the Chairman'.

With more than 300 companies and annual revenue of US$10 billion, the Salim Group is well and truly in the Asian superleague.[11] Employing more than 135,000 people worldwide, the group has interests in food and beverages, cooking oil, cement and other building materials, motor vehicles, commodity trading, property, chemicals, pharmaceuticals, textiles, financial services, distribution and telecommunications.

Liem's own wealth is put in the US$4.5 billion range – a far cry from the situation he faced as a 21-year-old arriving in Central Java from China in 1938 to work with his elder brother in an uncle's peanut oil shop in Kudus. With his savings, Liem was able to start his first business, selling coffee powder, during the Second World War.[12]

Today, he is generally regarded as one of the richest and most astute business identities in Asia. He is well connected politically to Indonesia's President Suharto [9] and his family – a legacy of Liem's background as a supplier of provisions and medical needs to Indonesian freedom fighters struggling against the Dutch for independence in the 1940s. In the 1950s, when Suharto was a young army officer, Liem first struck up an acquaintance which developed into a business relationship that has endured for 40 years. During the tense days after the 30 September–1 October coup attempt in 1965 that precipitated Sukarno's downfall and eventually brought Suharto to power, Liem was one of the people whom Suharto, by then a major-general, consulted.[13]

In the 1960s Liem established the first two companies that were to lay the foundations for the Salim Group: PT Bogasari Flour Mill, which eventually became the world's largest wheat-buying company, and PT Mega, which imported cloves under an exclusive concession from the government. That was followed in 1973 by PT Indocement, a veritable cash cow for the group through the fixed pricing system that applies to cement (and in flour, with the same effect for Bogasari). The Indonesian government holds 35 per cent of Indocement. Liem's listed flagship, PT Indofood Sukses Makmur, and Indocement dominate the Jakarta stock exchange, with a combined market capitalization of US$8 billion out of a total market capitalization of US$64 billion.[14]

Today Indofood is the world's largest instant-noodle maker and holds 90 per cent of the huge Indonesian market, where the population numbers 200 million. With disposable incomes in the world's fourth most populous nation continuing to rise – and much of the money spent on food and beverages – Liem's Indofood will continue to find rich pickings at home.

Similarly, Indocement is South-East Asia's largest cement company in a market that is expanding in line with the construction and home-building boom. In February 1995, Indocement sold its Bogasari Flour Mill to Indofood for US$600 million in a deal that was good news for Liem and his partners, but provided little joy for minority shareholders. Indocement said that the asset shuffle would let it concentrate on making cement, although it would continue to own 40 per cent of Indofood. For its part, Indofood's acquisition would allow it to diversify away from an over-reliance on noodles.[15]

Like Robert Kuok, Liem still sees plenty of growth left in the food industry throughout Asia. He controls the Kentucky Fried Chicken (KFC) franchise in Singapore (through United Industrial Corporation) and Indonesia (through Galeal Group), breeds and processes chickens and pigs in the Riau archipelago and has an abattoir in Singapore. In 1994 Liem bought a stake in Kuantan Flour Mills in Malaysia, apparently the better to link in with Robert Kuok's milling operations.

Liem's Indonesian business partners include several Suharto family members, including Suharto's cousin Sudwikatmono, who is president director and a major shareholder in Indofood and Indocement. Another partner has been Suharto's younger half-brother Probosutedjo, in the clove-import business, while Liem's youngest son and heir apparent, Anthony Salim, is close to Suharto's second son, Bambang Trihatmodjo. Bambang has a share of several Salim joint ventures on Batam island, where Liem is a major investor with the Singapore government in the 500-hectare Batam Industrial Park, part of the 'growth triangle' that links Indonesia's Riau archipelago with Singapore and the Malaysian state of Johor Bahru.[16]

Liem's Salim Group and the Singapore government are also partners in another 4000 hectare industrial park on the neighbouring island of Bintan, which is being developed both for industry and as a major tourist resort. In Singapore, Liem controls the listed United Industrial Corporation property group, which in turn has a majority stake in Singapore Land. Liem's other main Singapore company is Kabila Mandiri Persada (KMP) Pte Ltd, which has interests in food, finance, transport and property and is the major shareholder in UIC.

Liem moved his business headquarters from Central Java to Jakarta in 1952 where he set up a small bank, PT Bank Windu Kentjana, the forerunner to what became Bank Central Asia,

Indonesia's largest private bank with 400 branches. In the mid-1970s, with the help of banker Mochtar Riady [89], head of the Lippo Group, Liem was able to build BCA into the keystone of a formidable financial empire. BCA is owned 23 per cent each by Liem and his sons Andree Halim and Anthony Salim, 30 per cent split between Suharto's eldest son Sigit Harjojudanto (16 per cent) and eldest daughter 'Tutut' Siti Hardijanti Rukmana (14 per cent), while Liem's other son Albert Halim and daughter Macani hold the remaining less than 1 per cent.[17]

Anthony Salim, educated in Singapore and London, is the expected successor and the Salim Group's public face in the English-speaking world. He is the only Salim family member who talks to the media. Anthony heads the main Indonesian holding company, Salim Economic Development Corporation, and is group president and chief executive officer. His elder brother Andree is group vice-chairman, while Liem retains the chairmanship.

In February 1996, Anthony Salim told the *Asian Wall Street Journal*[18] that rice and clean water, two essential ingredients for the health of Indonesia's 200 million people, would figure high on the list of the Salim Group's development plans. He said that the group would cultivate between 100,000 and 300,000 hectares of rice on hitherto unused land in Kalimantan, the Indonesian part of the island of Borneo, at a likely cost of more than US$500 million. In a similar-sized investment, Salim would help supply clean water to the western half of Jakarta, in a joint venture with Lyonnaise des Eaux of France.

One of Liem's other major entities is Jakarta-based Waringin Kencana, which serves as a holding company for much of the group's activities in Indonesia and Singapore.

Much of the Salim Group's regional business now flows through the Hong-Kong-listed First Pacific Company, managed by a team of outside professionals led by managing director Manuel Pangilinan. A soulmate of Anthony Salim, Pangilinan scours the region looking for deals, and First Pacific is reckoned to account for about 40 per cent of the group's turnover. In March 1997 Pangilinan reported a 'year of substantial achievement' in 1996, with net profit of US$202 million on revenue of US$7.03 billion. Pangilinan said that the largest growth in profit contributions came from the group's marketing and distribution interests.[19]

In January 1995 First Pacific struck the jackpot in the Philippines, where its 60-per-cent-owned Metro Pacific led a consortium that picked up Manila's real-estate project of the decade: the right to develop the Fort Bonifacio military camp site, 214 hectares of prime downtown land. The Metro Pacific consortium, which included Liem's old mate Robert Kuok (through Kuok Philippine Properties) and two other billionaire members of the Fujian connection in Andrew Gotianun [63] (Filinvest Development Corp) and Lucio Tan [58] (Allied Bank), bid US$1.6 billion to beat off a host of rivals, including the heavyweight Philippines 'old money' group, the Ayala Corporation. Kuok, who bought a 2 per share of Bonifacio Land, later sold out of the project to Metro Pacific.

Liem's Metro Pacific Corp holds 40 per cent and Gotianun's Filinvest Development holds 20 per cent of Bonifacio Land Corp, which owns 55 per cent of Fort Bonifacio Development Corp (FBDC). The other 45 per cent is held by the Philippines government agency, the Bases Conversion Development Authority.

The Fort Bonifacio project is destined to make the FBDC the biggest landowner in Manila. Although there was an initial view that Metro Pacific had overpaid at an effective price of about 57,500 pesos (US$2350) a square metre in January 1995, a year later the market saw things differently: the land was being quoted at around 150,000 pesos per square metre, well above what Metro said was its breakeven cost of 76,000 pesos. The Fort Bonifacio project is regarded as the Salim Group's single biggest investment offshore, although in time Liem's China play could outstrip it. In the same month as the Fort Bonifacio bid was accepted, the Salim Group signed up another big deal – this time with Japan's Nippon Telephone and Telegraph to work on a telecommunications project in Manila.

The Salim companies in the joint venture are Metro Pacific, First Pacific and its Philippines telecoms offshoot, Smart

Communications, with NTT paying US$123 million for 15 per cent of Smart.

Besides property, Metro Pacific has a food and beverage stake that fits the Liem philosophy. It owns Metro Bottled Water, the leading distributor of distilled water in the Philippines.

Other products include health and energy drinks and an 'affordable' wine from the Philippines' first winery at Cavite. Also in the food business is 98-per-cent-owned Philippine Cocoa, the second biggest chocolate candy manufacturer in the country. Similarly, Hong-Kong-based First Pacific invested US$6 million to make dehydrated potato flakes in China's Liaoning province for sale to Japan.[20]

Liem is the premier *cukong*, an Indonesian term for a Chinese businessman who is a trustworthy supporter of the Indonesian *pribumi* indigenous power élite, primarily the military.

Besides his Suharto family connections, Liem's partners include a string of native Fujianese businessmen, including Djuhar Sutanto [56] and his cousin Henry Pribadi; banking ally Mochtar Riady [89] who heads the Lippo Group; Eka Tjipta Widjaja [25] (Oei Ek Tjhong) who heads Indonesia's second largest conglomerate, the Sinar Mas Group (and like Liem was born in Fujian province); Prajogo Pangestu [49] of Barito Group, who looked after Liem's timber interests; Ibrahim Risjad (one of the original 'Liem investors' from Aceh in northern Sumatra); and of course, fellow International Association of Fuzhous executive, Robert Kuok, with whom Liem shares an interest in hotels, commodity trading and a US$1 billion sugar-cane plantation in Sumatra.

In China, where the Salim Group has indicated that it will invest up to US$1 billion in Fujian province over a five-year period, Liem's KMP and Singapore Land are investing in the Singapore-backed Suzhou Township development consortium. Liem also made a sizeable donation in his home district of Fuqing in Fujian province, with infrastructure and investments in the silk and shoe industries.[21] Other Chinese investments include a cement factory and bonded zone in Wuhan, housing in Tianjin, and cooking-oil, hotel and property interests.

Liem and Kuok also share an interest in the media. The Salim Group owns a television station in Indonesia, while Kuok has become a significant figure in Hong Kong's boisterous newspaper environment. Through Kerry Media, Kuok is chairman and 34.9 per cent owner of South China Morning Post Holdings, which publishes Hong Kong's leading English-language daily newspaper. His frequent business partner and fellow Malaysian Chinese entrepreneur, Khoo Kay Peng [90], who controls Malayan United Industries, owns 22.15 per cent of SCMP. While there was initial speculation that Kuok would enforce a more pro-China editorial line at the *South China Morning Post* after Rupert Murdoch's News Corporation sold out its stake in the paper in 1993, this has not proved to be the case to date.

In another media play, in June 1996, after a four-month tussle with Shaw Brothers, controlled by Hong Kong movie tycoon Sir Run Run Shaw [96], Kuok's SCMP took over TVE Holdings, a property, publishing and entertainment group, for HK$1.15 billion (US$150 million). TVE, which publishes Chinese-language magazines, had been 30 per cent held by Shaw Brothers.

Throughout his career, Kuok has been the consummate dealmaker – whether it be in food, property or the media. And as he has shown over the last half-century, he has been happy to look to the Fujian ancestral connection for partners: when like-minded men like Liem Sioe Liong are ready and willing to deal anywhere and anytime in Asia, Kuok's Fujian connection rolls on and on.

4

Filipino Money-Go-Round

I want to become the biggest home builder in the world.

C&P Homes founder Manuel Villar, August 1995[1]

AT THE BEGINNING OF AUGUST 1996, A 17-YEAR-OLD FILIPINA MAID named Sarah Balabagan sobbed on the shoulder of Philippines Foreign Minister Domingo Siazon as she faced a media blitz at Manila Airport. Sarah, convicted in 1994 of murdering her 85-year-old employer in the United Arab Emirates after he allegedly tried to rape her, was returning home to the Philippines, courtesy of an early release by the President of the UAE, Sheikh Zayad bin Sultan al Nahayan. The act of clemency had been painstakingly negotiated by Philippines President Fidel Ramos. After 100 lashes, spending two years in jail and at one point facing a death sentence, it was clear that Sarah was glad to be home.

Responding almost incoherently to the barrage of questions about how she felt, she thanked President Ramos for not abandoning her and then gave thanks to Filipinos for amassing a 2 million peso fund (about US$80,000) to help her. Among her benefactors was one William Gatchalian, a 48-year-old Filipino-Chinese who rocketed to prominence in the mid-1990s as one of Manila's new breed of property developers. Gatchalian put up 1 million pesos so Sarah would be able to continue her schooling, and also paid 'blood money' to her late employer's family as compensation.[2]

Gatchalian had good reason to be generous to Sarah and the three million other Filipinos who work offshore, mainly as maids in Japan, Hong Kong and the Middle East. It is their billions of dollars of remittances every year that have fuelled the relentless growth of real estate in the Philippines and turned Gatchalian and others like Manuel Villar *[41]*, Jose Go and Andrew Tan into a newly emerging young rich.

For much of the postwar era, Filipino-Spanish 'old money' families like the *illustrados* – the Ayala, Lopez and Soriano clans – along with an older generation of Filipino-Chinese tycoons like Henry Sy *[52]*, John Gokongwei *[85]*, Alfonso Yuchengco *[86]*, George Ty and Lucio Tan *[58]*, dominated the big land developments in Metro Manila. They were the brains behind the shopping malls, the Makati office towers and, more recently, the massive US$1.5 billion Fort Bonifacio project that is changing the face and focus of downtown Manila.

The other dimension to the Filipino land boom is best seen from the perspective of William Gatchalian and Manuel Villar. Millions of low- to middle-income families – often with savings swelled by remittances from offshore workers – have their sights set on a house to call their own, and this is the market on which Villar in particular focuses.

Manuel Villar is something of a surprise packet in the Philippines real-estate race: a 40-something Congressman from Metro Manila, who like most of his competitors started from scratch. But unlike the Filipino-Chinese tycoons who keep their business dealings as private as possible, Villar lets it all hang out.

Foreign investors targeting the Philippines just cannot get enough of C&P Homes, the low-income-housing developer controlled by Villar and his wife, Cynthia. Villar's sensational rise to international prominence began when the company's initial public offering (IPO) in mid-1995 was more than 10 times over-subscribed after a two-week roadshow through the United States, Europe and Asia. It was the second biggest IPO on the Philippines stock exchange (after national oil company Petron) and suddenly the Manila-based Congressman was the focus of foreign interest. Offshore buyers took more than 60 per cent of the 7.2 billion peso (US$300 million) IPS for 566 million shares (representing 20 per cent of its stock) and, after C&P Homes listed on 31 July 1995, they bought up virtually all of the rest. Company executives said that most of the offshore interest came from pension funds and emerging market funds.[3] With profits up 150 per cent in 1995 and consumer demand outstripping C&P Homes's initial plans to build 27,000 houses in 1996, the foreign investors' enthusiasm was understandable.

Another reason was that chairman and chief executive Manuel Villar was guiding the company's destiny. At 46, Villar has become the new darling of the international property industry and a man who aspires to be the world's biggest builder of homes. For the past 20 years, he has focused on the low-income bracket (where a house costs from US$8000 to $25000) but is starting to raise his sights as demand for bigger houses flows from a growing middle class in the Philippines.

With his wife Cynthia, Villar still holds 80 per cent of C&P Homes, which had a market capitalization of more than US$2.1 billion in early 1997. This, along with a land bank in the Metro Manila environs valued at about US$2 billion, has rapidly propelled the Villar family to the top ranks of the Philippines rich list.

Villar's rise is the tale of a Manila boy made good. One of eight children, Villar delivered shrimps for his mother as a youngster (his father was a public servant), studied for an accounting degree at the University of the Philippines and later joined SyCip Gorres Velayo (SGV), one of the nation's top accountancy practices.

But eager to make his mark as an entrepreneur, Villar got into the building game in his mid-twenties and started the forerunner of C&P Homes. By focusing on housing for low-income earners and providing all the paperwork needed to get a government loan, Villar's company soon found its market niche. Owner-occupiers made for safe mortgages, and C&P Homes also tapped into the three-million-strong network of Filipino overseas workers and their strong urge to buy a house and land for their families with the money they make offshore.

Today, more than 90 per cent of the houses sold by C&P Homes go for less than Ps500,000 (about US$25,000), with the most popular design being a 35 square metre house on a 50 square metre block of land. But rising incomes are pushing up demand in the US$50,000 range, where a 100 square metre property is available. The company said that it expected demand for its bigger houses to double to about 10 per cent of the 27,000 homes it planned to build in 1996.

Villar, who was re-elected to the House of Representatives in May 1995 as Congressman for suburban Las Piñas, said that support for housing had been a consistent policy of all governments in the Philippines.[4] This was unlikely to change, and as C&P Homes sold to people who lived in their houses, rather than to speculators, there was little likelihood of the company being hurt in a cyclical downturn in the property market.

Not long after C&P Homes listed on the Philippines stock exchange and it was clear that Villar was in the billionaire class, he told *Asiaweek* magazine that he wanted to set an example to Filipino entrepreneurs. 'A lot of our people believe that Filipinos by nature can't make it in business, that only the Chinese have the capability. I have shown that it can be done,' he said.[5] With the stock riding high through 1996–97, Villar could afford to be confident. Foreign investors who watched C&P Homes's performance hoped that the next year's profit figures would back up Villar's proud claim.

Villar had indeed shown it could be done, but the Filipino-Chinese grip on real estate shows no sign of weakening. Villar's main rival, William Gatchalian, like so many other big fish in the Chinese diaspora, hails from Xiamen in China's Fujian province. The other high-flyer targeting the low end of the property market, Jose Go, is a 48-year-old Filipino-Chinese (also with family roots in Xiamen), who has developed the concept of discount malls to an art form. His Ever-Gotesco Grand Central mall on the northern

Household incomes above US$1000, 1995–2000

Market	1995 Households in millions and % of total		2000 Forecast households (m) and % of total		Annual average market growth (%)
Japan	49.6	91	53.2	96	1.4
South Korea	11.1	79	12.4	85	2.4
Taiwan	5.6	85	6.2	90	2.1
Hong Kong	1.3	73	1.4	77	1.1
Singapore	0.8	78	1.0	88	4.4
Malaysia	0.8	15	1.8	30	17.5
Philippines	0.4	2.5	1.1	6	20.9
Thailand	0.8	4.5	2.0	11	20.9
Indonesia	0.9	1.8	2.5	4.5	22.2
China	6.8	1.8	20.8	5	25.0
India	4.5	1.9	16.6	6.5	29.8

Source: EIU Country Forecasting Service

outskirts of Manila is for cheap-as-chips shoppers; Go wants volume, volume, volume, so that he can keep prices way down for his customers. With per capita income still only US$1100 a year – compared with US$4000 in neighbouring Malaysia and US$2700 in Thailand – Go figures that the Philippines' 70 million people will have a large low-income component for many years to come.

Go and Gatchalian provide a striking contrast to Villar. Where Villar has had a single-minded desire for the past 20 years to become the world's biggest home-builder, Go and Gatchalian have seen a life outside property. Both have a fascination with aviation: Go has his own helicopter for flitting between his six shopping malls and his own slice of the upscale action – the Evercrest golf resort outside Manila and the Evercrest White Cove beach resort in Batangas province.[6]

For his part, Gatchalian launched into aviation with Air

Philippines in March 1995. He set up the domestic carrier for a tilt at one of the Philippines' biggest taipans: Lucio Tan (another Xiamen immigrant), who controls the long-established Philippine Airlines. Another domestic carrier with overseas aspirations, Grand International Airways, appeared at about the same time. One year later, there was even more competition for Tan and Gatchalian in the shape of John Gokongwei, who established Cebu Pacific Air as a low-cost, no-frills airline, with a declared ambition to be PAL's main rival within five years. The competition from Gokongwei was an interesting counterpoint. Gatchalian holds a sizeable stake in Philippines Commercial International Bank, which is controlled by John Gokongwei and media tycoon Eugenio Lopez [69].

Gatchalian's business spread is nothing if not diverse: besides property, aviation and banking, his interests extend to plastics, energy, exploration and cocoa estates. His land bank includes low-cost housing estates in the provinces of Cavite, Bulacan and Cebu, and more upmarket projects in central Manila such as the 37 hectare New City Plaza commercial centre.

Gatchalian is yet to crack the billionaire status, but claims to be closing fast on his property role models like Gokongwei and the other mall-master, Henry Sy. Fujian-born Sy, acknowledged as the nation's retail king with nine department stores and five malls in his flagship SM chain, built the Philippines' first mega-mall, SM City in 1985. That was such a huge success that he quickly followed with more, including the SM Megamall in Manila's Mandaluyong city. At 1500 metres long and six storeys high, it is Asia's biggest mall; more than 300,000 people drop in daily to gawk, shop and play. Sy pulls the crowds with a combination of entertainment (cinemas, video game halls, ice-skating), a huge range of goods and relatively low prices.[7]

It wasn't always like this for Sy. In 1937, aged 12, he emigrated from Fujian with his parents, worked in the family store in Manila and later, while studying at university, made his first business foray with a shoe-selling operation after the war. In 1948 he opened his first shoe store and by 1960 had created ShoeMart –

the forerunner of his SM empire today that includes the listed SM Prime Holdings (operator of the malls) and listed SM Fund, which he said in March 1996 would be transformed from an investment fund into a property and development company to be known as SM Development. A third listed company is Fortune Cement. Sy took SM Prime public in June 1994, raising 4.7 billion pesos in an initial public offering. The Sy family still holds a massive 83 per cent of the shares, worth more than US$2.0 billion on SM Prime's market capitalization of US$2.6 billion in early 1997. Sy's main vehicle is his 100-per-cent-owned holding company, SM Investments Corp, which covers a spread of more than 25 companies in seven main business sectors: retail merchandising; malls; banking and finance; securities; real estate; manufacturing; and tourism and entertainment.

Sy, like most of his entrepreneur colleagues, has a controlling interest in a bank. In his case it is Banco de Oro, but in addition he has amassed a controlling 14 per cent stake in China Banking Corp, and smaller stakes in Far East Bank & Trust Co (controlled by Gokongwei) and Philippines National Bank. He also holds part of the property-based Ayala Corporation.[8]

Sy's six children (four sons, two daughters) all have a specific role in the business. Henry Jr looks after real estate, while the eldest child and Sy's apparent successor, Teresita Sy-Coson, 43, is president of Shoemart Inc and Banco de Oro. While Sy's offshore investments include a property development in the family's ancestral home of Xiamen in China's Fujian province, the Philippines remains his focus. In May 1996 he announced four new malls to open in 1997–98, including three in Metro Manila and one in Iloilo in the central Philippines. At the SM Group's Manila Bay reclamation project, Sy said that he would build his biggest mall yet – the Mall of Asia, destined to be the centrepiece of the 60 hectare commercial and residential 'Boulevard 2000' project along Roxas Boulevard.[9]

Despite newcomers like Jose Go and William Gatchalian, Sy's main competitor in the mall wars has always been John Gokongwei, the Cebu-born ethnic Chinese tycoon who built his first mall in Manila in 1987, two years after Sy's SM City. In the turbulent days after the fall of President Ferdinand Marcos in 1986, real estate in the Philippines was cheap but there were few takers. Gokongwei saw the potential and bought land in the now-booming Ortigas business district, where he built his Robinson's Galleria mall. Today, it draws 40 million shoppers a year.

Gokongwei was born in 1927 into a wealthy trading family originally from China.[10] Gokongwei's grandfather Pedro Gotiaoco set up Gotiaoco Hermanos in the nineteenth century and built it into one of the biggest enterprises in Cebu. But the family fortune was lost during the war and by the 1940s it was Gokongwei's responsibility to feed six siblings during the difficult years of the Japanese occupation. He started his business career as a small wartime trader, buying and selling rice, cloth, scrap metal – anything he could get his hands on. After the war, he moved into food processing, initially setting up a cornstarch factory called Universal Corn Products with his brothers. From there he ventured into textile production, property development, retailing and, later, banking, aviation, petrochemicals, infrastructure and telecommunications. Along the way, Gokongwei managed to give himself a decent education, with an MBA from De La Salle University, and attendance at Harvard Business School's advanced management program. Gokongwei even made a tilt at the nation's biggest blue-chip corporation, San Miguel, in the 1970s, but was rebuffed by the controlling Soriano family after building – and later selling – a 4 per cent stake.[11]

His holding company for a host of subsidiaries and affiliates is the listed JG Summit, which had a market capitalization of US$1.2 billion in early 1997. Other companies in the Gokongwei stable are listed Universal Robina Corp, listed Robinson's Land Corp, PCI Bank, PCI Insurance Brokers, PCI Capital Corp and Philippine Commercial Credit Card Inc. In 1993, Gokongwei moved quickly when an opportunity opened up to grab the 40 per cent stake of British-based Cable and Wireless in the new phone company Digitel Telecom. He built that into a controlling 57 per cent stake and the presidency of Digitel, which he said in August

1996 had an expanding subscriber base that would make it the nation's second largest carrier after Philippine Long Distance Telephone (PLDT).[12] His power and oil interests are through 20 per cent stakes respectively in First Philippine Power Corp (with old partner Eugenio Lopez) and Oriental Petroleum and Minerals Corp. Gokongwei's latest property developments include Robinsons Tower, a 30,000 square metre block in Makati, and the 81,000 square metre PCIB Tower in Ortigas.

Gokongwei's brothers Henry, Ignacio, Johnson and James and sister Lily work in the business with him in Manila and at home base in Cebu, as do his children, including daughter Robina, after whom his food company Universal Robina Corp is named. His son, Lance, born in 1966 and a graduate of the University of Pennsylvania's Wharton School of Finance in the United States, is senior vice-president of JG Summit and heir apparent. The Gokongwei family fortune is reckoned to be around US$1.3 billion.

With about the same level of wealth and aspirations as the Gokongwei clan are Andrew Gotianun Sr [63] and his family, who control the nation's seventh largest listed company, Filinvest Development Corporation (FDC). Gotianun has a lock on one of the Philippines' biggest property developments: a joint venture deal with the government, covering a 244 hectare site 15km from Makati at Alabang (between Metro Manila and the rapidly indus-trializing Calabarzon area to the south), where it will build a glam-orous 'Corporate City'. This massive development, predictably enough, includes a 3 billion peso, 20 hectare shopping mall called Festival Supermall, designed to win business from Henry Sy and John Gokongwei in the continuing mall wars of the 1990s.

Gotianun describes Filinvest Corporate City (80 per cent owned by FDC) as the company's flagship effort and by far its largest project to date.[13] But equally important in the revenue stakes could be Filinvest's 16 per cent stake in the massive Fort Bonifacio Global City project, which is converting an old military camp in the heart of Manila into prime commercial and residen-tial property. Leader of the consortium which successfully bid US$1.6 billion for Fort Bonifacio in January 1995 (ousting the

Ayala clan's bid along the way) was Metro Pacific, controlled by Indonesian tycoon Liem Sioe Liong's Salim Group. Along with Gotianun, Metro Pacific's partners included another substantial Filipino-Chinese tycoon, Lucio Tan. Fort Bonifacio Development Corporation chief executive Ricardo Pascua, formerly with Metro Pacific, said that the Global City project would eventually be three times the size of Makati, with more than 9 million square metres of office and residential space.

Almost two years after winning, Pascua recounted how the consortium came to bid the precise amount of 33,283.88 pesos per square metre. With help from First Pacific's Cantonese treasurer, David Wong, the group worked out some 'nice numbers' in Cantonese that gave the bid the highly focused meaning of 'business-business-easy-money-business-money-money'.

So, despite the traffic gridlock and inadequate services that hinder Manila's development, the property race is on between Fort Bonifacio, Gotianun's Corporate City at Alabang, and Henry Sy's Boulevard 2000 along Roxas Boulevard.

Gotianun, who started in business in 1955 by financing used cars, moved into other areas of consumer financing in the 1960s, and in 1970 started the Family Savings Bank. By the time the family divested it 14 years later, it had grown into the largest savings bank in the Philippines. The Gotianuns now control a commercial bank, the East-West Banking Corp.

In May 1996 Andrew Gotianun Sr, who had been appointed chairman of Fort Bonifacio Development Corporation early in 1995, decided that Alabang would need his full-time attention in his capacity as FDC chairman and president. He resigned the presidency of FDC's 70-per-cent-held real-estate subsidiary Filinvest Land Inc in favour of his wife Mercedes, so that he could concentrate on FDC.[14]

Amid the frantic pace of Filipino-Chinese real-estate projects, the conservative Ayala Corporation [34] seems to be almost glacial in its approach, even with a youthful president, Jaime Augusto Zobel de Ayala II, at the helm.

Harvard-educated Mr Zobel, or JAZA, was just 36 when he

took over from his father, Don Jaime Zobel de Ayala, in a smooth transition at the start of 1995.[15] That is simply the style of this oldest and richest of the *illustrados* families. Through its 160-year history, the Ayala Corporation has had to steer through some rough political and commercial waters, but has always managed to do so with a minimum of fuss.

Even when Ayala Land Inc (ALI) lost out to Metro Pacific early in 1995 in the Fort Bonifacio 'deal of the century', Mr Zobel was not too concerned. 'No regrets' was his simple summary of the result. A year later, he had good reason to be pleased: Ayala Corporation reported a record net profit in 1995 of US$209 million, mainly on the strength of a massive US$120 million profit contribution (up 44 per cent) from Ayala Land. The 1996 result was even better – group net profit rose 14 per cent to US$236 million.

Mr Zobel's father, Don Zobel, spent 36 years with Ayala Corp, including an 11-year term as president that covered the difficult years of the Benigno Aquino assassination, the fall of Marcos and the economic disasters of the late 1980s. Just before he stepped down, he called for a greater sense of teamwork in the private business sector.[16]

The Ayala family (estimated net worth US$2.3 billion) has interests in real estate, banking, hotels, agribusiness, financial services and insurance, electronics, aviation and telecommunications. The group's 15 subsidiaries include Ayala Land, BPI, Pure Foods Corp, Globe Telecom (a joint venture with Singapore Telecom), Ayala Life Assurance and Ayala Systems Technology.

Ayala Land (market capitalization US$6.6 billion in early 1997) is expected to remain the biggest contributor to the family's wealth. It is developing a complex of high-tech office buildings, starting with Tower One, called the Ayala Triangle in Makati, the glamour financial district that it largely transformed from swampland into Manila's most prestigious address. And long term, Ayala is eyeing a large tract in Canlubang, 50km south of Manila, for a showpiece residential estate. As always, this oldest of clans takes the long view when it comes to creating wealth in the Philippines.

5

Hong Kong's Land Barons

In our society, yesterday's hawker can be today's millionaire; and if he over-reaches his cashflow and is forced back to his street stall to begin all over again, nobody will think the worse of him but will admire his courage for trying that hard.

Sir David Ford, Hong Kong Chief Secretary, 1987–93[1]

WHILE THE FILIPINO-CHINESE WERE FAST REDEVELOPING METRO Manila and its environs, their relatives in Hong Kong were contemplating property developments and infrastructure projects of staggering size, such as the US$5 billion airport railway station project in the Hong Kong central business district.

Infrastructure kings like Cheng Yu-tung *[37]*, Lee Shau-kee *[4]* and Li Ka-shing *[6]*, while targeting the emerging Chinese market, found that Hong Kong still had plenty to offer. The Chek Lap Kok airport, due to open in 1998, and the associated road, rail, tunnel, bridge and office space projects that go with it, have created one of the biggest building opportunities of the 1990s. The developers who stood ready to share in the spoils of Hong Kong's appetite for advancement in the 1990s had themselves grown large from a succession of postwar land booms and busts.

These land barons knew the secret: buy position and buy amid turmoil, when those around you fear a falling market.

Hong Kong's first land baron, a luckless British naval officer by the name of Captain Charles Elliot, preceded the billionaire developers of the late twentieth century by more than 120 years.

In 1839 Elliot was Superintendent of Trade – the senior British Government representative – in the southern Chinese city then known as Canton (Guangzhou) when the new Chinese Commissioner, Lin Tse-hsu, laid siege to the foreign factories for six weeks. Commissioner Lin, in a bid to stem the illegal but lucrative opium trade into China, demanded that the foreigners surrender their opium stocks. He surrounded their factories, cut off their food and forbade anyone to leave. In the end, Lin got what he wanted – 20,283 chests of opium were surrendered and destroyed.[2]

Predictably, Lin's action infuriated the British Foreign Secretary, Lord Palmerston, who demanded either a commercial treaty to regulate the trade relationship with China, or a small island which could serve as a home for the British, free from harassment.

Palmerston's demands precipitated the first Opium War (1840–42), during which the island of Hong Kong was ceded to the British under the treaty of Chuenpi on 20 January 1841. Elliot took possession of the island and by June was selling off the first plots. Thus began foreign settlement on the barren rock which had seen evidence of human activity – mainly maritime based – for 6000 years.

Although the Chinese Emperor had ceded Hong Kong to Britain's Queen Victoria 'in perpetuity', Palmerston was not happy with the deal achieved by Elliot. Hong Kong was not the island of his dreams – he saw it simply as a 'barren island with hardly a house on it'. For his sins, Captain Elliot was replaced in 1841 and admonished by the imperious Palmerston, who declared: 'You have treated my instructions as if they were waste paper.'[3]

Waste paper or not, Elliot's successor Sir Henry Pottinger held on to the island and ensured that it would become the main trading post with China. By 1860, after the second Sino-British war, land on the Kowloon side had also been ceded to Britain, and in

1898, the New Territories were leased for 99 years.

From just over 30,000 people in 1851, the population rose to 880,000 in 1931 – 97 per cent of whom were Chinese. The southern advance of the Japanese into China in the late 1930s sent 750,000 more refugees streaming into Hong Kong between 1937 and 1939, so that by the time Hong Kong itself was attacked by the Japanese in December 1941, 1.6 million people were in the colony. By war's end the population was down to 600,000, but it rapidly built up again in the late 1940s. When the communists gained the upper hand in the Chinese civil war with the nationalists, another wave of humanity reached Hong Kong.

Hundreds of thousands of refugees fled from Shanghai, Guangzhou and other big cities along the South China coast, boosting Hong Kong's population to more than 2 million by 1950.[4]

Then the real work began, of developing a city that could sustain this population. One of the keys to its entrepreneurs' success in those early years was their ability to tap into funds – gold and cash from family sources, or from clan, guild and dialect networks, and even from the formal financial world represented by banks like the Hongkong and Shanghai Banking Corporation.

By 1996, Hong Kong was home to 185 licensed banks, including 81 of the world's top 100 banks. Despite misgivings about the July 1997 handover to China, business confidence generally was high, and top bankers like Vincent Cheng downplayed any threat to Hong Kong's pre-eminence as the region's financial centre. Shanghai, he said, could never adopt Hong Kong's way of life.[5]

Cheng, the Hongkong Bank's executive director, sat in his office overlooking Victoria Harbour in mid-1996 and ticked off the slings and arrows of Hong Kong's outrageous fortune over the preceding half a century.

It was a sobering list: riots in 1954 and 1957; a bank crisis in 1964; the spillover of the Cultural Revolution in 1967; an energy crisis in 1975; a loss of confidence during the Sino-British talks of 1982–84; the stock-market crash of 1987; the Tiananmen Square massacre of 1989; and the political arguments of 1993–95.

'The point is, we have seen ourselves weather all these

problems, but economic growth continues. In the same way, we will get through 1997 because the economic fundamentals are still sound,' Cheng said.

Adaptability and a willingness to change have been the secrets of Hong Kong's steady rise to a position where it has the highest per capita income in Asia after Japan.

In the early 1950s the Korean War embargo on China cost Hong Kong most of its trading activity, but it adapted by becoming a manufacturing centre. From the 1970s, services assumed more importance, and the opening up of China in 1978–79 enabled Hong Kong to move much of its manufacturing to nearby Chinese provinces like Guangdong.

'We make our future. We always have,' Mr Cheng declared. He might have added, and banks like us have helped make a bright and shiny future for billionaire entrepreneurs like Li Ka-shing.

On the slopes of Hong Kong's swish Mid-Levels, Li Ka-shing annoyed the neighbours for much of 1995–96 with the noisy construction of a very special gift: a HK$1 billion showpiece building for China's Foreign Affairs Ministry for the post-July 1997 period. As rockdrills and piledrivers hammered away on the 20-storey complex in Macdonnell Road, Li was busy elsewhere, spinning off a new corporate vehicle for his China plays – Cheung Kong Infrastructure.

Li, known as 'Superman' to Hong Kong's residents, is not the territory's richest tycoon – that distinction oscillates between the Kwok family [2] (which has a controlling 45.6 per cent stake in property developer Sun Hung Kai Properties, market capitalization US$29.6 billion) and Lee Shau-kee, who holds 68.2 per cent of Henderson Land Development (market capitalization US$16.2 billion) and a stake in Sun Hung Kai Properties as well. Depending on the state of the market, Lee and the Kwoks each have estimated net worth of US$11 to $13.5 billion. Poor Li languishes in third place on a miniscule US$8 billion. Or does he?

In January 1997, Li unveiled a major reorganization of his corporate empire, designed, he said, by eldest son Victor to streamline the companies' operations, deliver greater profits to shareholders and make it easier for Li to pass control to Victor and Li's younger son, Richard. It was an offer of '24 carat gold at copper prices', he said. The one thing immediately clear from the complex deal was that Li and his sons would be better off by several hundred million dollars.

Before the reorganization, Li controlled four key listed entities in Hong Kong: his flagship Cheung Kong (Holdings) Ltd (held 33.6 per cent); the ports and telecoms conglomerate Hutchison Whampoa (45.6 per cent, almost all through Cheung Kong); Hong Kong island's monopoly electricity supplier Hong Kong Electric Holdings (35 per cent through Hutchison); and the newest, the China power and roads play Cheung Kong Infrastructure (CKI), listed in July 1996 and held 70.66 per cent through Cheung Kong and 3.93 per cent through Hutchison. In Li's proposed three-stage deal, Cheung Kong moves to 50.17 per cent control of Hutchison; Hutchison ends up with 84.6 per cent of CKI and CKI holds up to 50 per cent of Hong Kong Electric. The market voted with its feet – a rush to Cheung Kong (Holdings), the company closest to Li and described as existing solely for the benefit of the Li family.

The market value of his stake in Cheung Kong (Holdings) alone is more than US$6.6 billion, but that represents only the most visible portion of Li's asset spread. And these days, he keeps his shares in Cheung Kong safely tucked away in the Cayman Islands – like any good tycoon concerned for the financial well-being of his sons and heirs Victor and Richard, to save on inheritance taxes. Victor Li is deputy chairman of Cheung Kong (Holdings) – which turned in a 1995 profit of US$1.44 billion – and an executive director of Hutchison Whampoa. In November 1996, Cheung Kong (Holdings) and Hutchison Whampoa announced that they would spend more than US$1.2 billion in 1997 on land premiums and acquisitions, following by one day a similar announcement of a US$1.2 billion land spending spree by Henderson Land's Lee Shau-kee. Li also holds 20 per cent of construction company Paul Y-ITC Construction.

Li Ka-shing's rise to great wealth began in the 1940s.[6] Born in the coastal city of Chiuzhou in southern China's Guangdong province in 1928, Li moved with his family to Hong Kong in 1940. His father, schoolteacher Li Wen-kin, died of tuberculosis two years later and so Li got a job to support his mother and two siblings. He sold plastic flowers, toys and watch bands, gradually building up a fighting fund of HK$50,000 that would allow him to start his own plastics factory in 1950 in Hong Kong. He set up Cheung Kong in the mid-1950s and presided over 40 years of growth that saw it listed on the Hong Kong exchange in 1972, and reach a market capitalization of US$23 billion in early 1997.

In the 1960s, Li moved into property development and cement manufacturing, but his first real step towards regional prominence came when he bought a 22 per cent stake in Hutchison from the Hongkong Bank in 1979. Thus he became the first Chinese major shareholder in one of the old British *hongs*, or trading companies, in Hong Kong. Since then, he has lifted Cheung Kong's stake in Hutchison Whampoa to 45.6 per cent (and rising) and taken control of a range of other international investments, including Husky Oil in Canada, and the telecommunications company Orange plc in the United Kingdom, which he started in 1994 as a joint venture with British Aerospace.

Orange, a mobile phone operator which suffered heavy set-up losses in its first two years, began trading on the London Stock Exchange in March 1996 after an initial public offering by Li's Hutchison raised US$666 million. This left Hutchison with a 50 per cent stake in Orange valued at US$1.9 billion.

It looked like Li's US$1.1 billion investment in Orange would pay off – it became the fastest-growing mobile-phone service in Britain, with sales projected to reach more than US$780 million in 1997. Stealing market share from competitors like Vodafone and Cellnet, Orange was likely to have 25 per cent of Britain's US$4 billion cellular market by 2000.

Apart from Orange, Li also holds almost 10 per cent of Canada's largest bank (by assets), the Canadian Imperial Bank of Commerce, and Hutchison Whampoa has almost 10 per cent of China Strategic Holdings, the well-connected Hong-Kong-listed company run by Oei Hong Leong. Oei is the son of Eka Tjipta

Widjaja [25], the billionaire founder of Indonesia's second largest conglomerate, Sinar Mas.

But not everything pans out perfectly for 'Superman' Li. Since late 1994, work on a US$1.5 billion shopping and office complex that Li aimed to build in downtown Beijing under the title Oriental Plaza had been stalled by a series of 'technical problems'. Apart from a change of heart by Beijing city authorities about the size of the development, one problem was that the massive site near busy Wangfujing Street included Beijing's most popular McDonald's restaurant, a 700-seater which opened in April 1992. In November 1994 there was talk that the restaurant would have to go, to make way for Oriental Plaza, whose consortium members included the Beijing municipal government. But even Li's high-level Chinese connections could not overcome the consumer appeal of the Golden Arches; it took two years for the world's biggest, busiest burger joint to succumb. On Monday 2 December 1996, McDonald's finally closed the Wangfujing Street store, after resisting a removal order on the grounds that it held a 20-year lease. It will rebuild elsewhere, giving the long-awaited green light for Li's Oriental Plaza development, so long a forlorn and moribund site in the heart of Beijing.

Still, Li has built a string of business alliances in China that he expects to bear fruit. He is a leading member of the Teochiu (dialect group) chamber of commerce in Hong Kong, and funded the establishment of a university in Shantou, the ancestral home of the Teochius (many of whom, such as the Sophonpanich clan of Bangkok Bank fame, migrated to Thailand).

Like his colleague and occasional business partner Lee Shau-kee, Li is an adviser to the Chinese government on Hong Kong matters. In the early 1990s, authors Evelyn Huang and Lawrence Jeffery interviewed Li for their book, *Hong Kong: Portraits of Power*. When they quizzed him about his thoughts on China, he told them: 'My present commitment to China represents 20 per cent of the total assets of my company. And that will grow.'[7]

Huang and Jeffery also described the scene of their interview with Li: 'The most striking feature in the office is a bank of four

televisions arranged against the wall facing his desk. Three of
these show views of the approach to his office: the lift, the waiting
room and the hall. A popular Chinese soap opera is playing on the
fourth.' Perhaps that fascination for television screens was shared
by his youngest son, Richard, who had emerged as a media player in his own right by the mid-1990s.

Li's wife Amy died in 1990. His sons Victor Li Tzar-kuoi, born
in 1964, and Richard Li Tzar-kai, born in 1966, both studied at
Stanford University and spent a considerable time in North
America. Victor, a Canadian citizen, graduated from Stanford in
1985, married Cynthia Wong in 1993 and is Li's heir apparent.
Richard, after time at Stanford, studied at the London Business
School, where he would have watched the emergence of BSkyB,
the UK satellite broadcaster controlled by Rupert Murdoch's News
Corporation. With a stake of about US$125 million from Hutchison
Whampoa and his father's blessing, Richard set up Asia's first
regional satellite television network, Star TV, in 1991 and then two
years later did the sort of deal that would make his father proud.
He sold off a 63.6 per cent stake to Murdoch's News Corporation
for US$525 million in 1993. As one of Richard Li's executives was
to observe a few years later in Hong Kong, it was a 'top deal' for
the young businessman.[8] Whether Murdoch thought he also had a
top deal was not clear, until News bought the rest of Hutchison's
stake in Star TV for US$300 million in 1995. Murdoch was buying
a unique, front-running and very large piece of Asia's media
future, and was prepared to pay the premium.

While his father and elder brother concentrated on Cheung
Kong (Holdings) and Hutchison Whampoa, Richard Li established his own Pacific Century group in 1993, with an initial focus
on telecommunications and financial services. Over the next three
years, he built up a US$500 million war chest (boosted by the sale
to Hutchison Whampoa of his telecommunications business for
US$75 million in November 1995 to avoid 'potential conflict of
interest') and began expanding into property and infrastructure
projects, including in China. While there was speculation that
Pacific Century's Singapore-listed unit Pacific Century Regional

Developments was a vehicle to help diversify the Li family assets out of Singapore, this was denied by company executives.

Li senior had his own China infrastructure vehicle ready for action. His spin-off of Cheung Kong Infrastructure from his Cheung Kong (Holdings) flagship in mid-1996 followed a trail already pioneered by the Cheng family's New World Development and Lee Shau-kee's Henderson Land Development, both of which have been big investors in China.

One of Li's first moves was to take a 50 per cent stake in the proposed 40km ring-road project in the southern Chinese city of Guangzhou, put forward by Hong Kong's embattled 'Mr Infrastructure', Gordon Wu [78] of Hopewell Holdings. Wu's part of the stalled road project runs east, south and west of the city. In contrast to Wu's experience of delays and problems with finance and approvals, Cheng's New World Development completed its 22km northern section of the ring road by January 1994 and immediately began generating revenue from it.[9]

New World is one of the most aggressive Hong Kong investors in China – and one concerned about the future of China's offshore relations and image. When Hong Kong's business community thought the outside world was getting too nervous about the transition to Chinese sovereignty in July 1997, the tycoons got together to do something about it, with the Cheng family leading the way.

The business leaders set up the Better Hong Kong Foundation in 1995 to boost business confidence in Hong Kong, with a membership list like a roll call of the territory's monied élite – Li Ka-shing, Lee Shau-kee [4], Cheng Yu-tung [37], Peter Woo [26], Stanley Ho [42] and Robert Ng were just some of the 20 tycoons who agreed to serve as trustees. Apart from the prestige of their names, they also each chipped in HK$5 million (US$650,000) for a fighting fund to take their message to the world.

The post of chairman of the foundation's advisory council went to Henry Cheng Kar-shun, 48-year-old son of the New World Development group's founder and chairman, Cheng Yu-tung.

Inside an ornately decorated office in the New World Tower on Queen's Road in Hong Kong's Central district, Henry Cheng exudes confidence. Despite the big money he has riding on the future, he is as relaxed as the tropical fish swimming lazily in a large tank that dominates his office.

'Our objective is to present a more accurate picture of Hong Kong, one that gives the whole facts. We want to boost confidence in the investment environment here,' he said.[10]

Cheng took a business delegation to Beijing in January 1996 to meet the Chinese Premier, Li Peng. He was, he said, heartened by the positive response he got from the Chinese leadership. 'They are sincere about Hong Kong's future under the one country, two systems model.'

Cheng said that New World was showing by its investment actions that it believed in China. 'We are one of the largest investors there, with close to US$2 billion invested, mainly in infrastructure, low-cost housing and real estate.'

Other interests include management of New World hotels in the Chinese cities of Guangzhou, Shanghai, Beijing, Harbin and Shenyang, and Ramada hotels in Wuhan and Qingdao.

'No one can predict what changes may happen, but I have full confidence that Hong Kong will not be in distress, and any impact can be overcome,' he said in an interview in mid-1996.

Henry Cheng is putting both the family's money and his own reputation on the line in China. Until recently Cheng was seen as being too much under his father's thumb, the legacy of some deals that went wrong when Cheng Yu-tung briefly retired. The old man came back and took control. But Henry is the China player: success with the hotels, roads, bridges, power plants and residential property he is developing there will cement his place as a second-generation tycoon. If he falters, can Cheng senior come to the rescue again, or will Henry's younger brother Peter take over? One thing is clear – Henry Cheng will never know the same life as his father.

Cheng Yu-tung was born in Guangdong province in 1925,[11] moving to Macau in 1939 to work in a gold shop, then on to Hong

Kong at the war's end to run his uncle's jewellery store, Chow Tai Fook Jewellery. The post-war years were difficult in Hong Kong, but the family business survived. Cheng senior eventually bought the jewellery business, prospered and moved into real estate, surviving the riots that shook Hong Kong during the spillover of the Cultural Revolution in 1967. The Tai Fook name survives, in the jewellery business, in a financial services company and in the vehicle that Cheng uses to control New World: the privately held Chow Tai Fook Enterprises. Cheng went on to develop one of the prime sites in Hong Kong – a vast slab of the Kowloon side waterfront near the Star Ferry. This became the group's first signature development: the New World Centre. And after dabbling in China since 1980, Cheng began investing there seriously in the wake of the 1989 Tiananmen Square massacre. He and son Henry are confident enough to put 20 per cent of New World's assets into China.

One family which does not fully share the same avid enthusiasm for China is the Kwok clan [2], led by brothers Walter, Thomas and Raymond. With an estimated net worth of US$13.5 billion through their 45.6 per cent stake in Sun Hung Kai Properties, the Kwoks are regarded as Hong Kong's richest family.

Sun Hung Kai Properties was founded by their late father Kwok Tak-sing. Kwok senior, who died in 1990, came to Hong Kong from Guangzhou in 1946 and went into partnership with another property entrepreneur, Lee Shau-kee, to establish the company in 1963.

The Sun Hung Kai group, which develops residential land mainly in Hong Kong's New Territories, annually rates as the best-run and most dynamic entity in Hong Kong. Among its office developments on Hong Kong island, Sun Hung Kai built the 78-story Central Plaza building at Wanchai, the tallest office block in Asia until its eclipse in 1996 by the 88 storeys of the Petronas Twin Towers in Kuala Lumpur.

In March 1996, the Kwok family and Lee Shau-kee combined to head a consortium that won a plum Hong Kong development: the new airport railway station in Central. There, they intend to build the tallest tower in Hong Kong: at least 80 to 85 storeys high and, at 400 metres plus, a rival to the 88-storey hotel and office block planned to rise above the future Kowloon station. The Kwoks still have a large stake in Central Plaza, which rises 374 metres above Wanchai.[12]

The three Kwok brothers were educated in the UK and the US. Walter, the eldest and family spokesman, trained as a civil engineer and is chairman and chief executive officer of the company. Thomas and Raymond both carry the title vice-chairman and managing director. Unlike their father, who worked seven days a week, the brothers work 'only' six days a week, and like to go boating on Sundays or dine *en famille*.[13]

Their frequent partner and a significant shareholder in SHK Properties is Lee Shau-kee [4], the property and finance magnate who chairs Henderson Land Development. Lee was born in 1928 in Shun Tak county of southern China's Guangdong province.

Married with five children, Lee is generally regarded as Hong Kong's richest individual, with a fortune estimated at up to US$11 billion. He arrived in Hong Kong from southern China in 1947, where his father was a banker. His first job in Hong Kong was as a dealer with a finance and foreign exchange company, and in 1956 he was one of a group of eight investors to found Eternal Enterprises. Among his co-shareholders was the Kwoks' father, Kwok Tak-sing, with whom Lee founded Sun Hung Kai Properties to develop extensive real-estate interests in Hong Kong.[14]

Today SHK Properties is the largest developer in Hong Kong, with a market capitalization of US$29.6 billion. Lee's flagship is Henderson Land, the company he set up on his own in 1976, while keeping his pivotal role in SHK Properties. In terms of market size, Henderson Land ranks third among Hong Kong's big developers, behind Li Ka-shing's second-ranked Cheung Kong (Holdings).

Lee's interests today, in addition to Henderson Land and SHK Properties, include a string of companies such as Hong Kong & China Gas, Hong Kong Ferry, Miramar Hotel & Investment, and property investments in China, Singapore and North America.

His children work in his companies, with son Peter serving as vice-chairman of Henderson Land. As a member of the Preparatory Committee and the Better Hong Kong Foundation, Lee Shau-kee naturally says that he is looking for a 'smooth transition' for the territory in 1997.

Any transition waves will immediately be felt on the Hong Kong Stock Exchange, where the share register is dominated by half a dozen big names: Li Ka-shing, Keswick, Swire, Kadoorie, Lee Shau-kee, the Kwoks. Together they control more than 40 per cent, or US$120 billion, of the market, while the next 10 families hold 15 per cent. Under existing law in Hong Kong, companies have to offer only 25 per cent of their shares to the public – and this rule has been waived sometimes if the float is big enough.

For example, the initial public offering from Robert Kuok's Kerry Properties in July 1996 was for only 15 per cent. There is a move by the Hong Kong Institute of Company Secretaries to raise the public float to 45 per cent in a bid to break the top families' stranglehold on the market. But it is clear that the way in which the big Hong Kong players are prepared to join forces and form consortia to bid for property-development and infrastructure projects means that they will control the market for years to come. The only change in the near future is the chance that 'Superman' Li may be missing from this line-up. In November 1996 he announced that he would step down from business in 1998 to do more social good deeds, particularly in medicine and education. His donations have already helped various schools and hospitals in Hong Kong and China. That early statement of intentions should give Victor Li, the low-key elder son, plenty of time to take a fitting for his own Superman costume.

6

Star Wars – the Thirst for Water and Information

In this world there is nothing softer or thinner than water. But to compel the hard and unyielding, it has no equal.

Chinese philosopher Lao-Tse, circa 600BC

INSIDE THE MASSIVE BOARDROOM AT THE HONG KONG HEADQUARTERS of Richard Li's Pacific Century group, an executive juggles the controls of the touch-screen panel that pulls in satellite signals from around the globe. 'If we sell the technology, Richard likes us to use the technology ourselves,' the executive explains. And that approach is what is helping propel the youthful Richard Li towards the billionaire stakes in his own right.[1]

As the younger son of Hong Kong property-development tycoon Li Ka-shing, Richard Li had a good start in business. But he quickly showed he had inherited his father's money-making skills when he took a start-up satellite operation called Star TV and sold a large chunk of it for a fabulous profit to global media player Rupert Murdoch. He sold another, final tranche to Murdoch in 1995, bringing in funds so that he could pursue a new vision: delivering business communications that are not dependent on government-owned telecom services.

The view from Richard Li's boardroom towards the harbour is

dominated by the city's two architectural monuments to Big Money: the I.M. Pei-designed Bank of China glass tower and the Hongkong & Shanghai Bank's Lego-like structure. But the real focus of the view from Pacific Century is on the satellite dishes on these buildings, and their proven ability to shift business data quickly and securely.

Perhaps more than any other of the up-and-coming billionaires, Richard Li has recognized that the two most important commodities in Asia today are good information and good clean water. The opportunity lies in the fact that the two are out of kilter – access to information is streaking ahead of access to physical infrastructure like water-supply lines. The result: people in many of Asia's mega-cities (defined as having more than 10 million inhabitants) have a better chance of watching Star TV than they do of drinking clean water or breathing clean air.

The acceleration of information access, powered by cheap silicon chips, is changing the way in which people think about the quality of their lives. This is having a fundamental impact on urban development in Asia, where a satellite dish not much bigger than a dinner plate is ubiquitous.

While dish sizes and prices tumble, competition for water is intensifying. The International Rice Research Institute has warned that the conflicting needs of urban consumers, industry and farmers will cause severe water problems by 2025.

Late in 1995, the then mayor of Shanghai Xu Kuangdi told a group of international business visitors that the city's main drainage channel, Suzhou Creek, was a 'black and choking silthole'.[2] No-one who ventured close to the creek would doubt the accuracy of his pungent description, nor his commitment to give Shanghai good-quality air and water, and a green belt that would separate the city's heart from industrial zones on its outskirts.

Cleaning up Asia's mega-cities dominates debate among urban planners, and those visionary business people who see money in muck. By 2020, according to the Asian Development Bank, Asia is likely to have 17 mega-cities, including three, Tokyo, Shanghai and Bombay, with populations approaching 30 million.[3]

World's largest urban agglomerations, 1995–2015

City		1995 Population in millions	2015 Estimated population in millions	
1	Tokyo	26.8	Tokyo	28.7
2	São Paulo	16.4	Bombay	27.4
3	New York	16.3	Lagos	24.4
4	Mexico City	15.6	Shanghai	23.4
5	Bombay	15.1	Jakarta	21.2
6	Shanghai	15.1	São Paulo	20.8
7	Los Angeles	12.4	Karachi	20.6
8	Beijing	12.4	Beijing	19.4
9	Calcutta	11.7	Dhaka	19.0
10	Seoul	11.6	Mexico City	18.8

Source: Global Report on Human Settlement 1995

But the amazing story of Asia in the 1990s is that as these cities struggle to meet their physical infrastructure needs – roads, bridges, power, water, affordable housing – their citizens are shifting from being the information poor to the information rich, amid a flowering of satellite dishes.

Behind this is the flood of affordable integrated circuits coming out of Lee Kun Hee's [20] Samsung plants in Korea and Malaysia, or Wang Yung-ching's [11] similar operations in Taiwan. New factories in China, Vietnam and Indonesia are adding to the supply, as Asia's billionaires scour the region for sites, in competition with American players like Texas Instruments and Motorola, and Germany's Siemens.

Taiwan is now the world's biggest producer of computer motherboards. Japan and Korea dominate the semiconductor field, particularly in 16-bit DRAM chips. In China, it seems that almost every month there is an announcement from makers like Motorola, NEC or Siemens about a semiconductor plant or a cellular phone factory.

The demand is certainly there. China, growing at a rate of 700,000 units a year, already has 2.5 million mobile phones, ranking fourth in the world after the United States, Japan and the United Kingdom. Korea's mobile phone market may reach 3 million units in 1997 as demand for the new code division multiple access (CDMA) handsets catches on.[4]

The latest World Bank figures say that spending on infrastructure during the next 10 years in Asia could hit US$1.5 trillion, with about half of that needed in China alone. The bank says that China needs US$200 billion for power, $140 billion in telecoms, $300 billion in transport and $100 billion in water and sanitation.

Of course, these are guesstimates at best. As the World Bank itself says, the requirement is massive but 'there is much uncertainty about these forecasts'. Only a proportion of that US$1.5 trillion could ever be spent in Asia; there is just not enough money in the global system to fund all that the region needs. Some places and projects will miss out; they will be the ones with the least attractive environment for investors.

Creating an investment environment is where information plays its fundamental role, by raising expectations of citizens through exposure to outside information.

It is no surprise that the Asian countries with the lowest television penetration rates are among the least attractive to infrastructure investors, including Asia's billionaires. In Burma, there is one TV to every 500 citizens. In Bangladesh and Laos, the figure is 170, followed by Cambodia with 120.

The natural hunting grounds of Asia's billionaires are the hot investment economies such as China (one TV to every 32 citizens), India (28), Vietnam (24) and Indonesia (16). While these TV penetration rates are much higher than those of, say, Burma, Laos and Cambodia, they are still well short of Japan's figure of 1.6.

The information flow out of a particular country is also crucial in making investors comfortable. Media images of violence in South Asia do not help countries such as Pakistan, Bangladesh and Sri Lanka attract business and infrastructure investors, even though the large populations make for a potentially good target market.

Television, radio, fax, the mobile phone, the personal computer, the modem, the Internet and the coming NetTV form the hardware that makes information accessible. But it is the software – the news, quiz shows and lifestyle programmes, the music, the home pages on the Internet, the voice and data traffic that flows back and forth to Asia – that really drives change.

This access to information and images from other societies conditions the demand for infrastructure in new ways.

It is why middle-class Indonesians and Filipinos are flocking to air-conditioned mega-malls put up by billionaires like the Riady family *[89]* in Jakarta and Henry Sy *[52]* in Manila, why slum dwellers in Bombay will pay a few rupees for illegal power to watch Channel V, and why a major goal for Shanghai's army of fast movers in business is to have a mobile phone.

Along with Richard Li, Henry Sy and the Riady family, a select group of Asia's billionaires have worked out that they should go with the new information flow, diversifying into telecommunications, media, software, financial services, health and tourism. They have discovered that where information leads, other profitable businesses like property development, housing, transport and other infrastructure can follow.

Thailand is the classic example of this, where telecoms and computers are the preferred areas of business for the new breed of billionaires thrown up by Thailand's scintillating economic growth in the 1990s.

A decade ago, four Sino-Thai banking families, dominated by the Sophonpanich clan *[30]* of the Bangkok Bank, ruled the financial roost. But while the Sophonpanich, Lamsam *[43]* (Thai Farmers Bank), Ratanarak *[68]* (Bank of Ayudhya) and Tejapaibul *[83]* (Bangkok Metropolitan Bank) families still wield immense power, they have been joined in the billionaires list by names like Thaksin Shinawatra *[40]* (Thailand's Deputy Prime Minister in 1995–96), Boonchai Bencharongkul *[61]* and Adisai Bodharamik *[62]*, all of whom made their mark in high technology.

The best known internationally is Dr Thaksin Shinawatra, 47, a former police colonel with an estimated net worth of 60 billion baht (more than US$2.1 billion).[5] Part of a well-connected family from Chiang Mai in Thailand's north, Thaksin graduated top of his class at the Police Cadet School and won a scholarship to study in the United States. He earned a master's degree in criminal justice from Eastern Kentucky University in 1974, and followed that in 1978 with a PhD from Sam Houston State University in Texas. In between, he returned to Thailand and served in the police force until the early 1980s. He quit the force to strike out on his own, running a cinema for a while in Chiang Mai, before starting Shinawatra Computer Co in 1983 as an agent for IBM.

His break came a few years later when he won a 20-year mobile-phone concession and then, in 1990, a licence to run a domestic satellite service. Since then, he has put up three satellites, Thaicom 1, 2 and 3 (with the last launched in March 1997), and seen the capitalization of Shinawatra Computer & Communications hit US$3.8 billion in 1995 before a general downturn on the Bangkok Stock Exchange cut that figure in half early in 1997. The company and its subsidiaries turned in a 1996 profit of about US$100 million.

Thaksin cut his stake in the group to less than 50 per cent and stepped down from any executive role when he entered politics in 1994, joining the Chuan Leekpai government as Foreign Minister under the Palang Dharma Party's quota. He later became leader of the Palang Dharma and in 1995 took his party into the coalition government of Prime Minister Banharn Silpa-archa, where he held the post of Deputy Prime Minister.

But in August 1996 he quit the coalition, angered by the extent of corruption allegations involving Banharn. He took no part in the November 1996 poll which saw the ousting of Banharn and the emergence of General Chavalit Yongchaiyudh as Thailand's new coalition leader. After Thaksin's unsatisfactory experience with politics, it was clear that he saw more rewarding challenges back at the helm of his Shinawatra group.

In Thailand's fast-growing cellular market, Shinawatra Computer's 56-per-cent-held mobile-phone subsidiary, Advanced Info Service, goes head to head with Boonchai Bencharongkul's

United Communication Industry subsidiary, Total Access Communication plc. UCOM holds 72 per cent of Total Access.

Boonchai began a swag of ventures in the mid-1990s, including a stake in Motorola's US$5 billion Iridium global satellite project. This involves the launch of 66 low-earth-orbit satellites from 1997 onwards to create a system capable of handling cellular phone calls almost anywhere in the world – one reason that a UCOM subsidiary is funding a study of a possible satellite launch site at Gunn Point, near Darwin in Australia's north.[6]

Space Transportation Systems Ltd, the Australian consortium which UCOM joined, won 'special project' status from officials, putting it on the fast track for government approval. If it goes ahead, the launch site could involve an investment of around US$630 million. With a market capitalization of about US$1.6 billion in early 1997, UCOM made a profit the previous year of US$110 million.

In comparison, the results for Jasmine International, owned by the third Thai telecoms billionaire, Adisai Bodharamik [62], were much more modest, with a profit of just US$52 million. Jasmine began in 1982 as an engineering company but now runs a domestic satellite network and mobile radio service. It also installs fibre-optic cables. For Adisai, potentially the most lucrative operation is likely to be 20-per-cent-owned Thai Telephone & Telecommunication, with its concession to install 1.5 million phone lines in Thailand's information-hungry rural areas.

Thailand's richest family, the US$5.5 billion Chearavanont clan which runs the agribusiness combine Charoen Pokphand Group (see Chapter 2), is likewise no stranger to telecoms. When CP started to diversify some years ago, chairman Dhanin Chearavanont [12] had the vision to get into the local phone business.

With US telecoms operator Nynex on board to provide technical know-how, Dhanin won the country's first private contract for phone services and set up TelecomAsia Corp in 1991. By mid-1996, it was Thailand's second largest fixed-line telephone operator and a major contributor to CP's profitability. It had a concession to install and operate 2.6 million lines in Bangkok in what is likely to be a US$4 billion investment.

TelecomAsia won the right in 1996 to operate a new limited mobile-phone service, the personal handiphone system (PHS), thereby increasing competition for Shinawatra's Advanced Info and UCOM's Total Access. CP Group, whose extensive China interests are run by Dhanin's elder brother Sumet Jiaravanon (an alternative spelling for Chearavanont) in Hong Kong, also has a share of Hong-Kong-based APT Satellite with Singapore Telecom and the Chinese government.

Apart from the state-owned Telephone Organisation of Thailand, CP's biggest competitor in fixed lines is TT&T, the joint venture between Adisai's Jasmine International and Loxley, a company linked to the Lamsam family, who run Thailand's third-largest bank, Thai Farmers Bank.

Even more of a multimedia newcomer is magazine and newspaper publisher Sondhi Limthongkul, whose regional aspirations extend to satellite broadcasting, in addition to print titles that include *Asia Inc, Asia Times* and *The Chinese*. Sondhi's M Group controls Asia Broadcasting and Communications Network, which hopes to be operating a direct-to-home satellite network when its two US-built L-Star satellites are in orbit by the end of 1998.

Sondhi, another of the Sino-Thai media players to have emerged in Thailand in the past decade, has stitched up a 30-year concession deal with the government of Laos to use an orbital slot belonging to Laos. In turn, the government has taken a 20 per cent stake in ABCN's satellite operating company. Another shareholder in ABCN is Boonchai's UCOM, keen to gain more exposure and experience with satellites as the much larger Iridium project picks up steam from 1997 onwards.

Motorola expects all 66 of the Iridium low-earth-orbit satellites to be in place by September 1998. The first five were launched aboard a Delta II rocket from Vandenberg airforce base in California in May 1997. Other Asian partners in Iridium with UCOM (which holds its stake through Thai Satellite Telecommunications) include Korea Mobile Telecommunications Corp, Nippon Iridium Corp and China Great Wall Industry Corp

– which builds the Chinese Long March launch rockets that had an unhappy launch record in 1995–96.

Iridium predicts a global market of 650,000 cellular-phone subscribers and 350,000 paging subscribers. Iridium's slogan neatly defines its goal: 'One World ... One Telephone'. But with half the world's population yet to make a phone call, fulfilment of that ambition is still some way off.[7]

7

Malaysia's Power Plays

Hollywood is the undisputed movie capital of the world; working together, it may be possible to expand this to other realms... The themes may be universal, but Asians increasingly will prefer entertainment that has localised languages, myths, characters, music, allusions and locations.

Dr Mahathir Mohamad, promoting his Multimedia Super Corridor concept
in Los Angeles, 14 January 1997[1]

WHEN THE LIGHTS WENT OUT IN MALAYSIA IN AUGUST 1996, IT was a US$100 million loss to the economy, but an even bigger blow to national pride. A furious and embarrassed Prime Minister, Dr Mahathir Mohamad, asked television viewers: 'Where are we going to hide our faces?', after a circuit breaker glitch at the Paka power plant in East Terengganu state tripped switches all down the country, and turned out Malaysia's lights for almost 12 hours on 3 August 1996.

As Saturday evening shoppers and commuters turned on their lights to negotiate their way along Kuala Lumpur's packed freeways, the Doc fumed and recalled his promise of 'never again' after a similar blackout struck the country in 1992.

One thing was clear – this time heads would roll in the country's state-owned power provider, Tenaga Nasional. Within a week, Tenaga's executive chairman, Dr Ani Arope, was told that he would be replaced when his term expired at the end of that month. His replacement, Dr Ahmad Tajuddin Ali, head of the Standards and Industrial Research Institute of Malaysia, said that his immediate task was to re-energize staff morale at Tenaga.[2]

Coming a year after a fire knocked out power to Malaysia's electronics manufacturing centre of Penang, the 3 August blackout was Dr Mahathir's worst nightmare. Only 48 hours earlier, in front of an audience of foreign investors, the Malaysian leader had launched with great fanfare his ambitious 'multimedia super corridor', designed to link Kuala Lumpur with the new international airport at Sepang, 45km to the south.

Among those to advise him on the 'super corridor', and a significant beneficiary of Malaysia's multimedia aspirations, was T. Ananda Krishnan [67], the enigmatic billionaire Tamil who launched the country's first satellite, MEASAT-1, in January 1996. But Krishnan, a graduate from Melbourne University and Harvard Business School, had more on his mind than just multimedia and satellites. On blackout night, one of the few buildings that commuters could see against the night sky were the twin peaks of Krishnan's massive Kuala Lumpur City Centre development, a US$3 billion project that features the world's tallest building, the 88-storey Petronas Twin Towers. The towers, standing 450 metres tall and built for Malaysia's national oil and gas company, Petronas, are just one part of the development in the heart of Kuala Lumpur that will continue for a decade. It includes 1.67 million square metres of commercial, retail and entertainment space, plus a 645-room luxury hotel, the Mandarin Oriental, which will be the largest in the country.[3]

It took Krishnan a decade to bring his KL City Centre concept to reality, consolidating the site late in the 1980s and then convincing Petronas to take a large part of the towers' office space.[4] From an observation platform high in one of the towers, topped out in February 1996, the immense scale of the project becomes clear: it covers 39 hectares of what was once the Selangor Turf Club, in a prime downtown site at the junction of Jalan Ampang and Jalan P Ramlee. Also standing tall on the Kuala Lumpur cityscape is the 421 metre Kuala Lumpur Telecommunications

Tower, officially opened in October 1996 and described by Dr Mahathir as 'the most beautiful tower ever built' and the direct result of privatization in the telecoms arena.

The Kuala Lumpur City Centre project provides some of Krishnan's cash flow for the broadcasting and cable television services he plans. At the heart of this is the MEASAT-1 satellite, launched in January 1996 by Binariang, the unlisted multimedia and telecoms company that Krishnan controls.

American telecoms company US West, which paid US$230 million for 20 per cent of Binariang in 1994, promised that it would transfer technology to Binariang for commercial multimedia services. The Malaysian government was also keen to be involved. Its investment arm, Khazanah Nasional, bought 15 per cent of MEASAT Network Systems so that it could foster high technology in the country.

Some of the applications for the MEASAT (Malaysia East Asia Satellite) series is to provide direct-to-home television broadcasts, distance learning and remote-area telephony services. Binariang began transmitting subscription-based television programmes over MEASAT in the second half of 1996, with plans to extend its service, known as All Asia Television and Radio Co (Astro), to India and South-East Asia. By late 1997 the service could include home shopping and banking, and Internet access. Krishnan sees even more potential in telephony; he plans to invest US$2 billion to develop satellite-based telecoms and a digital mobile network known as Maxis GSM that will allow roaming in most of Asia.

Binariang, which Krishnan may list in 1997 along with KLCC and MEASAT, aims to launch Malaysia's first micro-satellite by December 1997 for remote sensing, environmental control and other applications.

Krishnan also controls the listed lottery and racetrack operator Tanjong plc, which continued to pile up the cash in the late 1990s. It lifted net profit to US$64 million for the year to 31 January 1996, despite an 11 per cent drop in revenue to US$496 million. The company said that revenue dropped because the government reduced the number of days on which it could conduct lotteries.

Krishnan, whose estimated net worth is US$1.4 billion, is not alone in Malaysia's crowded telecoms and multimedia sector. Three other billionaires – Tajudin Ramli [79], Vincent Tan [19] and Halim Saad [59] – all had a stake in the industry as Malaysia exposed Telekom Malaysia, 70 per cent state owned, to the forces of competition.

The most prominent is Tajudin Ramli, the well-connected former merchant banker who, at the age of 48, rose to national attention in 1994 when he took a controlling 33 per cent stake in the national carrier, Malaysia Airlines (MAS). That highly leveraged deal cost him M$1.8 billion, or around US$720 million.[5] Tajudin controls listed Technology Resources Industries (TRI), which owns Malaysia's largest mobile-phone operator, Cellular Communications (Celcom).

In mid-1996, Deutsche Telekom paid M$1.3 billion for a 21 per cent stake in Tajudin's TRI. Government approval for the sale was conditional on TRI increasing its *bumiputera* (Malay indigenous) shareholdings to at least 30 per cent by the end of June 1997. TRI reported a 14 per cent profit rise for the first half of 1996 to US$86 million, with its wholly owned subsidiary Celcom emerging as the main contributor to group revenue and profit. Outside of Malaysia, TRI operates a telephone network in Cambodia and has a joint venture in China. TRI is also a stakeholder in a low-cost miniature satellite system operated by US-based ORBCOMM, designed to allow users to send and receive short messages at sea and in mountainous areas via low-earth-orbit satellites.

Tajudin has not been shy in seeing the big picture, be it in telecoms or airlines. Soon after he took control of Malaysia Airlines in 1994 he said that he would spend US$4 billion on 25 new aircraft for MAS by 2000, along with US$4 billion in aircraft purchases that were already in the pipeline. He upped the ante in late 1996 when he said that MAS might become a launch customer for Boeing's super-jumbo 747-600X series, a 600-passenger airliner likely to cost US$200 million each.[6]

Tajudin, like many prominent Malaysian entrepreneurs, enjoys close relations with Prime Minister Mahathir and former finance minister Daim Zainuddin, now a key adviser to the government. Tajudin, who is regarded as a protégé of Daim's, built Celcom to its premier status after winning Malaysia's first mobile-phone licence (which came with a competition-free guarantee period of five years) in the late 1980s. In early 1997, Tajudin's estimated net worth was US$1.2 billion.

Along with Krishnan and Tajudin, ethnic Chinese billionaire Vincent Tan, 44, is another close associate of the Malaysian leadership and a telecoms player. One of Malaysia's richest men with an estimated net worth of US$4.5 billion, Tan built his empire on gambling enterprises and astute deal-making. He controls the diversified Berjaya group which includes listed Berjaya Sports Toto, the company he formed after acquiring the state-owned Sports Toto betting agency in 1985.[7]

Tan, an aggressive, predatory but not always successful investor over the years in such Malaysian stocks as Singer, Magnum Corp and Malayan United Industries, is described as the antithesis of older, conservative ethnic Chinese businessmen like Robert Kuok [28] and Khoo Kay Peng [90]. He heads a group of developers embarking on a US$4 billion project in Kuala Lumpur known as the Linear City – at 12km the world's longest building, straddling the Klang River which flows through the city. The project, involving office space, apartments, shopping malls, a theme park and a mass transit system called the Peoplemover, is going ahead with the support of the Prime Minister, Dr Mahathir.[8]

Aside from Linear World and his gaming, leisure, food franchises and healthcare interests, Tan is keen to get connected in the multimedia world. His vehicle is his private company Mutiara Telecommunications, which operates Malaysia's largest mobile-communications network with around 13,000 subscribers.

In July 1996 Swiss Telecom paid more than US$300 million for 30 per cent of Tan's Mutiara, on the strength of an international gateway licence which it held. Analysts were stunned by the high price, but a few months later, in October 1996, Mutiara announced that it was using the funds to commit to a US$480 million upgrade of its services by 1998, including a new earth station.[9] Market forces in Malaysia's crowded but fast-growing telecoms sector will determine if Swiss Telecom's investment is a good one and if Vincent Tan's wealth will continue to increase.

The other major entrant in the telecoms sector is well connected, likewise a Daim protégé, and a relative newcomer to billionaire status – Halim Saad, 43, who is linked to Malaysia's ruling United Malays National Organisation. Halim, a former accountant educated in New Zealand, controls the Renong conglomerate. Renong has done well from privatization, winning the lucrative construction and operating contract for Malaysia's 845km US$3 billion North–South Highway. Renong's infrastructure successes also include building the Malaysian side of the new US$900 million bridge with Singapore and a US$400 million contract to build a sports complex in Kuala Lumpur for the 1998 Commonwealth Games.[10]

Another part of the Renong group is listed Time Engineering, whose subsidiary, Time Telecommunications, also has a licence and operates payphone and mobile services. It is this unit which hopes to win a share of the expanding Malaysian telecoms market.

On the private front, however, the Renong chief executive Halim Saad had an unhappy year in 1996, with a protracted and messy attempted divorce from wife Norani Zolkifli attracting corporate and media interest. One reason was that, while Halim engineered her removal from the company's board in March, Norani still had an indirect interest through a 28.34 per cent Renong stake that was in her husband's name. Separately, Halim held another 5 per cent of Renong through a family trust. For onlookers, the most fascinating part of the divorce proceedings was the claim by Norani's lawyers that Halim had assets of more than US$2 billion.[11] In May 1997, a Malaysian Islamic court dismissed Halim's suit against Norani. Renong had a market capitalization of about US$3.8 billion in early 1997.

While Malaysia's mobile-phone market draws entrepreneurial bees to the honeypot, at a subscriber base of just 781,000 in 1995 it is by no means Asia's most substantial target. The biggest mobile-phone markets naturally enough are Japan, with 8.05 million subscribers in 1995, and China with 3.44 million.

But not far behind are Korea with 1.64 million subscribers and Thailand with 1.28 million. They are followed by Taiwan with 789,000, Malaysia 781,000, Hong Kong 688,000 and the Philippines 484,000. Growth prospects are phenomenal, with estimates for China to reach 4.82 million subscribers in 1997, followed by Korea 3.1 million and Thailand 2.31 million. Taiwan and Hong Kong could have 1.5 and 1.3 million subscribers each in 1997.[12]

The booming telecoms market is one reason that so much money has been poured into semiconductor production, with billion-dollar wafer-fabrication plants sprouting across Asia in environments as varied as Japan, Korea, Singapore, the Malaysian island state of Penang and Taiwan's Hsinchu science park.

The global market for silicon chips is around US$150 billion, of which Asia supplies about half. That comes largely from Japan and Korea at the high-value end, with Taiwan, Singapore and Malaysia further down the scale.

Taiwan, where the silicon-chip industry is worth US$4.2 billion a year, has its own special reasons for fostering communications technology, above and beyond the pure business drive of entrepreneurs like Stan Shih of Acer and Dr Morris Chang of Vanguard Corp. The Chinese missile tests in early 1996 reinforced the view in Taiwan that an increasingly uncertain strategic environment in the late 1990s required a high level of technological readiness. Communications – and, hence, silicon chips – would be of fundamental importance should things ever go awry across the Taiwan strait.

At its narrowest point, the Taiwan strait is only 140km wide – just a few minutes by F6 fighters or Su-27 fighter-bombers from bases in China's Fujian province. If hostile aircraft should ever appear over the Taiwan sky, command and control of the defensive effort will come in part from a specially 'dug-in' airbase where communications will be of paramount importance. This is Taiwan's ace defensive weapon: the Chien An No. 3 airbase at Chia-shan, near the resort city of Hualien on the northeast coast.[13]

Under the lee of Taiwan's central mountain range, where the

highest peaks are more than 3500 metres, is the Taroko National Park – home to the magnificent tourist site, Taroko Gorge and, tucked away nearby, the biggest, most sophisticated underground airbase in the region. Here, up to 200 aircraft are stored deep below ground in hardened bombproof sanctuaries. Lifts take them to tunnels that open on to the runway, where a sophisticated microwave landing system means that the base can launch and receive multiple waves of aircraft. With its bombproof doors, underground power and enough food, fuel and military supplies for several months, Chien An No. 3 represents a formidable target. Because of the high mountains of the central range, the base is safe from a missile attack from the mainland – for the time being. Hostile aircraft would have to come at it from the east. Most importantly, the base gives Taiwan a credible second-strike capability in the event of an aircraft or missile attack on other parts of the island.

But in the view of most defence experts, China is unlikely to attack Taiwan – which it regards as a renegade province – in the immediate future. Apart from the damage to its own commercial interests, a prime reason is that the Chinese armed forces are not yet strong enough to overcome Taiwan's defences. A specialist on the offensive capabilities of the Chinese People's Liberation Army (PLA), Dr Lin Chong-Pin, vice-chairman of Taiwan's Mainland Affairs Council, said in September 1996 that he believed Taiwan was safe from attack for some years to come.[14]

Because of defensive factors such as the Chien An airbase, he said that China would need cruise missiles for a surgical strike against Taiwan. Even if it had these by 1998, it would need time to deploy them effectively. The US experience in the Persian Gulf with cruise missiles had shown their limitations.

Dr Lin said that by 2000 it was quite possible that China would have cruise missiles with a range of 1800km – but again, it would need another 10 to 15 years to be able to use them effectively, or to build a 20,000-tonne aircraft carrier with better fighters that would offer a similar offensive capability. By then, the political and economic situation might be a much changed one.

But Dr Lin said it was also true that beyond 2000, the picture was one of uncertainty. The PLA's capabilities would increase to the point where, by 2005–2010, depending on the nature of the regime in Beijing, there might be something to worry about.

Dr Lin said he took comfort from the fact that in July 1996 a Visa card was issued in the name of the Chinese President, Jiang Zemin. He saw it as symbolic of the rapid changes in China and the frantic pace of its economic development.

Much of the credit for that rapid development goes to thousands of Taiwanese entrepreneurs who have poured between US$25 billion and US$50 billion into investments on the mainland.[15] One of the key business figures in what is known as the cross-straits dialogue is billionaire Koo Chen-fu [65], founder of the Koos business group in Taiwan, and chairman of the Straits Exchange Foundation. Koo stepped down as chairman and chief executive of Chinatrust Co, the Koos Group flagship, in 1989 at the age of 72 so that he could devote more time to national responsibilities, including serving as a presidential adviser.

The group is headed now by Koo's nephew, Jeffrey L.S. Koo, an internationally prominent banker and businessman who revels in the title 'Mr Taiwan'. While much of the family's fortune has been built on banking, insurance, other financial services and heavy industry such as cement, plastics and petrochemicals, the Koos have also seen the value of getting connected in the world of telecommunications.

In August 1996, the Koos Group and the US telecommunications company Sprint Corp agreed to invest more than US$360 million in a new cellular-phone network in Taiwan. The Koos Group will hold a majority interest, while Sprint will hold 20 per cent. Taiwan's mobile-phone market is expected to reach 1.5 million subscribers by 1997, and more than 2 million early in the twenty-first century.

Like the four Malaysian billionaires Ananda Krishnan, Vincent Tan, Tajudin Ramli and Halim Saad, Taiwan's Jeffrey Koo was betting on big growth in telecommunications. He would have been cheered by the results of a Gallup survey in September 1996 which predicted that the world's telecommunications market would be worth US$650 billion a year by 2000. Coupled with information technology, it is now the world's biggest industry – all the more reason why Asia's billionaires find it such a happy hunting ground.

8
Korean Car Wars

I am merely a rich labourer who, through his labour, produces commodities.

Chung Ju Yung, founder of Hyundai and patriarch of Korea's richest family,
estimated net worth US$6.2 billion[1]

BILLIONAIRE PHILOSOPHER, PATRON OF KOREAN CULTURE, American movie buff, quality-control fanatic, indicted on charges of bribing a former Korean president, and the leader who exhorted his 190,000 employees in the Samsung Business Group to 'change everything except your wife and children!', Lee Kun Hee [20] is the sort of businessman who knows how to get what he wants. Lee, gunning for automotive glory, might have added, 'and change your taste in cars, too, because Samsung is getting into the car business fast'.

Lee and the other super-rich industrialists who run much of Korea Inc – men like Kim Woo-choong [51] of Daewoo, Chung Mong Koo of Hyundai and Kim Suk-won [74] of Ssangyong – share one common aim: they covet a place among the world's top 10 automakers by early in the twenty-first century. Never mind that the Japanese, European and American carmakers see no room for the Koreans at the top; if there is one characteristic that the Koreans have in spades, it is determination. It is what has driven them from a dirt-poor war-ravaged former Japanese colony in

Korean car wars: the road ahead

Manufacturer & chairman/CEO	Motor vehicle production, 1995	Production target, 2000
Hyundai Chung Mong Koo	1,213,000	3,600,000
Daewoo Kim Woo-choong	631,000	1,500,000
Ssangyong Kim Suk-won	50,000	350,000
Samsung Lee Kun Hee	0	500,000

Source: Korea Auto Manufacturers Association, October 1996

1946 to a nation 50 years later that excels in shipbuilding, construction, heavy engineering, petrochemicals and, more recently, consumer electronics and semiconductors. Now the top rung of the car industry is in the Koreans' sights.

When they back determination with aggression and a breathtaking willingness to invest billions of dollars in emerging automotive markets in Eastern Europe, Africa, India, China, Vietnam and elsewhere in Asia, the Korean carmakers become a formidable competitive force for companies like Nissan, Toyota, Mercedes-Benz and General Motors – their past and present technology partners.

To understand the Korean billionaires' passion for global recognition and for setting targets that seem staggering in their audacity – Samsung, for example, has yet to build a car, but Lee is determined to win a top 10 slot by 2010 – it is worth a one-hour drive out from the Korean capital Seoul to gain some historical perspective.

Sixty kilometres northwest of the city, where the Han river flows into the Western Sea, the serene island of Kanghwado stands as a perennial guardian of the capital. It was here in the thirteenth century that the Korean kings set up their first line of defence against foreign invaders, and it was just south of Kanghwado that General Douglas MacArthur led the United Nations troops in the Inchon landing in 1950, turning the tide of the Korean War and recapturing Seoul from the communist forces.[2]

Today, buses from Seoul take picnickers to the island, to explore the old fortifications and buy some ginseng or rush mats from local farmers. There is a mood of tranquillity in the elegant temples and 4000-year-old burial grounds found on the island. Most of all, there is the whiff of history on the sea breeze; folk legends link the island to Tangun, son of a bear-woman and the mythical founder of Korea. Myths aside, in the early thirteenth century Kanghwado became both a refuge from the Mongol invaders and the site of one of the most remarkable literary endeavours in human history: the creation of the Tripitaka Koreana, the world's most important set of Buddhist scriptures.

Kojong, one of the Koryo dynasty kings, fled to Kanghwado during a Mongol invasion around 1237. To invoke Buddha to come to the aid of the Koryo people and drive out the Mongol invaders, Kojong commissioned the carving of 81,258 wooden blocks, containing the complete Buddhist scriptures and a history of Korea. Unfortunately, Kojong died on the island and the entreaties to Buddha were to no avail. But the 16-year effort by a team of Buddhist priests and scholars to create the Tripitaka Koreana between 1237 and 1252 was an unparalleled literary achievement.

Today, those 750-year-old wooden blocks are preserved in a naturally ventilated storage room at the Haeinsa Temple, near the southeast Korean city of Taegu. While the blocks remain in perfect shape, access to them has been limited. But in his role as philosopher tycoon, Samsung's Lee Kun Hee funded a US$1.6 million project to transfer the 53 million characters of Chinese text found on the blocks to CD-ROM so that Buddhist scholars throughout the world would have access to the Tripitaka. The two-year project, completed in January 1996, was a triumph of Korean determination (and a technological boost, naturally, for Samsung Electronics): it required devising a whole new typeface and digitizing into a common format thousands of characters with identical meaning but different forms.[3]

That determination epitomizes the way in which Lee and his billionaire colleagues approach their global business wars, where technology and historical perspective come into play. Lee funds Korean domestic cultural projects to the tune of hundreds of millions of dollars a year. Nor is Lee shy with funds for worthy causes outside Korea. In 1996, when the Nobel Foundation came knocking for US$10 million to help set up the US$100 million Nobel Museum by 2000, Samsung was quick to say yes. It was smart tactics on the part of the Nobel Foundation to declare that it would ask only the world's 10 largest business groups for US$10 million each.

Lee is alleged to have made another donation (said to be US$13 million) that has brought even more attention, unwelcome though it may be. Like many of Korea's richest identities, Lee lived through interesting times in the 1980s and 1990s, when the links between politics and business were exceedingly close. In December 1995, he paid the price when he was one of eight leading business executives (along with rival Kim Woo-choong of Daewoo) indicted on bribery charges related to former Korean president Roh Tae Woo. Although suffering the initial opprobrium of being indicted, Lee and the other business leaders were spared arrest because of the perceived harm which this would have done to the Korean economy.

In an even more pragmatic demonstration of the billionaire's importance, Lee was still able to dine with Korean President Kim Young-sam a few days later, and accompany the president on a Korean investment swing through India, where Samsung has major business plans. But in August 1996 the wheels of justice ground out the verdicts: 22½ years' jail for Roh Tae Woo and the death sentence for another former president, Chun Doo Hwan, on treason and corruption charges; a two-year suspended sentence for Lee, and a two-year jail term for Daewoo chairman Kim Woo-choong. An appeal kept Kim out of jail for the time being, and a few months later, on 16 December, the Korean system kicked in with the result business was hoping for: the appellate court com-muted Chun Doo Hwan's death sentence to life imprisonment, reduced Roh's jail sentence to 17 years, and suspended Kim's sen-tence (along with those of two other business leaders). Korea Inc breathed a sigh of relief and got on with the business of tackling global competitors in motor vehicles and electronics.

Lee, born in 1942, is still young enough to be regarded as one of the new breed of business leaders. In fact, he didn't really want the top job at Samsung. Lee is the third son of Samsung founder Lee Byung Chul. But because Lee senior did not get on with his No. 1 son, Lee Meng Hee, the leadership of the Samsung group passed to Lee Kun Hee in 1987.

Until then, Lee Kun Hee had had little to do with running the group, but he threw himself into the challenge with a passion that has since driven Samsung to pre-eminence among the Korean *chaebol*, or conglomerates.

Lee comfortably headed the list of dividend payments to own-ers and managers of Korea's top 30 *chaebol* in 1995. His US$16 mil-lion dividend cheque was a healthy gain on the US$9 million he earned the previous year, reflecting in particular the record-breaking performance of the group's listed flagship, Samsung Electronics.[4] As demand for computer chips soared, net profit for Korea's biggest electronics maker (and the world's largest pro-ducer of semiconductors) rose 165 per cent in 1995 to US$3.2 bil-lion, on sales of more than US$20 billion.

Indeed, Samsung Electronics, with exports of US$14.6 billion (mainly in consumer goods such as TVs, VCRs and other home appliances), accounted for 12 per cent of South Korea's total exports of US$125 billion in 1995. Samsung's telecommunications and information systems products also contributed to the result.

The dividend payouts from that performance helped swell the

US$3.2 billion Lee family fortune, ranking it third behind Hyundai's Chung family (US$6.2 billion) and Lotte group founder Shin Kyuk-ho [17] (US$4.5 billion).

Lee, a graduate of Tokyo's prestigious Waseda University and George Washington University in the United States, has been keen to create a climate of change at Samsung, urging workers to arrive and leave early, and to focus on quality. He exhorted people to make sweeping reforms, to 'change everything except your wives and children'.

'In 1993 I changed the work hours from the old 9am to 6pm to 7am to 4pm. Employees now have part of their afternoons free to develop themselves,' he said recently. Lee brings a missionary-like zeal to the search for quality, claiming that 'making defective products is a crime against the customer'.[5]

'I tell my people that product defects are like a cancer. Ulcers are curable, but cancer is progressive. If it is not eradicated early, it will return in a few years and kill,' he said in 1996, reviewing the achievements of Samsung since his 'Frankfurt declaration' of 1993. At that time, Lee says that he had felt a strong sense of crisis and impending doom within Samsung. The company was plodding along in a 'two-dimensional' fashion. He feared what would happen if Samsung were to collapse in the face of competition. He was angry and disappointed, and those emotions had welled up into an impromptu address to Samsung staff during a visit to the group's European headquarters in Frankfurt.

'I emphasized putting an end to the quantity-oriented business approach and having the entire Samsung group put the priority on quality,' he said. But the impressive business results of the mid-1990s still had not delivered satisfaction.

'We have made some progress, but the group as a whole has not been able to get away from quantity-centred priorities of the past. This extremely dangerous force of past habits is controlling the group,' he warned in an address in April 1996.[6]

Recalling the grim days of 1993, Lee said that his Frankfurt declaration had not been rehearsed, nor had he discussed it in advance with any of his staff. 'At the time, I felt extremely isolated. The speech was filled with a sense of mission, prompted by an enormous feeling of crisis. Although the Frankfurt declaration was meant for Samsung in a narrow sense, I believe it pertains to all Koreans, and ultimately to all people,' he said.

To follow up the Frankfurt declaration, in early 1996 Lee took his senior managers to San Diego, California, for a 'second period' strategy meeting. There he sketched out the future of the Samsung group. While Samsung Electronics, with its US$21 billion annual revenue, would remain the group's flagship, over the next five years Samsung would invest US$75 billion to nurture the next generation of business in fields such as multimedia, bio-engineering and LCD-TFT (liquid crystal display–thin film transistor). This, Lee declared, would be the post-semiconductor era. At the same time, he renewed the group's commitment to a place at the automakers' top table.

This fits with the latest research on global auto trends by the Economist Intelligence Unit, which found that the increasing use of electronics in cars will help companies like Samsung which manufacture both chips and motor vehicles.

Lee, whose family interests control about 48 per cent of the Samsung Group, has embarked on expansion plans to lift revenue for the group's 24 companies well above the 1995 figure of US$80 billion.

These include investment decisions designed to take advantage of emerging market opportunities in Asia and South America and to consolidate Samsung's stake in high-value markets such as Europe and North America. One example is a new focus on strategic partnerships. In March 1996, for the first time in Korea's industrial history, Samsung and its chief rival, Hyundai, formed a joint venture in telecommunications. The following month Samsung Electronics signed a joint-venture agreement with India's Larsen and Tonbro to produce and sell telecoms equipment. This is part of a planned investment of around US$800 million in India by 1999.

Despite Lee's high business profile and 'can-do' image within Korea, he showed some vulnerability when he fell foul of

President Kim Young-sam during a visit to Beijing in 1995. At the time, he made the mistake of describing Mr Kim's administration as 'second class';[7] what followed was an apparent government freeze on Samsung's business interests, including its push for a piece of the automotive action. But the setback proved only temporary, with the group's record-breaking business performance showing that it was strong enough to survive the pressure. Still, it was enough to show Lee and other business leaders that criticism of the political leadership was unwise.

Lee also was wrongfooted over his passion for movies (his home collection is said to number 6000 titles), coupled with a misreading of American business culture. Lee foresaw, correctly, that while hardware in the form of VCRs, CD-ROMs and semiconductors was still going to provide a strong income stream, part of the new business future for Samsung lay in multimedia software. Like other potential media tycoons the world over, he believed the mantra 'content is king'. In 1994–95 Lee wanted to bid for a share of Hollywood and thought that he had found his partner in DreamWorks SKG, the studio founded by the talented trio of *ET* director Steven Spielberg, former Disney Studios boss Jeffrey Katzenberg and record company chief David Geffen. But somehow, the chemistry just wasn't right. When Lee spoke to Spielberg about taking a share in DreamWorks, Spielberg came away knowing no deal could be done. As he told a US magazine later, there was too much talk of semiconductors.[8]

One part of the Lee family *was* sympatico to the Americans: Lee's niece 'Mikey' Lee Mee Kyong, 38, and nephew 'Jay' Lee Jae Hyun, 36. They started talking to Spielberg.

As Lee Kun Hee noted in 1996, 'The coming age is one of separation and unification, of global illumination, of free-flowing information – the perfect drama.'[9] But separation, illumination and the perfect drama had already arrived in the form of a good old-fashioned family feud, involving money, power and prestige.

Jay Lee Jae Hyun is Lee Meng Hee's eldest son and the first grandson of Samsung founder Lee Byung Chul. He now heads Cheil Foods and Chemicals, which spun itself off from the

Samsung group in 1994 – although Cheil is still tied up with Samsung because of price difficulties in disposing of the various stakes it holds in Samsung group companies. Its biggest stakes include 15 per cent of the Samsung Lions, 11.5 per cent of Samsung Life and almost 10 per cent of Samsung Petrochemicals – all unlisted companies. To be regarded as a separate group to Samsung by the Korea Stock Exchange, Cheil must cut its holdings in Samsung companies to less than 1 per cent. Until both sides can agree on the right buyout price, that can't happen.

Despite the price problems, the spin-off meant that the Cheil Food branch of the Lee family was cashed up and ready to spend. In April 1995 Jay and his older sister Mikey outlaid US$300 million for an 11.1 per cent stake in DreamWorks SKG. For that, Jay got a seat on the 10-member board, Mikey became one of five members of the DreamWorks executive managing committee, and Cheil got access to DreamWorks' product for distribution in Asia. While Samsung downplayed reports of rivalry between Lee Kun Hee and his energetic niece and nephew, it was clear that Jay and Mikey were ecstatic at their coup. The Korean plunge into Hollywood was underway, with a smart, sassy, US-educated team at the controls. Mikey Lee in fact was born in the United States in 1958, the first grandchild of Lee Byung Chul. She did a master's at Harvard, after first studying at Seoul National University and later Japan and Taiwan. Some Korean analysts saw it as the beginning of a Lee family war, with control of the entertainment software business the ultimate prize. But the real Korean war is not with families; it remains where it has always been – first with the Japanese and then with the rest of the world, be it in semiconductors, cars or multimedia.

In early 1996, with the DreamWorks tie-up under his belt, Lee Jae-hyun announced a new name for his Cheil Food group, Cheiljedang, and a new mission: to be Asia's top multimedia group.[10]

Apart from its ambitious stake in DreamWorks, Cheiljedang also has a distribution joint venture with Golden Harvest, the Hong-Kong-based movie company that first rose to fame through the martial arts action flicks of the late Bruce Lee, and later hit the big time with action superstar Jackie Chan. Golden Harvest boss Raymond Chow is an old family friend of the Lees. Golden Harvest and Australia's Village Roadshow are partners with Cheil in a plan to build multiplex cinemas in Korea.

While this family sideshow plays out over the next few years, Lee Kun Hee still has his automotive goals to kick. To do that, he has entered into a joint venture and technology-transfer agreement with Nissan of Japan. And he keeps roaming the world looking for good investment sites and deals; while Daewoo rival Kim Woo-choong ploughs new ground in eastern Europe, Lee prefers the more predictable fields of western Europe. In February 1996, a beaming Lee stood alongside Britain's Queen Elizabeth II as she announced a US$2 billion investment in a new Samsung semiconductor plant that would bring jobs and new skills to the United Kingdom. It made Samsung the single largest investor in the UK.

Nissan's giant car plant at Sunderland in England's gritty northeast is the sort of operation which Samsung will seek to replicate with its own car plants, now under construction in Korea. Plant productivity rests on a teamwork approach that closes the gap between management and labour: no timeclocks, no management privileges in the car park, one canteen, the same blue uniforms for all levels, and the same sickness benefits and performance-assessment systems for every worker. Only the salary sizes differ.

But Lee Kun Hee must ponder whether he has made the right choice of partner. Globally, Nissan lost US$818 million in the year to March 1996 on sales of US$55.9 billion. The loss was an improvement on the US$1.53 billion that Nissan lost in 1995, but Lee will be looking to do better than that with Samsung.

Lee can take some solace from the fact that within Japan, Nissan returned to profitability in 1996, posting pretax profits of US$300 million, compared with a loss of US$565 million the previous year.

Ultimately the biggest challenge yet to Nissan may come from its joint-venture partner, Samsung, which hankers for the best technology it can buy and a rapid sales rise when it starts producing. Samsung has had the auto industry in its sights for some time: in 1993 it started buying stock in Kia Motors Corp, then Korea's second-largest carmaker behind Hyundai, as a way of entering the industry. But the government of Kim Young-sam was not keen on the move at that time and Samsung was forced to put its plans on hold for a while.

Now, however, it has got the green light. Samsung Motors plans to produce its first passenger cars in 1998 from its US$2.2 billion plant in Pusan, the port city on the southern tip of Korea. By mid 1997, Samsung expects to be testing four models in the 1.8 litre to 2.5 litre engine range. Samsung aims to produce 10,000 small cars in 1998, and expects to expand capacity to be producing half a million cars by 2002. By 2010 it aims to rank among the world's top 10 carmakers – an aspiration shared by its major home-grown competitors Hyundai and Daewoo.[11] Like its rivals, Samsung will target the North American, Latin American, Asia-Pacific and European markets.

Samsung also is negotiating with Nissan to introduce the 1.3 and 1.5 litre Sunny small car and the 3.0 litre Cima large car for the domestic market, where Japanese models have long been forbidden. While some marketing experts wondered how the new auto name would be received at home, thousands of Koreans proceeded to vote with their wallets. Since May 1996, a steady stream of Korean consumers have signed up for one of Samsung's credit cards, which will let them build up funds towards the purchase of a new Samsung car, sight unseen. Yet in production capacity, marketing skills and technology, Samsung is behind its major competitors, Hyundai, Daewoo and Kia, and way, way behind the technological leader, specialist maker Ssangyong, which gets its know-how from shareholder Mercedes-Benz.

At about the same time as Nissan was building its Sunderland plant, some 350km away to the south at Oxford University a young man named Chung Mong Kyu was reading for a master's in politics, philosophy and economics. On lazy summer days when Mong Kyu's mind drifted from Machiavelli, Bacon and Keynes, perhaps he mused about building Korea's first world-standard Formula 1 race track, or of emulating Honda and its highly successful foray into motor sport.

In January 1996 at the age of 33, Chung Mong Kyu got his chance to start putting some reality into those dreams, when he became the youngest chairman of one of the most important companies in Korea: Hyundai Motor Company. As part of the Chung family, Korea's richest (estimated worth US$6.2 billion) and most powerful business dynasty, Chung Mong Kyu's elevation put new verve into the giant Hyundai Business Group and touched off talk of another bust-up within the family.

With intense competition already from Daewoo and Kia locally, and Samsung set to join the auto battle by 1998, Chung Mong Kyu had the task ahead of him. But he obviously was in tune with his new role and the need to boost Hyundai's global brand recognition. Among his first pronouncements was his decision to spend US$20 million or more to build a Formula-1-standard race track at Hyundai's Namyang Bay proving ground. Hyundai, he said, would also launch a four-wheel-drive bid for the World Rally Championship, evoking memories of Mitsubishi's image-making push in its Pajero 4WD.[12]

To make sure the rest of the world was listening, Chung Mong Kyu said that Hyundai had another surprise on the way: a 4.5 litre V8 engine to power its luxury car competitor for BMW, Mercedes-Benz and Lexus by 2000. Also part of the 2000 target: global production to double from the 1995 figure of 1.2 million to reach 2.4 million units, with half of that to be exported. This would put Hyundai into the world's top 10 automakers, a decade ahead of Samsung's goal.

But Chung Mong Kyu knew that it would not be easy selling to a world that knows Korean cars only as cheap, technologically outdated clones of Japanese and American models. He told journalists visiting Korea in 1996 that image was the biggest problem facing the company.

'We have to improve our quality and our image in export

markets,' he said.[13] That quest for quality, shared with Samsung's Lee Kun Hee, also found an echo in the new Hyundai group chairman, Mong Kyu's iron-willed cousin, Chung Mong Koo.

Chung Mong Koo, 25 years senior, is the eldest surviving son of Hyundai founder Chung Ju Yung *[10]*. Mong Koo was the major beneficiary of the momentous changes announced by Hyundai in December 1995. Describing the shake-up as the biggest personnel change in its history, Hyundai named Mong Koo, then 57, to succeed chairman Chung Se Yung, younger brother of Chung Ju Yung and father of Mong Kyu.

Chung Mong Koo immediately set a tone that followed his father's aggressive field-oriented management style, with words like 'patrol of subsidiaries'. Chung Mong Koo had some other ideas too – mainly to do with 'value management'. In the intensely tough car wars that swept across Korea in the mid-1990s, Chung adopted the slogan in 1996 of 'a year of open sales cultures', warning that only the best automakers would survive the onslaught of international competition as Korea's own market opened up to outsiders. 'The best approach to tide over this situation,' Chung said, 'is to give the maximum extent of satisfaction to our customers.'[14]

In his inaugural speech in January 1996, Chung Mong Koo said that Hyundai (1995 revenue US$78 billion) would not be taking any backward steps, within Korea or abroad. Specifically, he said that Hyundai would actively pursue steel production, with the construction of an integrated steel mill using blast furnaces. This activity, a long-held dream of Mong Koo's father, would put Hyundai into competition with one of its major suppliers and long-term Korean giant, Pohang Iron & Steel Co (Posco), which is one-third state controlled. Hyundai expects to need 5 million tonnes of steel a year by 2000 to support its carmaking, shipbuilding, construction, engineering and electronics activities. If Mong Koo's high-stakes gamble pays off and Hyundai becomes a competitive steelmaker, it will further boost the group's carmaking abilities. But Hyundai's ambitious steelmaking goals so far have not found favour with the Korean government, mindful of its stake in the highly profitable Posco.

Within a few months of taking on the chairman's role, Chung Mong Koo embarked on an epochal mission designed to cement Hyundai's business ties with the mother of all markets: China. In June 1996 he journeyed to Beijing to pay a courtesy call on Chinese President Jiang Zemin and tell him of the group's plan to invest US$2.3 billion in China. With China in desperate need of more and better infrastructure, what Chung Mong Koo had to say was music to the Chinese leader's ears. Chatting with Jiang inside the National People's Congress Hall, Mong Koo said that he was looking for ways to accelerate business ties between Hyundai and Chinese enterprises. So far, Hyundai had invested a mere US$250 million in China's manufacturing and high-tech sectors. Now the Hyundai chairman wanted to see that figure multiplied tenfold. He identified projects in the automotive, electronics, machinery, rolling stock and information communications sectors and said that these investments would be in place by the beginning of 1999. One of the first joint ventures would be to produce and sell sub-way railcars. Hyundai's China card was played and on the table for all the other Korean business leaders to see.[15]

It was a classic performance by Chung Mong Koo, one worthy of his aged father, who remained group honorary chairman and patriarch of the Chung family.

Chung Ju Yung was born in November 1915 into a rice-farming family in a small village in what is now North Korea. The area continued to fascinate him long after the Korean War split the peninsula, putting his village just on the northern side of the demilitarized zone (DMZ). Before the Second World War, the family lived in a cardboard home in Japanese-occupied Seoul. As a teenager, Chung Ju Yung left home to seek his fortune, working as a labourer, delivery boy, car repairer and then in the construction industry. In his book *There are Difficulties, But No Failures*, Chung Ju Yung described himself thus: 'I am merely a rich labourer who, through his labour, produces commodities.' Chung had four brothers and one sister; the youngest brother, Chung Se Yung, born in 1928 and educated at Korea University, Seoul, has been the other major participant in running Hyundai, which Chung Ju Yung founded in 1947 as a construction company. It was Se Yung's only son, Mong Kyu, who moved up to chairman of Hyundai Motor in January 1996.

Chung Ju Yung had always been one step ahead in picking markets and opportunities. In the 1970s, Hyundai became Korea's largest engineering and construction company on the strength of a domestic boom and offshore work, notably in the Middle East. Hyundai also ventured early into the automotive business in the late 1960s. While its first efforts were crude copies of Japanese models, by 1995 Hyundai had lifted quality to exportable levels and was making 1.2 million cars and commercial vehicles a year. About 500,000 of them were exported, mainly to North America, Europe and Australia. In November 1996, it rolled out its 10 millionth car, a subcompact Accent model from its Ulsan plant.

Chung Ju Yung's nephew and new chairman Chung Mong Kyu said in 1996 that Hyundai Motor's next target markets would be India, Latin America, Africa and the Middle East. As part of that plan, he announced in mid-1996 that Hyundai would build a large auto plant in India with annual production capacity of 100,000 subcompact Accent cars.[16] Hyundai has plants operating or under construction in Venezuela, Indonesia, Thailand, the Philippines, Vietnam, Pakistan, Turkey, Egypt, Zimbabwe and Botswana. Its 1996 production goal was 1.4 million cars and commercial vehicles, of which 600,000 would be exported.

A younger brother of Chung Ju Yung, Chung In Yung, born in 1920, fell out with him in 1976 and left to create his own group, Halla, which now ranks 15th by sales among Korea's top conglomerates. Its core business is heavy industrial.

Ironically, a proposed steelmaking venture in Australia known as Asia Iron could deliver to Chung In Yung the integrated steel mill that his elder brother so covets. While heavy industry is the stuff of Chung In Yung's life in the late 1990s, he came to business by a circuitous route. An avid reader of English-language books at home in Seoul, he polished his skills later at Aoyama Gakuin university in Tokyo. This helped him become a journalist with one of

Korea's leading newspapers, the *Dong-A Ilbo* newspaper. He also worked as an interpreter with the US army during the Korean War, building up a network of valuable contacts that he was able to put to good use in business later.[27]

Elder brother Chung Ju Yung had another passion besides business – he wanted global recognition for Korea and thought that the sporting arena was one route to success. In 1981, after assiduous lobbying around the world, Chung won the right for Korea to host the 1988 Olympics in Seoul.

In Zurich on 5 June 1996, it was a case of family *déjà vu*, when FIFA announced that the right to host the 2002 soccer World Cup would be shared by South Korea and Japan. The president of the Korea Football Association and the man who had racked up 1.5 million kilometres of frequent flying during his three-year bid to get the World Cup was Chung Mong Joon, sixth son of Chung Ju Yung.

Old man Chung Ju Yung was forced to step aside from the reins of power after a disastrous run-in with South Korean President Kim Young-sam. The Kim administration harassed Hyundai with tax audits because Chung Ju Yung ran against him in the 1992 elections. This culminated in a court decision on 11 July 1994, when Chung Ju Yung, then 78, was given a three-year suspended sentence for spending more than US$65 million of Hyundai company money on his unsuccessful 1992 presidential bid. His younger brother Chung Se Yung had taken over as group chairman in 1987 and was named honorary chairman of Hyundai Motor in the December 1995 reshuffle that delivered the top job to Chung Mong Koo. Mong Koo's younger brother, Mong Hun, became group vice-chairman.

There was speculation that the meteoric rise of Chung Mong Kyu to the helm of Hyundai Motor could signal a split in the family, with Chung Se Yung and his only son taking control of all the automotive businesses in the Hyundai empire. But there could be no room for family rivalry in the late 1990s: watching for any sign of weakness was Hyundai's fierce carmaking competitor Kim Woo-choong [51], chairman of the Daewoo Business Group.

Kim, a chain-smoker who likes to relax playing Paduk, the chess-like game that the Japanese know as Go, is different from his tycoon colleagues in one key respect: there are no sons or daughters in key managerial positions at Daewoo. In fact, he expressly forbids it. One son is an architect, the other is a professional golfer. Kim, born in Taegu in the southern part of Korea in December 1936, has said that his successor will come from among the professional managers in the Daewoo group.[28]

For much of the 1980s and 1990s, Kim Woo-choong (estimated family worth US$1.9 billion) could do no wrong with both his business and cultural constituencies. His 1989 book written for the Korean younger generation, *Every Street is Paved with Gold*, was a runaway bestseller and was translated into 10 other languages.

By early 1996, however, the streets of Seoul were not so inviting. After charges over allegations of bribery involving Roh and other politicians late in 1995, Kim took himself off to Eastern Europe and a series of negotiations that led to Daewoo opting for massive new investments in the auto industry there. There were suggestions that he would not be coming back; with a 1994 suspended jail sentence already standing against him for an earlier bribery conviction, involving a former Korean trade minister and a nuclear power plant project, Kim might not relish the prospect of going to jail. In August 1996, Kim was given a two-year sentence, later suspended by an appeals court, allowing him to continue his peripatetic search for offshore investment openings.

Despite Kim's high profile, Daewoo is the weakest of the big conglomerates. There was some fear in the mid-1990s that the highly leveraged group could collapse if something unfortunate happened to Kim Woo-choong, but by early 1997, with the chairman still free to circle the globe, those fears had receded. Kim, sometimes described as Korea's most admired business leader, has been known to get down on the factory floor at any time of the day or night to check the quality of Daewoo cars. In a keynote speech in the United States late in 1996, Kim explained how he goes about his globalization and localization strategy in cars:

To improve our technical competitiveness, Daewoo is developing a network of advanced research centres in fully industrialised nations. We are establishing production bases, through highly calculated risks, in periphery nations largely shunned by OECD nations because of uncertain market growth potential, weak infrastructure and the time required to train labour. We consider localisation the key to success in these nations.[19]

Kim's 1989 book, with its Korean title meaning *It's a Big World and There's Lots to be Done*, struck a chord with Korean readers, who bought more than a million copies. Kim was regarded as an inspirational entrepreneur; even the name he gave to his company, Daewoo, which means 'great universe', reflected a breadth of vision destined to take him to the top.

After graduating in economics from Yonsei University in 1960, Kim spent a year with a Korean government organization, the Economic Development Council. Then followed five years with Hansung Industrial Company, where he rose to become a director before resigning in 1967 to set up his own business, Daewoo Industrial Co, as a small textile company with just five employees.[20]

Today, Daewoo has 100,000 employees worldwide and 1996 sales figures of more than US$60 billion. It consists of 24 companies, of which 9 are listed and 15 are closely held. Its business areas include general trading, motor vehicles, construction, heavy equipment and machinery, textiles, telecommunications, consumer electronics and financial services.

In February 1995, Kim decided that he would focus his attention on motor vehicles. In a shake-up designed to foster efficiency (and free himself up for the big tilt at the world's auto markets), he named 10 new chairmen to have full responsibility for the group's other main companies, including Daewoo Corporation, Daewoo Electronics, Daewoo Telecom and Daewoo Heavy Industries.

While Daewoo has global aspirations in motor vehicle sales, its technology is old-fashioned and based on outdated General

Motors designs. Daewoo entered into a joint venture with GM in 1979, but the partnership split in 1992 because of differences about marketing. Kim subsequently bought out GM's 50 per cent stake in Daewoo, and now also uses technology from Japan's Suzuki and Isuzu.

Daewoo Motor Co produced more than 630,000 motor vehicles in 1995 – mainly passenger cars in the 1.5 to 3.2 litre range. In April 1996 Daewoo said that it would invest US$1 billion in a $2 billion joint venture with Chinese partners to make automotive components – including engines and transmissions – in several locations in China. Two months earlier, Kim announced that Daewoo would invest up to US$5 billion over five years in India, mainly in car manufacturing, electronics, heavy industry, ship-building, construction and finance.

Kim's Vision 2000 strategy calls for the Daewoo group's total sales to reach US$134 billion by 2000, with $26 billion of this coming from motor vehicles, $28 billion from electronics and $36 billion from general trading.

Lee of Samsung, Chung of Hyundai and Kim of Daewoo all recognised that access to world-class technology would ultimately determine the success of their bid for a ranking among the world's top 10 carmakers. The one Korean company with access to just such technology is a comparative outsider; like the rhinoceros that gave its name to its flagship motor vehicle, the Musso four-wheel drive, Ssangyong had some hard charging to do. But even with a mountain of debt and a government-induced change in April 1995 at the top of the controlling Kim family (estimated worth US$1.3 billion, unrelated to Kim of Daewoo), Ssangyong was still in with a good shot.

Ssangyong's trump card in the Korean car war was its relationship with the German automaker Mercedes-Benz. In 1991, Mercedes-Benz took a 5 per cent stake in Ssangyong, and two years later, the stunningly competitive Ssangyong Musso four-wheel-drive station wagon, powered by Mercedes-Benz engines and transmissions, made its debut in Korea. Until then, Ssangyong had made only trucks and buses. Its Musso was viewed as a strong competitor to the Toyota Landcruiser, the

Mitsubishi Pajero, the Landrover and the Jeep in the 4WD category, largely on the strength of its Mercedes-Benz technology.

Like all the Korean conglomerates, Ssangyong (which means 'twin dragons') was not afraid to aim high. Although it ranked only sixth among Korea's business groups, with 1995 assets of US$17.4 billion and revenue of US$19.3 billion, it threw off its conservatism and declared that it would be one of the world's top 50 enterprises by 2000.[21]

The leadership change in April 1995 was a political order from the government of Kim Young-sam. Kim Suk-won [74], the eldest son of Ssangyong founder Kim Sung-kon, stepped down as chairman and was replaced by his younger brother Kim Suk-joon, then 42. Kim Suk-joon, who joined Ssangyong in 1977, had studied business administration at the University of Hartford in Connecticut, US. He was made vice-chairman in 1990.

His elder brother Kim Suk-won had guided the group for 20 turbulent years, building it into Korea's sixth largest business group with activities ranging from cement, oil refining, engineering and construction, general trading, financial services and, more recently, motor vehicle manufacturing. He also took Ssangyong to the point where it was ready to develop high-tech industries in electronics and fine ceramics.

Auto enthusiast Kim Suk-won said that he would remain an adviser to the group on its automotive business affairs, but essentially would devote himself to politics, by heading the Taegu branch of the ruling Democratic Liberal Party. Kim Suk-won's move into politics was a case of history repeating itself. His father, who died in 1975 after founding Ssangyong in 1939 as a soap-manufacturing firm, was an influential adviser to the late President Park Chung-hee during the 1970s and a leading member of Park's Democratic Republican Party. Park, who came to power as President in December 1963 after leading a military coup in May 1961, was assassinated on 26 October 1979.

While automotive business would be the top priority for Ssangyong's new leader, Kim Suk-joon said that the group would also concentrate on cement, fine ceramics, oil and petrochemicals in its bid to become a world-class enterprise.[22]

Ssangyong Group set up its first oil refinery in Korea in 1980 in a joint venture with the Iranian National Oil Company. The group includes Ssangyong Cement, one of Asia's largest cement producers (15 million tonnes a year) and operator of the world's largest cement plant on the east coast of Korea.

But with US$6 billion earmarked for investment in new auto plants over the five years 1995–99, it is this sector which exemplified the group's ambitions for the future.

The company's first passenger car is scheduled to hit the Korean market in late 1997. The mid-size sedan, again powered by Mercedes-Benz and likely to be based on the previous E-class Mercedes, will compete with Hyundai and Daewoo in the 3 litre class. Ssangyong's main Chagwon plant, built in 1994 with the help of Mercedes-Benz, will boost capacity to 250,000 units by mid-1998, while a 350,000-unit plant is under construction at Taegu and should come on stream in 1999. But by mid-1997, Ssangyong's rapid expansion was taking its toll. Ssangyong Motor had total debts of US$3.2 billion and said it was trying to sell up to 49 per cent of the company to a foreign automaker.

By 2000, the battle lines in the Koreans' global car wars will be well and truly drawn: four billionaire families, representing four of the most powerful business dynasties in Asia, want to squeeze into a space already occupied by names like Ford, GM, Toyota, Nissan, Volkswagen, Renault, Mercedes-Benz, Mitsubishi and Chrysler. Something has got to give.

9

Singapore Laps up the Luxury

We made a big mistake in market research.

Star Cruise chief executive Eddy Lee, October 1996[1]

FOR A FEW BRIEF WEEKS IN OCTOBER 1996, THE UNSPOILT Vietnamese island of Phu Quoc found itself playing host to several hundred wealthy visitors from Singapore, Malaysia and Thailand. They were guests aboard the luxury liner *Star Pisces*, a sleek, multi-decked palace of pleasure that cruised from the Thai port of Sri Racha to Phu Quoc and back. But with capacity running at only 50 per cent and no permanent port to give the passengers easy access to the island's delights, Phu Quoc quickly died a marketing death. The *Star Pisces* pulled out and headed north for Hong Kong, to serve the booming Hainan–Xiamen route in China.

The Phu Quoc experiment was a rare mistake for the Chinese Malaysian tycoon Lim Goh Tong *[13]*, whose Genting Group owns Star Cruise, operator of the *Star Pisces* and four other cruise boats.

Lim – who, like so many of Asia's billionaires, hails originally from Xiamen in China's Fujian province – made a fortune betting that the human desire to gamble ran so deep and so strong that it would triumph in almost any circumstances. He built Malaysia's first legal casino in the Genting Highlands in 1971 and, despite a sometimes treacherous 75-minute commute from Kuala Lumpur, watched the punters flock to his flamboyant eyrie of hotels, golf courses and funparks. In a country where the official religion, Islam, frowns on gambling, Lim's success is both stunning and sustained.

Twenty-five years later, Lim is betting on another irresistible human urge – a love of luxury – as he mixes gambling with the latest Asian leisure activity, high-style cruising.

Lim's Genting International paid about US$250 million in 1995 to acquire a small fleet of upmarket cruising ships, including the 2200-passenger *Star Pisces*. And despite the unprofitable Vietnam experiment, Lim wants more. In December 1995 he placed a US$700 million order for two 75,000-tonne super cruise ships, the *Superstar Leo* and the *Superstar Virgo*, that will take cruising in Asian waters to new heights of luxury. With 2800 passengers, 1000 crew and a 22-knot service speed, these German-built super cruisers will join Lim's fleet in 1998 and 1999.[2]

That will take Star Cruise from the eighth largest cruise line in the world to the fifth largest, and the largest in Asia. As the chairman of Genting International, Lim's son Lim Kok Thay, told shareholders in mid-1996, 'It is Star Cruise's vision to transform South East Asia into the new cruise region in the world.'[3]

The confidence that the Lim family expresses in this new business field reflects a recognition that luxury cruising is one of the new status symbols for Asia's wealthy élites in Singapore, Kuala Lumpur, Bangkok and Hong Kong. From a market that barely existed at the start of the 1990s, Singapore's cruise industry has leapt to 1 million passengers a year, equal to a sixth of the world market. Malaysia shows a similar spectacular growth rate.

Luxury is something that Singaporeans can well afford – the latest projections by a Japanese research institute, the Japan Centre for Economic Research, suggest that Singapore may be the world's wealthiest country by 2020, with a per capita gross national product of more than US$145,000 – ahead of current leaders like Switzerland, Scandinavia, Japan, the United States, Germany and France.[4]

Singapore's Inland Revenue Authority reported in November 1996 that the country had 386 millionaires, based on taxable earnings for the 1994 fiscal year – almost triple the number three years earlier – with another 1200 taxpayers closing fast on millionaire status.

That propensity to make money and spend it on life's little luxuries has not gone unnoticed by two Singapore-based billionaires, Kwek Leng Beng [22] and Ong Beng Seng [98], who between them have made a full-scale assault on some of the world's plushest hotels and consumerism's most alluring brand names.

Kwek, the Ferrari-driving figure who teamed up with Saudi Arabia's Prince Al Waleed bin Tahal bin Abdulaziz Saud to buy 80 per cent of the Plaza Hotel in New York in 1995 for about US$325 million, heads City Developments and the Singapore arm of the diversified Hong Leong Group, which has property, finance, industrial and trading interests.

The Plaza was just one of many five-star acquisitions in the 1990s by the peripatetic Kwek; his roll-call included the Gloucester and Britannia Hotels in London, the Grand Hyatt in Taipei, the Plaza in Manila, the Regent in Kuala Lumpur and the Nikko in Hong Kong. With the Singapore Government Investment Corporation as a potential partner, Kwek was thought to have his eye next on the Marriott Hotel in Hong Kong. Kwek's CDL Hotels International has rapidly built itself into one of the top 10 global hotel owners, with a mixed bag of 57 properties in East Asia, Australia, New Zealand, the United States and Europe.[5] In Britain, properties in his Millennium & Copthorne chain, floated on the London Stock Exchange in April 1996, are being refurbished and rebranded in 1997 as part of a push for greater identity on the luxury hotel scene. When Kwek took a breather from his buying spree at the start of 1997, he was said to be on the lookout for a strategic alliance with a luxury hotel operator, such as the Toronto-based Four Seasons/Regent group, to bring some top-flight management expertise to the hotels.

For his part, Ong Beng Seng has been a shade more modest than Kwek with his hotel purchases, although his Singapore-listed Hotel Properties Ltd (HPL) controls a line-up that includes the Four Seasons in Singapore, the Four Seasons Resort in Bali and the Four Seasons Hotel Milano. On Australia's Gold Coast, Ong plans to build a US$250 million five-star hotel that would be the biggest in the country, with 1570 rooms. And in London, HPL is a joint venture partner with Canary Wharf Ltd in a US$500 million development on the river Thames that will include luxury condominiums and a hotel.[6]

Ong's HPL is better known in Singapore for its residential apartment complexes, particularly after an unsolicited discount offer on the purchase of four condominiums by Singapore's elder statesman and Senior Minister, Lee Kuan Yew, and his son, Deputy Prime Minister Lee Hsien Loong, turned into a public relations disaster for Ong in April 1996. The Lees were cleared of any wrongdoing by the Singaporean Prime Minister, Goh Chok Tong, but Ong was censured by the Stock Exchange of Singapore for not being forthcoming with information about the discounts.[7]

After defending the unsolicited discounts as 'totally transparent' commercial transactions, Ong got on with the business of making money from his string of other luxury-related interests: the Giorgio Armani, Bulgari and Donna Karan/DKNY labels – including a joint venture with Donna Karan Japan to open about 30 stores in Asia – and franchises in various parts of Asia for the Planet Hollywood, Hard Rock Café and Häagen Dazs names. Ong's wife, Christina, is involved in some of these ventures, including the Armani and Bulgari names in Britain and her own Club 21 fashion line in Asia. HPL's 10 per cent stake in Nasdaq-listed Planet Hollywood International Inc proved Ong's bargain of the year; his US$30 million investment was worth more than US$190 million when the shares made their trading debut in April 1996. He followed that up by getting Lee Kun Hee's Samsung conglomerate to be his powerful ally in selling the Donna Karan and DKNY apparel labels to Korea's fast-growing upper–middle-income market.

Luxury is never far from Ong's mind: HPL's corporate structure includes ownership of Luxury Holdings, which in turn owns

Luxury Hotels, Luxury Properties and Luxury Complex.[8] More down to earth was Ong's ownership of the Australian music and retail group, Brash's, which did not prove hugely successful. After a US$7 million loss in 1995, Ong disposed of 49 per cent of Brash's in January 1996 to Japanese consumer electronics retailer Daiichi Corp for about US$25 million.

While HPL is the public vehicle for the high-flying Ong, much of the family money cycles through Kuo International, the oil and commodities trading company which Ong's father-in-law, Peter Fu Yun Siak, controls. Together with her father and brother Peter junior, Christina Ong runs the upmarket fashion store Club 21 in Singapore's Hilton Shopping Gallery, owned, naturally enough, by husband Ong Beng Seng's Hotel Properties Ltd. Club 21's own fashion lines and hot international brand names like Donna Karan and Calvin Klein are making it one of the outriders of the Asian luxury boom.

The third key Singaporean billionaire, Ng Teng Fong [27], made his first millions in local property deals, to the point where Ng is Singapore's largest landlord after the government. But in recent years Ng and his son, Robert Ng Chee Siong, have chosen to concentrate on the more lucrative property plays to be found in Hong Kong, where their Sino Land is now one of the heavyweight developers with assets of more than US$12 billion.

Sino Land is behind the massive new Gold Coast residential development, about 40 minutes by fast ferry from Hong Kong Central, while the Ngs' hotel arm, Sino Hotels, teamed up with parent Sino Land to outlay almost US$150 million for an 80 per cent stake in Hong Kong's five-star Conrad Hotel. Sino Land also paid US$300 million early in 1997 for a prime 18-storey building in the heart of the Tsim Sha Tsui tourist precinct. One reason for the Ng family's Hong Kong focus is to be found in a comparison of retail rents; in 1996 the world's most expensive shop rents were in Causeway Bay on Hong Kong island. At around US$8000 a square metre per year, they were almost three times the price of Singapore's Orchard Road shopping strip, where the top rents peaked at around US$2800.

Still, the prime commercial and shopping precinct around Orchard Road has been a happy hunting ground for Ng Teng Fong. Along with property developments in the area like Lucky Plaza, Ng's listed hotel/restaurant company, Orchard Parade Holdings (OPH), operates the Orchard Parade Hotel. Ng used OPH and his privately held development company, Far East Organisation, to win a bitter tussle in 1995 with financier Quek Leng Beng – the Malaysian cousin of Kwek Leng Beng – for Singapore food and beverage company Yeo Hiap Seng. One reason Ng wanted Yeo Hiap Seng was to get access to the land where its factories are now sited. Those plants are due to move in 1998, freeing up the land for potential redevelopment.

Ng, Ong, Kwek and Malaysia's Lim are just some of the Asian tycoons to have targeted luxury properties inside and outside the region. In 1989, Cheng Yu-tung's [37] New World Development paid more than US$500 million for the Ramada hotel chain and turned it into a profitable operation. By the time the Hong-Kong-based Cheng family agreed to sell its 54 per cent stake in Renaissance Hotel Group to US company Marriott International Inc in February 1997 in a deal that valued the chain at US$1 billion (pipping an offer by Doubletree Corp a month earlier of about US$850 million in cash, stock and debt), New World had more than 140 Ramada and Renaissance properties in North America, Australia and Asia.[9]

In August 1996, a consortium of investors from Singapore and Hong Kong, led by Lim Por Yen's Lai Sun Development, paid US$190 million for New York's posh Four Seasons Hotel – the equivalent of US$514,000 a room for its 370 rooms. The 52-storey hotel, built in 1993, was designed by I.M. Pei, responsible for such landmarks as the Bank of China building in Hong Kong.

Yet another New York property to end up in Asian hands was the former Helmsley Palace (now the New York Palace), snapped up by the world's richest man, the Sultan of Brunei, for US$200 million in November 1993. The Sultan also owns the Beverly Hills Hotel in Los Angeles, which he bought in 1987 for US$185 million and then spent another US$100 million restoring it over four years to its 'Hollywood landmark' status.

Poet and reluctant businessman Seiji Tsutsumi, half-brother to Japan's richest man, Yoshiaki Tsutsumi [3], controls the Inter-Continental chain from his base in the ultra-exclusive Seiyo Hotel in Tokyo's Ginza, while Bangkok's top hotel owner, Chanut Piyaoui of the Dusit Thani group, acquired her controlling interest in Germany's Kempinski chain late in 1994.

These acquisitions in just one luxury field, five-star hotels, confirm what the economic statistics already suggest: while Europe now has more seriously rich people (1.7 million, controlling assets of US$4700 billion) than the United States (1.6 million, controlling US$4500 billion), both will be overtaken by Asia (now US$4200 billion) within 10 years.[10]

And even after years of recession in the wake of the 'bubble economy' excesses of the late 1980s, Japan still has the greatest membership of Asia's wealth club. There are at least 40 billionaire families in Japan; while some are new-age financiers and real-estate speculators, a good proportion are 'old money' names like Toyoda (founders of the Toyota Motor Corporation), Saji (of Suntory fame), Yoshida, who began the YKK group, and Takenaka, whose construction company has borne the family name for generations.

In the 1980s and early 1990s, Japan was synonymous with conspicuous consumption of luxury goods, particularly brand names like Gucci, Versace, Chanel and Dior. But most of the consumption took place offshore, with tourist destinations like Hawaii, Hong Kong, Europe and Australia benefiting from a surge of cashed-up Japanese visitors. It was almost obligatory for young Japanese women – known as 'office ladies' or OLs – to shop in Paris for their Louis Vuitton luggage and designer clothes, and for male retirees – known as 'silvers' – to buy their Jack Nicklaus or Greg Norman golf clubs in the United States or Australia. The strength of the yen made every purchase seem like a bargain.

Conversely, purchasing-power parity works against the Japanese billionaires at home – hence only a handful are listed in the top 100 because their domestic purchasing power is so much lower than that of their business rivals in India, Indonesia or Thailand. Put simply, US$1 billion buys a whole lot more in Bombay, Jakarta or Bangkok than it does in Tokyo or Osaka. But while the gap is closing, the largest lump of accumulated Asian wealth will remain in Japanese hands well into the twenty-first century.

By 2020, the combined GDP of Asia (excluding Japan) will constitute 25.8 per cent of the world's GDP, ahead of North America's 23.9 per cent, western Europe's 22.1 per cent and Japan's 11.3 per cent. Within Asia, Singapore, Hong Kong, South Korea, Taiwan and Thailand are the fastest-growing sources of wealth, and Singapore is ranked the second most profitable country in the world (behind Switzerland) for business investment, just ahead of Japan and Taiwan.[11] From a long way back, China is beginning the inevitable sustained run that, barring catastrophe, will see its wealth eclipse that of every other nation by the middle of the twenty-first century. This alone should ensure a continued Asian love affair with luxury goods and services.

Another sign of the Asian times: in October 1996, a few months before his tragic death in a helicopter crash in March 1997, Malaysian billionaire Yahaya Ahmad [97] confirmed that he had bought 80 per cent of British sportscar maker Lotus in a deal valued at about US$80 million. Yahaya, whose DRB-Hicom group took a controlling 32 per cent stake in Malaysian national carmaker Proton in late 1995, said that he wanted Lotus for its research and development capability.[12] That brought another sportscar name under Asian control; the Italian marque Lamborghini was acquired by Indonesian interests, including Tommy Suharto, in the early 1990s. And buoyed by Yahaya's purchase of the Lotus name, Malaysia's Prime Minister, Dr Mahathir Mohamad, struck another blow for luxury spending in the name of technology transfer. Late in 1996 he announced that Malaysia would sponsor the Jackie Stewart–Ford team in the 1997 Formula 1 motor-racing season. A potential bonus down the track: Malaysia could host its own Formula 1 race in 1999.

Brand hunting, from hotels to car marques, watches, fashion

accessories and department stores, may well be the next big growth zone if Singaporeans like Kwek Leng Beng, Ong Beng Seng and Ng Teng Fong are any guide. And those cachet-carrying brand names are all the better to be seen with, when cruising through the South China Sea aboard one of Lim Goh Tong's luxury liners like the *Star Pisces*, or alighting from one of the low-slung Lotus sportscars that the late Yahaya Ahmad so dearly loved.

10

'First Family' Fortune – the Suharto Children

This is not robbery. The poor are entitled to demand something from those who are more fortunate and able.

> Indonesia's President Suharto, warning the country's rich that the government would force them to help the poor if they did not do so voluntarily[1]

IN EARLY 1997, WHILE AMERICANS FRETTED OVER THE FRIENDSHIP between their president and Indonesia's billionaire Riady family (founders of the Lippo Group), a much more fundamental and far-reaching saga of wealth and influence was being played out on the other side of the world. This had nothing to do with Asian contributions to the Democratic Party's 1996 presidential campaign funds, and everything to do with the future of Asia's most enduring leader – President Suharto *[9]* – and his business-minded family.

In a country of 200 million people where 3.5 per cent of the population (the ethnic Chinese component) controls 75 per cent of the wealth, Suharto's September 1996 warning to Indonesia's rich élites was almost a plea for self-preservation. But for once, few people seemed to be listening and the warning largely went unheeded. When a series of violent outbursts motivated by political, ethnic and socioeconomic rivalries convulsed parts of

Indonesia in 1996–97, threatening to tear at the stable platform for growth built so painstakingly by Suharto over the 30-year period, it was clear that the ageing Indonesian leader (and his family) faced a monumental challenge.

It began with a plan to share a little bit more of the wealth. Early in 1996, President Suharto called on all Indonesian individuals and corporations whose annual after-tax income exceeded 100 million rupiah (about US$43,000) to give 2 per cent of their income to a special fund for Indonesia's 25 million poor. The money was to go to the Sejahtera Mandiri Foundation, which the president himself would oversee. But the response during the year was less than overwhelming, prompting first a threat of compulsion and finally, in December, a presidential decree ordering a 2 per cent surcharge on wealthy taxpayers. Throughout the year and in the run-up to the May 1997 general elections, the country simmered with ethnic jealousies, the discontent of the have-nots and the protests of the politically marginalized.

The president's wealth fund is part of the Suharto paradox – concern for the poor, but when it comes to a financial dynasty in Asia, Indonesia's 'First Family' is in a world of its own. Between them, the ambitious sons and daughters of President Suharto are building billion-dollar empires in property, banking, industry, telecoms, media and transport, the like of which have never been seen before in Indonesia. Many of those businesses started and prospered on the strength of licences or special contracts handed out by the government, angering competitors and investors in the process. Despite the secrecy that veils much of the Suhartos' accumulation of assets, it is clear they may already represent the single biggest concentration of family wealth in Asia.[2]

The story of the Suharto family fortune goes back to June 1921, when Suharto was born to a poor peasant family in the village of Kemusu, near Jogjakarta in central Java.[3] After a conservative Islamic upbringing and a short stint as a bank clerk, Suharto entered military school in the Dutch colonial forces in 1940. He was just 19, at the start of a military career that would bring him eventually to centre stage. By early 1942, the Dutch forces in

Indonesia had surrendered to the invading Japanese and Suharto, who became an officer in 1943, served with the Japanese-sponsored Indonesian Volunteer Army until its collapse in 1945. Suharto was named a battalion commander and later a regimental commander with the Indonesian forces at Jogjakarta. When Indonesia declared its independence in 1945, he fought against the returning Dutch colonialists, aided with food and medical supplies by a trusted ethnic Chinese businessman named Liem Sioe Liong *[18]*.

As Suharto's star rose, so too did that of his friend Liem. By 1957, when Suharto had risen to the rank of colonel, Liem had moved his trading business to Jakarta and embarked on his own commercial journey that would seem him emerge in the 1980s as Indonesia's richest and most influential businessman at the head of the Salim Group. Suharto's military career continued apace, apart from a smuggling hiccup in 1959 that saw him lose his Central Java command and be sent to staff college at Bandung; he became a brigadier-general in 1960, and by 1962, as major-general, was in charge of operations against the Dutch in West Irian.

In December 1947 Suharto married Sitih Hartinah, who bore him six children (three sons, three daughters) and was his soul-mate, loyal companion, adviser and sounding board for almost 50 years.[4] It was an arranged marriage, but a long and fruitful one. Madame Tien Suharto, as she was later known, came from royal blood, a descendant of the Mangkunegoro sultans who once ruled central Java. She was active in the guerrilla war against the Dutch and won two medals for her exploits. From his humble beginnings as the son of a common farmer, Suharto was already making his mark as an army officer when they married. With Madame Tien at his side, he rose to become the most powerful and enduring leader in South-East Asia, the man who presided over a nation of 200 million people and a family that saw no bounds to the search for profits.

In 1965, Suharto played the decisive role in the most important political event of postwar South-East Asia – the coup attempt in Jakarta that led to the downfall of Indonesia's founding President,

Suharto family and friends

Family member	Main companies	Main business partners
First daughter: Siti Hardijanti Rukmana, married to Indra Rukmana	Citra Marga Nusaphala Persada, Citra Lamtoro Gung Persada	Prajogo Pangestu
First son: Sigit Harjojudanto, married to Elsye Anneke Ratnawati	Henurata Group, Humpuss Group, Nusamba	Younger brother Tommy, Mohamad Bob Hasan
Second son: Bambang Trihatmodjo, married to Siti Halimah	Bimantara Citra, Satelindo, PSN, Kanindo, Chandra Asri	Rosana Barack, Muhamad Tachril, Peter Gontha, Johannes Kotjo, Henry Pribadi, Anthony Salim
Second daughter: Siti Hedijanti Harijadi, married to Major-General Prabowo Subianto	Maharani Paramita	Hashim Djojohadikusumo
Third son: Hutomo Mandala Putra, married to Ardhia Pramesti Regita Cahyani	Humpuss Group, Sempati Air	Mohamad Bob Hasan, Kia Motors
Third daughter: Siti Hutami Endang Adiningsih, married to Pratikto Prayitno Singgih	Plantations, warehousing, transport and land reclamation, director of the Mekarsari Fruit Garden	Holds various stakes in elder siblings' ventures
Sudwikatmono (Suharto's cousin)	Indofood, Indocement, Mulia Land	Liem Sioe Liong
Probosutedjo (Suharto's half-brother)	Mercu Buana Group	Hardijanti Rukmana

Sukarno. In the terrible bloodletting that followed, perhaps half a million people were murdered as various vigilante groups led killing raids on communists, their political sympathizers, ethnic Chinese (*cukong*) and ordinary villagers. Although some of the *cukong* such as Liem Sioe Liong were already close to Suharto, the army chose not to intervene as waves of terror convulsed Indonesia for the next few months.

The coup attempt began on the night of 30 September and continued into the early hours of 1 October, when seven bands of soldiers entered Jakarta to kill or capture seven of Indonesia's top generals.[5] They were acting on the orders of Lieutenant-Colonel Untung, an officer of the palace guard, who was directing operations from the Halim air base outside Jakarta. Various members of the Indonesian communist party, the PKI, were on hand to support the coup. Sukarno, too, made his way to Halim, but the extent of his support has always been clouded in debate.

Overnight, the rebels captured and killed six of their targets. The seventh, Defence Minister General Nasution, escaped. Though the 44-year-old Major-General Suharto was deputy to the Army Chief of Staff, he was not on the plotters' list – a mistake that was to prove their undoing. Early on 1 October, Suharto was told of the killings and immediately set about isolating the coup plotters. With a flurry of calls from his office in central Jakarta, he sized up the situation, mobilized the loyal troops of his Army Strategic Reserve (KOSTRAD) and talked the commanders of the rebel forces into surrendering less than 24 hours after the coup began. The next day, his forces took the conspirators' headquarters, the Halim air base, after Sukarno had left Halim for his Bogor palace. In the deliberate steps that Suharto took, he neutralized Sukarno without ever actually taking presidential power away from him.

Over the next year Suharto progressively cut away Sukarno's support base, and by February 1967 he had assumed all real powers of government; the People's Consultative Congress appointed him acting president the following month and on 27 March 1968 he was formally appointed Indonesia's second president. Sukarno was left in isolation, first at Bogor, and later in the Jakarta house of his Japanese wife, Dewi. He died in a military hospital on 16 June 1970, a pathetic and lonely man.

Suharto, the pragmatic military man, had won. And with his cohort of economic rationalists – known as the Berkeley mafia for their US training – he embarked on a new economic course for Indonesia that would bring it stability and business opportunity, not least for the family and friends of the president. The army, with the *cukong* running its various business enterprises, had shown itself under Suharto's command to be the only force capable of maintaining order.

As the Australian author Bruce Grant wrote perceptively in 1966, 'Suharto's friends say that he does not see himself continuing indefinitely in the "strong man" role thrust upon him after 30 September 1965. But men do not give up power easily.'[6]

How true. More than 30 years later, Suharto was not inclined to step down, and the accumulation of riches by his six children, relatives like half-brother Probosutedjo and cousin Sudwikatmono, family friends like Liem Sioe Liong, Mohamad Bob Hasan [80] and Prajogo Pangestu [49], along with linkages to the Riady [89] and Djojohadikusumo [94] families, showed no sign of abating.

The Suhartos have an estimated net worth of at least US$6.35 billion – the real figure may be much higher. Three years ago, all the businesses were private and, while publicly traded companies like Bimantara Citra and Citra Marga have lifted the lid a little, there is a view that the best family assets are still tucked away out of sight.

In a sense, the death of Madame Tien accelerated the opening-up process and may yet prove the turning point for the Suharto family's fortune. Madame Tien died of a heart attack on 28 April 1996, aged 72, after more than 49 years as Suharto's wife. In the 1970s, when Indonesia's economy was sloughing off the negative growth impact of the Sukarno years, Madame Tien had become a prominent business figure. Her husband ran the country, and she ran their business interests. But in later years she stepped back to let her children pursue the family's fortune. Most of her time after that was spent developing a private charity, the Yayasan Harapan Kita (Our Hope Foundation), which was part of the family's business interests.[7]

Each of the six Suharto children has developed a variety of companies, with the eldest, first daughter Siti Hardijanti Rukmana (known as Tutut), and the second son, Bambang Trihatmodjo, presiding over the most diversified fortunes.

But will the children prosper in a post-Suharto world? That was the question most often asked in Jakarta, following the death of Suharto's wife and the president's own health worries that led to a quick trip to Germany for a check-up in July 1996. The riots late that same year and early 1997 added to the confusion. The result was a volatile stock market and a tendency for some of the *cukong* to look offshore for financial boltholes in Singapore, Australia and North America.

For the Suharto children, the art of mixing politics and business gained more importance as their father's sixth term neared an end. In May 1996, Suharto's second son Bambang, treasurer of the ruling Golkar Party, told reporters at a Golkar meeting in Jakarta that his father was not preparing any member of the family to be his successor.

Suharto himself has said that the People's Consultative Assembly, known as the MPR, should decide from a range of candidates.

But a few months later, in September 1996, Bambang and his elder sister appeared on a list of the Golkar Party's parliamentary candidates for the general elections at the end of May 1997. By the time the list closed, Suharto's third son, Hutomo Mandala Putra (known as Tommy), and second daughter, Siti Hedijanti Harijadi Prabowo (known as Titiek), had joined the Golkar list, along with Bambang's wife, Halimah Trihatmodjo.

Until the September announcement, only Tutut had shown political inclinations. Almost invariably clad in a Muslim scarf, Tutut appeared often at Golkar events, and was touted as a possible vice-presidential candidate if her father were to stand again for president in 1998, as seemed increasingly likely.

A few leading Indonesian figures were prepared to speculate on the post-Suharto era. General Soemitro, one of Suharto's comrades in arms from Generasi 45 – the Indonesians who fought for independence from the Dutch in 1945 – declared that, as Suharto's retention of the presidency beyond 1998 was 'all but guaranteed', the wisest course was to start talking about the transition of power 'that will inevitably take place after the 1998–2003 term, if not before'.[8]

Calling for a re-engineering of the vice-president's post, General Soemitro said: 'I am of the opinion that Mr Suharto, as the chief executive officer of Indonesia Inc, needs to share more of his power with whomever fills a position that should rightly be regarded as the government's chief operating officer. This recast executive vice president would no longer be the symbolic figure the VP is now, but would act on behalf of the president by orchestrating the day-to-day operations of the cabinet.'

One contender for an expanded vice-presidential role (and then on to the presidency) is Indonesia's Minister of Technology, Dr Jusuf Habibie, a Suharto confidant. Habibie, a technocrat rather than a military man, has already observed that Suharto will be 77 in 1998 and it would be unwise not to 'allow him to enjoy his retirement'.[9]

But before a new chief executive steps up to take over Indonesia Inc, he or she will have to fashion a strategy for dealing with the rest of the First Family and their future business plans. While details of their individual business activities appear in Part II of this book, on pages 179 to 184, what follows is a brief description of the six Suharto children.

Siti Hardijanti Rukmana, born in 1949, is the eldest child and known popularly as Mbak (sister) Tutut. She is married to businessman Indra Rukmana. Her listed company is toll-road operator Citra Marga Nusaphala Persada (CMNP), which had a market capitalization of about US$780 million in early 1997. But her main company, begun in 1983, is Citra Lamtoro Gung Persada, of which she owns 35 per cent. Her husband holds 20 per cent, and sisters

Titiek and Mamie also have shares.

Apart from her business activities, Tutut is head of the Indonesian Red Cross, active in the Indonesia Portugal Friendship Association and deputy chair of the central board of Golkar, the ruling political organization.

The eldest son in the Suharto family is Sigit Harjojudanto, born in 1951, and married to Elsye Anneke Ratnawati. Until the mid-1990s, Sigit had been a relatively low profile member of the family, involved in banking and plastics through his Hanurata Group. Like his elder sister Tutut, he held a 17.5 per cent stake in Liem Sioe Liong's Bank Central Asia. He also had a 40 per cent stake in Humpuss, the group he helped his younger brother, 'Tommy' Hutomo Mandala Putra, to establish. Like Tommy, he is also in business with Suharto confidant and golf partner, plywood king Mohamad Bob Hasan. Sigit and Hasan each hold 10 per cent stakes in Nusamba, an investment holding company that was involved in a share-buying move on Astra International, Indonesia's largest car assembler, in late 1996. Hasan emerged at the head of an informal group controlling more than 50 per cent of Astra.[10]

Sigit's second big move in 1996 was to sign on with the Canadian miner, Bre-X, to develop Busang, touted by its promoters as a vast gold deposit in Kalimantan reputedly worth US$30 billion. But after the mysterious death of chief geologist Michael de Guzman in March 1997, apparently in a fall from a helicopter, the Busang mine was eventually shown to be a huge, elaborate fraud. Before the scam was unmasked, Bre-X thought that having Sigit as a consultant and stakeholder would guarantee smooth passage. But heavyweight Canadian miners Barrick Gold and Placer Dome sought to be involved. While Bre-X had Sigit, Barrick had Sigit's elder sister Tutut as a potential partner. Finally, in February 1997, Sigit's partner Hasan engineered a whole new deal, bringing in the US miner Freeport McMoRan Copper and Gold: Bre-X got 45 per cent, Freeport 15 per cent, Hasan, Sigit and friends 30 per cent, and the Indonesian government 10 per cent.[11] Freeport's own due diligence investigations soon unravelled the monumentally embarrassing fraud. Busang had been salted by persons unknown.

Second son Bambang Trihatmodjo, born in 1953, had his own share of high-profile deals to do in the late 1990s. Bambang is possibly the best known of the Suharto children internationally, on the strength of his assiduous courting of US and European investors after taking his holding company Bimantara Citra public in 1995. He also listed his polypropylene company Tri Polyta in the same year.

Bambang has benefited hugely from a swag of government concessions and licences since setting up Bimantara in 1981. Today there are more than 100 subsidiaries in the group. The flagship is Bimantara Citra, a holding company with interests in broadcasting and telecommunications, the automotive and oil industries, and infrastructure, finance, electronics and entertainment.

Bambang, who started Bimantara with friends Rosano Barack, Muhamad Tachril and ex-Citibanker Peter Gontha, holds 41.1 per cent of the company (market capitalization US$1.4 billion in early 1997), while his brother-in-law Indra Rukmana, married to elder sister Tutut, holds a smaller share and is chairman of the group.

Bambang, with Salim Group associates as partners, had a stake in a US$500 million power project in East Java involving the US power company Enron, and also showed interest in another major infrastructure play in late 1996 – Jakarta's US$1.5 billion light rail project being developed by a billionaire in the making, *pribumi* (indigenous) businessman Fadel Muhamed. Fadel's Bukaka Teknik Utama company emerged in the late 1990s as one of the hottest new performers on the Indonesian corporate scene.

Second daughter Siti Hedijanti Harijadi, born in 1959 and popularly known as Titiek, is married to Major-General Prabowo Subianto, 45-year-old commander of the Kopassus special forces regiment, and a man tipped for high office – possibly even as Suharto's successor.[12] Titiek's main company is Maharani Paramita, which is involved in property, telecommunications, finance and forestry. She is also a business partner of Prabowo's billionaire elder brother, Hashim Djojohadikusumo [94], in the Paiton power project and a Jakarta shopping mall project.

The most flamboyant of the Suharto children is the third and youngest son, Hutomo Mandala Putra, known as Tommy. Born in

1962, Tommy is a pilot, rally driver and often seen in the company of starlets until his surprise marriage in April 1997 to a 22-year-old civil engineering graduate, Ardhia 'Tata' Pramesti Regita Cahyani, daughter of a shipping executive. Tommy started the Humpuss group in 1984, which covers about 70 companies in fields such as aviation, agribusiness, toll-road construction, oil, gas, commodities, manufacturing, media, petrochemicals and timber. Humpuss earns much of its revenue from oil shipment contracts with Pertamina, the state oil and gas corporation.

Tommy's biggest and most controversial business play is his joint venture with South Korea's Kia Motors to produce the Timor 'national car'. Tommy's father gave the project 'pioneer' status, meaning that it would gain a tax break of up to US$1 billion and a substantial price advantage over other carmakers in the Indonesian market such as Astra and Indomobil.

Tommy is also head of the Clove Marketing Board and his business partners include Mohamad Bob Hasan [80], who holds 20 per cent of Sempati Air (an Indonesian army foundation holds 22 per cent, Humpuss has a 14 per cent direct stake and an offshore investment company controlled by Tommy has 44 per cent).[13]

The youngest Suharto child is third daughter Siti Hutami Endang Adiningsih, born in 1964. Known as Mamie or Mimiek, she is married to Pratikto Prayitno Singgih. Her companies are involved in plantations, warehousing, transport and a land-reclamation project near Jakarta.

Other prominent relatives involved in the family fortune include Suharto's half-brother Probosutedjo, 66, who is deputy chairman of KADIN, the Indonesian Chamber of Commerce and Industry, and his cousin Sudwikatmono, 61, who holds board positions with the two largest of the Salim Group's listed companies, Indocement and Indofood. Apart from Liem Sioe Liong and Bob Hasan, a more recent business associate of the Suharto clan is Prajogo Pangestu [49], whose Barito Pacific group has extensive plywood and forestry interests.

While basic commodities such as food, tobacco, oil and timber figured prominently in the early business interests of the Suharto clan, it was Indonesia's massive power needs that began producing the most lucrative opportunities in the 1990s. With 200 million people and per capita income crossing the US$1000 threshold, power consumption has only one way to go – up. From 13,000 megawatts in 1996, Indonesia needs to lift its generating capacity to 50,000 megawatts by 2008, with about 20 per cent of this to come from independent power producers.

The biggest power project now underway in Indonesia is the twin 600 megawatt Paiton One plant in East Java, a US$2.5 billion project due for completion by late 1998. Naturally, there is a Suharto connection. The partners are General Electric and Mission Energy of the United States, Mitsui of Japan, and PT Batu Hitam Perkasa, the Indonesian coal company controlled by Hashim Djojohadikusumo and his sister-in-law by marriage, Suharto's second daughter, Siti Hedijanti Harijadi (Titiek).

Close by the Paiton project is another massive infrastructure play with the almost obligatory Suharto mark on it. This is the 1220 megawatt Java Power Plant, whose investors include Siemens of Germany, PowerGen of Britain and Bimantara Citra, the listing holding company of Suharto's second son, Bambang Trihatmodjo.

Not everyone believes that the Suharto children's activities have a totally negative impact on the Indonesian economic scene. In September 1996, Michael Backman, director of research at Jakarta-based investment research company The Castle Group, said that the business interests of Indonesia's First Family had been 'instrumental in breaking up some of the monopolies held by incredibly inefficient state-owned enterprises in Indonesia'.[14]

'The sons and daughters of the President have been the only group sufficiently highly connected, and powerful, to break up some of the monopolies – and in some instances, to force privatizations,' he wrote. 'The first family has reached its position by receiving substantial favours in its business dealings by virtue of its position. This may be unfair, but not necessarily bad economics.'

To counter the perception that when Suharto goes there will be a violent reaction against the business excesses of his children, the family has begun to take defensive measures. Tutut and Bambang have already taken public their main holding companies, Citra Marga and Bimantara Citra. Tommy was expected to list the Humpuss Group's partly owned airline unit, Sempati Air, on the Jakarta Stock Exchange and was said to be considering a partial float of Humpuss Sea Transport.

But the 2 per cent wealth tax may hasten the test of perceptions: Suharto has been critical of big business for not voluntarily supporting his foundation for the poor. As cracks begin to appear in this hitherto relatively stable society of a few 'haves' and many millions of 'have-nots', will Suharto's sons and daughters be seen to pay up, or will they invoke 'First Family' privilege?

11

A Sultan's Wealth Beyond Measure

It is important that everyone owns a house, for it is where everything begins. It is a place for 'ibadat' (acts of piety), character moulding and cultivation of pure values.

The Sultan of Brunei[1]

FOR A FEW BRIEF DAYS IN DECEMBER 1962, THERE WAS A CHANCE that eventual ownership of the richest house in the world might elude a shy 16-year-old student prince. Rebels were seeking to overthrow his father, Sir Omar 'Ali Saifuddien III, the 28th Sultan and the man known as the architect of modern Brunei.

Today, no such fears confront Hassanal Bolkiah [1], the 29th Sultan of the tiny oil-rich nation on the island of Borneo. Two wives, ten children, numerous palaces, 165 Rolls-Royces, 250 polo ponies, 300,000 subjects and an estimated wealth of US$30 billion are just some of the vital statistics that help define this absolute monarch.

When the Sultan turned 50 in July 1996, the celebrations in his capital of Bandar Seri Begawan were fittingly sumptuous for the man widely regarded as the world's richest person.

Three concerts by entertainer Michael Jackson, mammoth fireworks displays, the formal opening of a free Disney-like funpark as a gift to his people, and a guest list that included Britain's Prince Charles, helped swell the birthday bill to US$20 million.[2]

While 1996 was a gala year for the Sultan and his people, the mood in Bandar Seri Begawan had not always been so festive – particularly back in December 1962 when the young Crown Prince was heading home from studies in Singapore. He was forced to abort his journey when an armed rebellion broke out in Brunei's capital, then known as Brunei Town – a sleepy village of 60,000 people on the banks of the Brunei River.

The rebels were a mixed bunch: disaffected local politicians and external guerrillas from the North Borneo Liberation Army, opposed to Brunei's planned entry into the Federation of Malaysia and supported by Indonesia's then president, Sukarno.

Early on the morning of Saturday 8 December 1962, they attempted to overthrow the current Sultan's father, Sir Omar 'Ali Saifuddien, by cutting off power and attacking key points in the capital, including the police headquarters.

But rumours of an impending rebellion had reached Sir Omar a few hours earlier, and he was prepared for trouble. Following an appeal from the Sultan, British troops from Singapore flew in to help the local police put down the rebellion, and after about 10 days order was restored. Rebels who fled into the jungle were hunted down by tribespeople loyal to the Sultan, while those who escaped to Indonesia and Malaysia were effectively neutralized. The Brunei People's Party (Partai Rakyat Brunei, or PRB), which had earlier won 54 of 55 seats in the nation's first and only elections, was banned.[3]

A state of emergency declared by Sir Omar remains in force today, almost three decades after the present Sultan took over from his father. Despite occasional steps in the direction of a more liberal political regime, the Sultan shows no strong inclination to change the system of rule by decree. His subjects, he says, are not yet ready for politics again.

In 1996, the Sultan could well afford to indulge his subjects in some conspicuous consumption; the cost of his 50th birthday bash was equal to just three days' revenue from the steady stream of oil and gas that has given Brunei's inhabitants one of the highest per capita incomes in Asia.

But the Sultan, who doubles as Prime Minister and Defence Minister (and, since the resignation of younger brother Prince Jefri in February 1997, as Finance Minister), is acutely aware that the oil, first discovered at Brunei's Seria field in 1929, won't last forever. While the search goes on for new fields, the latest predictions are that with daily production of up to 180,000 barrels, existing reserves will be exhausted in the first half of the twenty-first century.

To ensure that consumption continues to come naturally to Bruneians long after the oil runs out, the Sultan has been pursuing a diversification programme that relies heavily on offshore investments. His purchase in the past decade of trophy properties may grab public attention, but the Sultan's real money-making machine is the Brunei Investment Agency, the overseas investment arm of the Brunei government.

It has an estimated US$30 billion to US$40 billion invested around the world in property, gold, securities, bonds and various businesses, and brings in revenues thought to be at least equal to the US$2.5 to $3 billion that comes from Brunei's oil and gas sales.

Managing Brunei's overseas investments brings together some of the best financial brains in the world. Names like Citibank, Morgan Grenfell, J P Morgan, Japan's Nomura and Daiwa, and Singapore's Government Investment Corporation advise on investment options (Singapore's Senior Minister, Lee Kuan Yew, is a long-standing friend of the Sultan's family).

Providing financial-management advice to the Sultan was the exclusive role of Britain's Crown Agents until 1978, when Brunei widened its pool of advisers to include Morgan Grenfell and James Capel, bringing in some fresh competition. It eventually terminated the Crown Agents' role entirely in July 1983, when it set up the Brunei Investment Agency, and since then has become one of the most desirable (and heavily targeted) clients for the cream of the world's investment advisers.

Apart from the Brunei Investment Agency, chaired until February 1997 by Prince Jefri, the sultanate's major companies include Baiduri Holdings and Singapore-listed QAF Holdings, established in 1982. The Sultan's other younger brother, Prince Mohamad Bolkiah, is Brunei's Foreign Minister. The Sultan's brothers are regarded as aggressive businessmen, with Prince Jefri's resignation clearing the way for him to concentrate even more on his business interests. Another company, Semaun Holdings, headed by the Minister for Industry and Primary Resources, Abdul Rahman Taib, was set up in December 1994 to function as the government's domestic investment arm and to promote foreign investment in Brunei in industries such as timber and wood products, fisheries and agriculture.[4]

Overseas investments are not just in trophy buildings. The Sultan's US$123 million purchase of a 13.4 per cent stake in the Australian merchant bank, the Macquarie Bank, in November 1996 through the Brunei Investment and Commercial Bank (a subsidiary of the Brunei Investment Agency), opens up the possibility of investment opportunities in Australian infrastructure such as tollroads, bridges and railway lines.

The Sultan is already a large landholder in northern Australia, where his three cattle stations and pastoral leases have a combined area of 6000 sq km – greater than the 5765 sq km of Brunei. They include Scott Creek and the adjoining Willeroo property in the Northern Territory, about 400km south of Darwin. The stations, acquired by Brunei in 1981, carry about 34,000 head of Brahman and Brahman-cross cattle. Most of the steers are sent to the Sultan's third station, Opium Creek, about 150km east of Darwin, to be fattened on its lusher pastures before their live export to Brunei. The Brunei government also has an interest in a *halal* abattoir run by the Brunei Meat Export Company at Batchelor, 100km south of Darwin.[5]

For the time being, oil and gas vie with investment income for pre-eminence in Brunei's finances. Brunei is a 50–50 partner with Royal Dutch/Shell in sharing the revenues from oil, while Japan's Mitsubishi group has a 25 per cent stake in the LNG plant at Lumut, one of the world's largest such facilities.

The other shareholders are Brunei (50 per cent) and Royal

Dutch/Shell (25 per cent). Almost all of the 5 million tonnes of LNG sold each year by Brunei go to three Japanese customers: Tokyo Electric, Tokyo Gas and Osaka Gas.

The importance of oil to Brunei can best be gauged at the coastal town of Seria, about 100km west of the capital Bandar Seri Begawan, where the Billionth Barrel Monument marks the steady steam of oil that has flowed from the Seria field. Oil was first struck there in 1929, 16 years after oil exploration started in a region described as 'oozing with hydrocarbons'. Today, scores of oil rigs, known as 'nodding donkeys', pump oil from hundreds of metres below the surface.

The Sultan wants to change that dependence on oil and gas; speaking at a ceremony to mark his 50th birthday, he outlined his aim to turn Brunei into a trade and tourism services hub by 2003. He followed that with the release in February 1997 of a five-year US$5 billion development plan that stresses diversification. He also says that he regards the East ASEAN growth area (which embraces Brunei and parts of the Philippines, Indonesia and Malaysia) as the 'cornerstone' of the country's economic development.

To all intents and purposes, what belongs to the Sultan and what belongs to Brunei are one and the same. The Sultan is absolute ruler of Brunei and, while he is advised by an 11-member council of ministers, he rules by decree – a legacy of the ongoing state of emergency declared by his father in 1962.

The upside of that situation is that citizens of Brunei pay no income tax, enjoy free medical and healthcare and education, and own one car for every two people. Brunei also sends about 2000 students abroad every year to study at universities in Britain, the United States, Australia and elsewhere. Almost half the population of Bandar Seri Begawan live on stilt houses in the water village of Kampong Ayer, complete with televisions, running water and garages on land for the family car.

The polo-playing Sultan, born in 1946 at the Istana Darussalam (royal palace), is the 29th of his line, which dates back to the fourteenth century. Since July 1965, he has been married to his cousin, the Raja Isteri (Queen) Saleha, and since 1981 also to Princess

Mariam, daughter of a customs official. Princess Mariam is a former flight attendant with Royal Brunei Airlines. The Raja Isteri lives at the official residence, the Istana Nurul Iman, while Princess Mariam lives in the Istana Nurul Izzah, a palace on the coast near Jerudong Park. The Sultan has six children by Queen Saleha (four daughters, two sons) and four by Princess Mariam (two daughters, two sons).[6]

It comes as no surprise that the Sultan's own main house, with 1788 rooms and two 24-carat gold domes, is not just the biggest and best in Brunei, but the largest residential palace in the world. Its throne room features 12 large chandeliers and arches covered in gold tiles. The main reception hall is a vast affair, while the royal banquet hall seats 4000 people. The palace, a low-slung complex on a hill overlooking the Brunei River, also serves as Brunei's centre of administration.

And when it comes to modern entertainment, the Sultan also wants the best. The Jerudong amusement park he has built as a gift to his people can accommodate 60,000 people and features the latest in high-tech rides. First opened in 1994 to coincide with the Sultan's 48th birthday, Jerudong is unique in that it is entirely free for all visitors.

At Asia's wedding of the year in August 1996, when the Sultan's eldest daughter Princess Rashidah married businessman Abdul Rahim Kemaludin and drove through the streets of the capital in a gold Rolls-Royce convertible from the royal car pool, entertainer Stevie Wonder was the star attraction for the public concert that followed.

With his own large jet, helicopters and a fleet of vehicles that includes 165 Rolls-Royces and Bentleys, plus other marques such as Aston Martin and Mercedes-Benz, the Sultan is not short of personal transport. The car pool would have been slightly bigger except for a disaster in October 1996, when a Russian Antonov 124 cargo plane crashed just before it was due to land at Turin, Italy. Five people died in the accident, which also destroyed the plane's cargo of 15 luxury cars, including another Rolls-Royce and a Bentley bound for the Sultan.[7]

The Sultan's property interests include the New York Palace Hotel, formerly the Helmsley Palace, bought in November 1993 for US$202 million. He picked it up after the husband-and-wife team of Harry and Leona Helmsley had lost control of the hotel in 1992 as a result of facing tax-evasion charges.

Six years earlier, in 1987, the Sultan bought the Beverly Hills Hotel for US$185 million from America's Marvin Davis, then spent more than four years restoring the 'pink palace' to its original 1912 glory. Elsewhere, the Sultan owns the Hyatt Hotel in Singapore and the Dorchester Hotel in London – bought in 1985 primarily so he could always be sure of getting the suite of rooms he wanted during his frequent visits to Britain.

After a long association with Britain as protector, Brunei regained full independence on 1 January 1984, and is a member of the Association of South East Asian Nations (ASEAN).

Britain keeps a 1000-member garrison in Brunei, including a Gurkha infantry battalion. The Sultan also has two battalions of Gurkhas as a reserve unit guarding the royal family and palace.

While religious freedom is guaranteed under the constitution, Islam is the religion of Brunei's Malay community, which makes up 70 per cent of the population, and in 1990 the government encouraged citizens to embrace Malay Islam Monarchy (MIB) as the state ideology. A striking manifestation of Islam's importance in Brunei is the gold-domed Omar 'Ali Saifuddien mosque, named after the Sultan's late father and one of the most visually stunning buildings in Asia. Linked to the mosque, and giving the impression that it is floating in a pond, is a concrete replica of a sixteenth-century royal barge.

But while the Omar 'Ali Saifuddien mosque dominates the city centre, it is not Brunei's largest mosque. That honour belongs to another magnificent gold-domed and much newer building, the Jame 'Asr Hassanil Bolkiah mosque in Kampong Kiarong, a few kilometres west of the city. It was built to commemorate 25 years of rule by the current Sultan in 1992.

In July 1996, the same month that Brunei's largest shopping complex, the Sultan Haji Hassanal Bolkiah Foundation Complex, opened, the Sultan said that he wanted Brunei to enjoy balanced development which catered for spiritual and religious needs, as well as material ones. He said that he would establish the Islamic Syariah code to the highest possible level.

The Sultan is a rarity on the world's list of billionaires in that he is also the ruler of a country. In a sense, what he owns belongs also to the 300,000 citizens of Brunei, although few have a chance to stay in the Sultan's overseas hotels.

But they can go to the Big House at home. At least once a year, during the festival of Hari Raya, the Sultan's palaces are open to the public and many thousands take the opportunity to visit and be greeted by the Sultan and his family.

12

India's New Money, Old Tensions

You must understand human psychology. Because not long ago I was just a riff-raff boy. People say: 'Who is this Dhirubhai?'... My skin, fortunately, is very thick!

Billionaire founder of India's Reliance Industries, Dhirubhai Ambani[1]

FROM THE INDIAN CAPITAL OF NEW DELHI, NATIONAL HIGHWAY 8 begins its tortuous, more than 1300km run west by south through the states of Rajasthan, Gujarat and Maharashtra to Bombay, India's great commercial centre on the Arabian Sea. Heavy with all manner of transport, from Tata trucks, old-fashioned Ambassador cars and Bajaj motor scooters to lumbering elephants, camels and donkey-carts, NH8 epitomizes the potential and the problems that are embedded in the Indian economic challenge. Six hours and 260km out of Delhi, packed passenger coaches pull into Jaipur, the City of Victory, to take a breath from the fearsomely combative driving conditions on NH8.

Here, in India's rose-pink city, the sandstorms that swirl in from the Rajasthan deserts are long gone by mid-year. The loo – the hot wind from the west – gives way to the monsoon rains of June and July. Gradually, as the months slip by, the humidity eases and the nights cool down. By the end of October, when it is time to celebrate the festival of lights known as Diwali, a steady stream of visitors descends on Jaipur. They come for the fireworks and to savour the elegant façades of Jaipur's palaces like the exquisite Hawa Mahal – the five-storey Palace of the Winds, where in another era ladies of the royal court could enjoy the breeze and the view of Diwali's flickering lights. The visitors also find pleasure in the appearance of Jaipur's ordinary houses, washed pink so that they too will glow in the sunset. And after the chaos of NH8, they marvel at the ordered, well-planned layout of the city, built in the eighteenth century by the Raja of Amber, Sawai Jai Singh II, a ruler noted for his skills as an architect, engineer and astronomer.

But after Diwali, there is little reason for the business visitor to tarry in Jaipur. The real target is still away to the south; 600km further down NH8 is Ahamadabad, commercial centre of Gujarat, the birthplace state of entrepreneurs like Dhirubhai Ambani [77] and the diamond-trading Shah brothers, Bharat and Vijay. Gujarat is the showpiece of India's heavy industry, and the focus for much of the foreign investment it seeks to attract. And from Ahamadabad, NH8 turns due south for the 500km run through the fertile coast of Maharashtra and into Bombay, home of such great business houses as Tata [84], Birla [50] and the scooter king, Rahul Bajaj. Here, where the Arabian Sea stretches into the western horizon and all manner of craft wait in the harbour, is India's beating business heart. And this is where the Indian diaspora begins.

Next to the Overseas Chinese, the greatest commercial network in Asia is run by the Indians. While the old business dynasties like Birla and Tata built vast domestic empires from their bases in Bombay, thousands upon thousands of small traders went beyond India's borders in search of their fortunes.

Over time, they gathered in communities in Singapore (venue for the first Global Indian Entrepreneurs conference in 1996), Arabia, Africa, Europe, Britain and North America, eventually coalescing into an economic force sometimes known as the non-resident Indians, or NRIs. In the late 1990s, tapping into the NRI network is almost as compulsory a market-entry strategy for India as hooking up with the overseas Chinese is for China.

In mid-1996, Singapore-based academic Dr Mukul G. Asher estimated that the Indian diaspora numbered between 15 and 20 million, with combined gross assets of US$300 billion (about equal to India's gross domestic product) and combined net assets of between US$40 and 60 billion.[2]

But not every non-resident Indian is comfortable with the NRI appellation; Srichand P. Hinduja, head of the richest Indian family in Britain, the Hindujas, prefers the term 'overseas Indians'.[3] The Hindujas are heavy investors back into India, notably in telecommunications, information technology, infrastructure, motor vehicles and, most recently, banking, with IndusInd Bank. Hinduja is a great admirer of the overseas Chinese networks; his bank is seen as one attempt to replicate the capital-raising power of those borderless connections.

While members of the Indian diaspora like the Hindujas and the Singapore-based Thakral Group see the economic potential of investing back in India, the rest of the world is not so sure. Red tape and memories of abrupt policy reverses make big potential investors like the Japanese nervous. Japanese banker K. Yoshizawa claimed early in 1997 that India attracted only US$2.5 billion in foreign direct investment in 1996, compared with US$40 billion for China.[4]

Yet India will have a larger population than China before the middle of the twenty-first century, and its legal system is more easily understood in the West. Even in the reform-driven 1990s, India's problem continues to be red tape and an attitude that goes back to the 'Licence Raj' when prices, profits and production were decided by bureaucrats in New Delhi, and good political connections could seemingly fend off any competitor.

One Indian billionaire who benefited from the Licence Raj was self-confessed 'riff-raff boy' Dhirubhai Ambani. A member of the Indian diaspora from the age of 17, Ambani served his time amid Arab oil merchants and textile traders in the port of Aden in the 1950s. After eight years, including five years with Burmah Shell, he returned to Bombay at the end of 1958 to begin his own business. The man later reviled by the Indian *Express* newspaper as head of an 'evil empire' started his Reliance company as a commodities trader, using his Aden connections to deal in spices with the Arab world.

By the 1960s he had moved into textiles, setting up his first mill near Ahamadabad in his home state of Gujarat. A government scheme in the 1970s in which rayon fabric exports were offset against nylon fibre imports gave Ambani the trading volumes to upgrade his machinery, ready for a plunge into the domestic textiles market. Ambani took the view that the traditional yarn traders and mill owners had misjudged the expansion capacity of the Indian market.

He took Reliance public in November 1977 and, to the delight of his investors and the distress of his opponents, doubled the company's sales between 1978 and 1980. Although constantly under attack from business rivals, the media and politicians for much of the 1980s and 1990s, Ambani remained a corporate hero to the 2.6 million small shareholders in his family's listed flagship, Reliance Industries. High dividends and bonus issues helped keep them happy. Even when the share price of Reliance slumped in the wake of a missing stock parcel scandal that saw the Ambani family subject to a hefty fine in 1996, there was little loss of faith among his legion of admirers.

Ambani's humble business origins as a labourer and small-time trader in Aden inspired a generation of Indian investors until then conditioned to believe that wealth could only ever flow upstream to the rich, never down to the poor. Ambani gave them hope that even a tiddler could one day make it to the top. His response was to keep the fires of hungry ambition burning; helped by government licences that Ambani exploited to the hilt, Reliance turned in record profits and mouth-watering dividends throughout the 1980s. Ambani drove Reliance to the highest reaches of India's corporate scene, sparking furious wars with textile rivals like Nusli Wadia, chairman of Bombay Dyeing. Even when he was waylaid by a stroke in February 1986, Ambani's sons

Mukesh and Anil kept Reliance on track in pursuit of world scale and excellence in petrochemicals and fibres.

In the three decades since Ambani returned from Aden, the Gujurat-born industrialist had built a substantial fortune and turned the Bombay-based Reliance Industries into India's largest private-sector company. Sales in 1995–96 topped US$1.6 billion, while market capitalization in early 1997 was US$2.3 billion. Ambani and his family control about 26 per cent of the company and have brought it to the point where it has ranged up on the outside of more favoured commercial runners like India's old money, the Tata and Birla empires.

Ambani's sons Mukesh and Anil began moving into new strategic business sectors in the mid-1990s, with one of their biggest decisions being to gear up for an assault on India's deregulated telecommunications sector in concert with Nynex of the United States.

Other new ventures for Reliance include a gas and oil exploration joint venture in the Arabian Sea off the coast of Bombay, with Enron Oil & Gas of Houston and India's state-owned Oil & Natural Gas Commission. But petrochemicals and fibres remained the group's mainstay; in October 1996 Reliance announced that it had completed construction of the world's largest polypropylene plant, with annual capacity of 350,000 tonnes, at its petrochemical complex in Surat, in western Gujarat state.

For Dhirubhai Ambani, big is usually better, and the results of his efforts speak for themselves. In her book *Business Maharajas*, Bombay author Gita Piramal reported how the Reliance chief saw no limits to the company's growth. 'I keep revising my vision ... I believe we can be a Rupees 300 billion [about US$8.5 billion] company by the end of the century,' he said.[5]

Another investor favourite of the 1990s carried its own magic, tragic name: Birla. Kumaramangalam (known as Kumar) Birla found himself unexpectedly thrust to the fore when his father, Aditya Vikram Birla, chairman of the Calcutta-based B.K.-Aditya Birla Group, died of prostate cancer on 1 October 1995 after several months in hospital in the United States. He was just a month short of his 52nd birthday.

Kumar, then 27, had to take the reins of a domestic and international empire that turned over US$4 billion a year and controlled such blue-chip stocks as Grasim Industries, Hindalco Industries, Indian Rayon and Indo-Gulf Fertilisers.

Fortunately, Kumar, a London Business School MBA graduate, had been well trained to take over eventually from his father, but it was a daunting initiation nonetheless. The elder Birla, who qualified as a chemical engineer in the United States, had chosen his industries well, building a diversified international conglomerate with assets of more than US$3 billion. When Aditya Birla's grandfather G.D. Birla died in 1983 after ruling the family empire for 60 years, Aditya and his father Basant Kumar (B.K.) inherited the bulk of the group's best assets, such as Grasim and Hindalco. B.K.'s two elder brothers, Lakshmi Niwas (who died in 1994) and Krishna Kumar (K.K.) were not happy with the outcome. Later it became the source of family friction, involving Lakshmi Niwas's son, Sudarshan (S.K.) Birla.[6]

With that head start from his grandfather and his own business acumen, Aditya's side of the Birla clan continued to prosper. From his home in Bombay's fashionable Malabar Hill, Aditya planned his domestic strategy and his offshore forays to set up textile and chemical plants in Thailand, Indonesia, Malaysia, the Philippines and Egypt. By the time he died in 1995, he had 17 companies up and running in 14 countries, including two, Thai Rayon and Thai Carbon, listed on the Bangkok Stock Exchange.

'No other Indian businessman can claim to even remotely match Birla's ability to build factories from scratch,' Gita Piramal wrote in 1996, noting that in the space of 25 working years, Aditya Birla had built 70 plants covering textiles, paper, various chemicals, aluminium, sponge iron, industrial machinery and a host of other commodities.[7]

As a non-smoking, non-drinking vegetarian like his long-lived grandfather and father, Aditya could have anticipated a lengthy business career. That was not to be. But Aditya's untimely death in October 1995 may have helped Kumar and his grandfather Basant Birla achieve a reconciliation with other members of the Birla clan who split in 1987. By the end of 1996, other Birla family members were serving as directors and had agreed on new shareholding arrangements.[8] It was a fitting legacy to the charismatic and sensitive Aditya Birla, whose talents as a musician and artist matched his commercial vision.

The other great name of Indian commerce is Tata, established by Jamshetji Tata in Bombay (now also known as Mumbai) in 1868. He was a Parsi, the followers of the Zoroastrian religion which entered India from Persia. The trading firm that he set up became Tata Sons, which today is the chief holding company, with Tata Industries, of the Tata business group.

At the head of the group is Ratan Tata [84], the US-educated chairman who took an enterprise left flat-footed by the rapid changes of the 1980s and oversaw its resurrection as India's most respected enterprise. The Tatas have always represented the most ethical side of Indian business; shady deals have never been their style. But that also left them open to shareholders' complaints of passivity and lack of aggression. Ratan Tata set about revitalizing the group to meet the competitive challenges of the 1990s.

Tata, who is also a director of the Reserve Bank of India, inherited the leadership in 1991 from his uncle, the late Jehangir Ratanji Dadabhoy Tata. JRD Tata, who died in November 1993 aged 89, had been at the Tata helm for half a century.

Ratan Tata, born in Bombay in 1937, studied engineering at Cornell University and business at the Harvard Business School's advanced management program in 1974–75. In 1995 Harvard honoured its former student for 'strengthening the collection of companies in your care'.[9]

That house of Tata collection is highly diversified. With group turnover of US$8 billion, Tata Sons has investments in about 27 listed companies and 19 private companies, covering activities such as steel, engineering, motor vehicles, tea, chemicals, telecommunications, household goods, cosmetics, computer software and financial services.

One of the key flagships is motor vehicle company Tata Engineering & Locomotive (TELCO) which, with sales in 1995–96 of US$2.2 billion, ranks among the top five private-sector companies in India. Along with another top five company, Tata Iron & Steel Co (TISCO), it accounted for about half the group's total revenue in 1996. A year earlier, car enthusiast Ratan Tata had vowed that TELCO would be a major automotive player. By 2000, he visualized it as a company with revenue of about US$5.6 billion, of which 20 per cent would come from export sales.[10] The need to go global weighed heavy on Tata's mind. In September 1996 he lamented to the *Far Eastern Economic Review* that the group's greatest missed opportunity was not having established 'substantial enterprises overseas in our core competence areas'.[11] He set about remedying that a few months later through a tie-up with US Steel and the German carmaker Porsche, to develop an ultra lightweight steel for use in car bodies.

When analysts questioned the viability of the Tata empire amid the heavy competition of a liberalizing economic environment, Ratan Tata's response was swift and decisive. He announced in late 1996 that the two unlisted firms which manage the Tata empire, Tata Sons and Tata Industries, would strengthen their strategic crossholdings.

It was the culmination of moves he foreshadowed in 1995, when he told *Business India* that it was conceivable that 'someone' could raid the group. 'If we are managing a company, our holding in it should be more than symbolic,' he declared.[12]

While Ratan Tata is very much the billionaire face of here-and-now corporate India, a host of lesser lights are poised to cross the billionaire threshold in the next decade. Indeed, when purchasing-power parity is taken into account, they may have already knocked on the door and been admitted.

Billionaire contenders from the country destined to vie with China for Asia's economic mantle in the twenty-first century include the R.P. Goenka family, who control RPG Enterprises; the Ruia brothers, Ravi and Shashi, who head the Essar Group; Rahul Bajaj of Bajaj Auto; and the multitudinous Modi brothers (KK, VK,

SK, BK and UK), whose breadth of industries and embrace of technology are symbolic of a family network destined to rule large parts of India's future corporate landscape.

Perhaps the closest to billionaire status is India's 'King of the Road', Rahul Kumar Bajaj, chairman and chief executive of motor-cycle and scooter specialist Bajaj Auto. A boxing champion at school, the Harvard-educated Bajaj has fought for almost 30 years to keep the Pune-based company pre-eminent in India, where its two- and three-wheel scooters and motorcycles hold about half the domestic market (1995 sales US$1.1 billion). In 1995, *Forbes* magazine estimated the Bajaj family fortune at US$500 million, or around US$2.5 billion on a purchasing power basis.[13] The Bajaj family holds about 51 per cent of Bajaj Auto and about 25 per cent of three-wheel maker Bajaj Tempo, which is controlled by the Firodia family – once allies of the Bajajs but now bitter rivals.

During the 1980s, Bajaj Auto grew faster even than that darling of small shareholders, Reliance Industries. In recent years, Bajaj Auto has moved into exports, developing markets in Africa, Latin America and parts of Asia. All it needs domestically is a tie-up with a foreign carmaker to exploit India's next big auto opportunity: four-wheel vehicles. But so far a suitable partner has eluded Bajaj. Still, Rahul Bajaj should have a few years left to make the connection and perhaps reach billionaire status in more than just purchasing power terms. Rahul, born in June 1938 in Calcutta, says that he will retire in 2001, by which time sons Rajiv and Sanjiv and their older cousin Madhur Bajaj should be firmly in control of the family's automotive fortunes for the twenty-first century.

13

Billion-Dollar Babies – the Next Generation

I planned to retire at 75, but it looks like I will go to 80.

Macau casino tycoon Stanley Ho, January 1997[1]

'FU BU GUO SAN DAI' RUNS THE CHINESE SAYING. ITS MESSAGE, THAT wealth does not last three generations, is as well known in the West as it is in the East.

At the end of the twentieth century, only a few of Asia's wealthiest families are testing the third-generation thesis. The explosion of wealth has been so dynamic and so breathtaking in its speed that many of Asia's billionaires are still relatively youthful.

At the very top of the wealth tree, young men and women like Victor Li, Beau Kuok and Peter Lee in Hong Kong, Robert Ng in Singapore, Teresita Sy-Coson and Lance Gokongwei in the Philippines, and Anthony Salim in Indonesia share a common thread – their fathers are the region's top billionaires, and they are being groomed to take over the family business.

Their fathers, starting mostly from ground zero as ethnic Chinese migrants in their adopted countries, today sit at the top of huge empires founded on banking, property, commodities, transport and scores of other activities. The billion-dollar babies' biggest concern is to ensure that the family business continues to flourish when they take over from their fathers, and that they pass on to their own children the Midas touch that will ward off the curse of the third generation, when wealth supposedly washes into the sands of youthful recklessness.

In the Philippines, Teresita Sy-Coson is diligently preparing to run SM Prime, the retail empire built by her father Henry Sy [52]. When SM Prime went to the European markets for money in late 1996, it was Teresita who led the roadshow and did the talking.[2]

But not all the billionaires' daughters are happy to follow in their father's footsteps. In Hong Kong, Josie Ho Chi-yee, youngest daughter of the Macau gambling magnate Stanley Ho [42], is trying to make a name for herself as a recording artist and television personality. She is adamant that she will create a career in the music business, free from family help, starting in the highly competitive world of 'Canto-pop' – Cantonese-language pop songs.[3] With an estimated net worth of US$2.3 billion, it would be easy for her 75-year-old father Stanley Ho to buy up her entire record output. But Josie Ho wants to make it on her own, so that is unlikely. And father Ho, who according to local legend arrived in Macau in 1941 with just HK$10 in his pocket, would surely understand.

Stanley Ho – 'big brother Sun' to Cantonese speakers – is to Macau what Wang Yung-ching [11] is to Taiwan and Dhanin Chearavanont [12] is to Thailand: the inspirational figures of their generation, men who have become billionaires from humble origins.[4] Ho's wealth has been accumulated over a 30-year period in which he virtually rebuilt the sleepy Portuguese territory of Macau into Asia's biggest gambling centre. Since 1962 he has held the gambling monopoly franchise there through his Sociedade de Turismo e Diversoes de Macau (STDM), which generates annual revenue of US$2 billion and an estimated US$500 million a year in profits. In Hong Kong, his flagship is Shun Tak Holdings; apart from real estate, hotel management and shipyards, it runs a fleet of high-speed jetfoils and catamarans that accounts for about 75 per cent of passenger traffic on the 60-minute run between Hong Kong and Macau. Stanley Ho has two daughters on the board of

Shun Tak: eldest child Pansy, 34, who was promoted to head the group's core ferry business in January 1997 (and thus is heir apparent) and Daisy, 32, who is responsible for property and finance. Another daughter, Maisy, also works in property, but youngest daughter Josie just wants to be a pop star.

A one-hour flight to the east of Macau lies Taiwan, home to half a dozen families that control much of the nation's wealth in industry and finance. One of these families is the fabulous Wang dynasty, headed by the Formosa Plastics founder and crusty industrialist, Wang Yung-ching. The frugal, workaholic Wang has 10 children, all of whom have roles in the business.[5]

Eldest daughter Charlene, 46, used her own money to set up a high-tech business, First International Computer Co, with her husband, Chieng Ming. With maths and science degrees from London University and the University of California, Charlene Wang had the right credentials to carve out her own niche in the new world. But the family pull was too strong. FIC is now part of the Formosa Plastics Group, which with annual revenue of US$10.8 billion in 1995 stands well clear of all other family conglomerates in Taiwan.[6] Charlene's 43-year-old brother, Dr Winston Wang, was also educated in Britain, earning an MBA from Middlesex Polytechnic and a PhD from Imperial College, London. Although he dropped out of favour in the mid-1990s after a romance with one of his university students, Winston was still widely seen as heir apparent to Wang Yung-ching. That view suffered a setback in November 1996, however, when Wang senior rejected the idea that Winston had corrected the 'errant ways' that led to his dismissal as executive vice-president of Nan Ya Plastics Co.

At 79, chairman Wang shows no sign of slackening in his discipline or his plans for the Formosa Plastic Group's development. On a strip of land jutting into the sea on the west coast of central Taiwan, Wang is building the crowning achievement of a spectacularly successful career – a US$10 billion petrochemical complex known as the Sixth Naphtha Cracker.

This massive project, regarded as the world's largest private investment, pits Wang's money and engineers against the stormy forces of nature and a vocal band of environmentalists. Along with the naphtha cracker and associated petrochemical plants, Wang's plan calls for a 2400 megawatt power plant, the reclamation of 2600 hectares of land from the sea and the building of a harbour to handle giant 200,000dwt tankers. His new harbour will have a strategic edge in the battle for market share on the mainland: it will be only 200km from ports on the China coast, plying a route that has been out of bounds to Taiwan shippers since 1949. Having once bowed to political pressure to cut back on a mainland power project, the integrated naphtha cracker and harbour may well prove Wang's masterstroke in the race for China's twenty-first-century riches.

Softly, softly...

There is another group of Asian entrepreneurs knocking at the door to the billionaires' wealth club; they are young, aggressive and willing to take risks in hot new fields such as multimedia, biotechnology, consumer services, luxury goods and new materials. Japan's Masayoshi Son [16], the man behind Softbank, is a shining example of this new generation.

The 'Asian Bill Gates' is the most common description of Masayoshi Son, the 39-year-old ethnic Korean president of Tokyo-based Softbank Corporation. The youthful billionaire, already the world's largest publisher of computer magazines through his purchase of Ziff-Davis Publishing Co for US$2.1 billion in 1995, has global ambitions that rival those of Gates.

Although he still has some way to go, Son is proving remarkably fast on his feet; after two more key acquisitions in 1996 and a string of earlier tie-ups with names that included Gates's Microsoft, Son predicted that his 1997 group sales would reach 340 billion yen (more than US$3 billion).[7]

His two biggest deals in 1996 covered content and hardware. In a 50–50 partnership with Rupert Murdoch's News Corp, Son took a 21.4 per cent stake in Japanese television network TV Asahi in

June 1996 for 41.75 billion yen (about US$380 million), then followed that up in August by splashing out US$1.5 billion for an 80 per cent stake in California-based Kingston Technology, the world's biggest supplier of memory-board products. In December 1996, Son and Murdoch formally announced what they had foreshadowed in their June deal: a 50–50 joint venture, Japan Sky Broadcasting Co Ltd (JSkyB), capitalized at 20 billion yen (about US$177 million) and which will start full-scale broadcasting in April 1998 when the JSAT-4 satellite becomes operational.[8] But in a surprise twist in March 1997, Son and Murdoch said they would sell their TV Asahi stake to the Japanese newspaper publisher Asahi Shimbun for the same amount, 41.75 billion yen, that they had paid for it. The pair recovered from that programming setback when in May 1997 they brought two new Japanese partners, Sony Corp and the large commercial TV network Fuji Television, into their JSkyB project. Each of the four held a 20 per cent stake, with the remaining 20 per cent split among some minor shareholders.

Son, whose 61.4 per cent stake in Softbank Corp was worth US$3.6 billion in early 1997, started his company in 1981 as a software distributor after returning to Japan from studying in the United States. Over the next decade, the computer wizard built Softbank into the biggest wholesaler of software, systems and peripherals in Japan. Then, with the personal computer riding high on the blossoming of the Internet and a call for ever more information and software, Son decided that it was time to take on the rest of the world.

After taking Softbank public in 1994 with an IPO that raised more than US$600 million, Son had the money he needed to pay for his first acquisition of choice – Comdex, the computer trade show business founded by Sheldon Adelson of the United States. He paid US$800 million for Comdex and laid out an ambitious growth strategy to lift the number of trade shows from around 50 events a year to 300.

Son followed that with the US$2.1 billion purchase of the Ziff-Davis computer magazines, which included market-leading titles such as *PC Magazine, PC Week, PC Computing* and *MacUser,* then added the television content component with his joint venture jump into TV Asahi, and the hardware link through Kingston Technology.

The aborted TV Asahi venture and the subsequent deal with Sony and Fuji TV were designed to tap into a stream of Japanese-language content for the 150 satellite channels that Murdoch and Son aim to beam into the Japanese market from 1998 onwards.

Son moved quickly when he heard that Murdoch had plans for a digital satellite broadcasting service, to be called JSkyB, in Japan. At a June 1996 press conference to announce the joint venture, Son said that he had approached Murdoch only a week earlier and urged him to 'hook up with me'.

Son reached a rapid rapport with the News Corp chief executive; he said that he met Murdoch for the first time in Los Angeles earlier in 1996, when the two discussed the concept of a global television channel dealing with personal computer topics.[9]

By December 1996, details of the 50–50 joint venture had been formalized, with Murdoch named founding chairman of JSkyB and Son named founding president. The pair also planned to set up a broadcaster, Sky Entertainment, to deliver 12 channels on an existing satellite, JSAT-3, and switch to the JSkyB service on JSAT-4 in 1998. To enable JSkyB to operate a core service of 150 channels, Murdoch and Son agreed to set up another 12 licensed broadcasters each able to operate 12 channels, with News and Softbank each holding a maximum 10 per cent interest.

The deal will put the Japanese market to its first severe test. While satellite broadcasting has been part of the Japanese media scene for more than a decade with services by the national broadcaster NHK and commercial operators, no one has ever offered content on the scale of the 150 channels that Murdoch and Son envisage. Subscribers to existing digital satellite broadcaster PerfecTV! are expected to be able to pick up JSkyB signals once the Murdoch–Son joint venture is operating.[10] After its shaky start with TV Asahi, the Murdoch–Son alliance recovered when the pair won the backing first of Sony and then Fuji TV, two of Japan's premier brand names. Sony Corp said it was keen to participate in JSkyB with hardware, content (a reference to its Hollywood movies and music) and an equity stake.

Across the Pacific in the United States, Son is betting with his Kingston Technology play that the market for computer memory boards will continue to grow at more than 30 per cent a year. That is a fair assumption, given that from just a standard 1 megabyte of random access memory (RAM) at the end of the 1980s, personal computers raced swiftly to 4, 8 and 16 megabytes of RAM as software such as Windows 95, Netscape Explorer and Office 97 gobbled up memory space. Before 2000, 32 megabytes will be standard on home PCs as users strive to see and do everything that the Net promises them. Kingston Technology, already the world's largest maker of PC memory boards, can expect to take a large share of that growth. The co-founders of California-based Kingston, David Sun and John Tu, will stay on to run the company and keep a 20 per cent stake worth almost US$400 million.

Son described Kingston as a perfect fit with the growth strategy he had in mind for his existing businesses.[11] That strategy is to bring global scale to the task of delivering information in a digital format. And while he has a powerful media ally in Murdoch and strategic stakes in Internet service firms such as US-based Yahoo! Inc, CyberCash Inc (with Dentsu, Japan's biggest advertising agency) and Hong Kong-based Asia On-Line, Son knows that competitors like Gates and Marc Andreesen of Netscape have their own visions of global dominance that see no serious place for a trans-Pacific rival. In that sense, Kingston was the right move, buying into a hardware market that everyone believes can only expand.

But by early 1997, Softbank was carrying a heavy debt load. To fund its US$1.5 billion stake in Kingston, Softbank planned to raise around 46 billion yen (about US$420 million) through a new share issue. The worry for Son remained the strength of the Tokyo over-the-counter share market, and the reluctance of the Japanese economy to shake off the recessionist mood that prevailed through the mid-1990s. Analysts observed that if the market turned down too sharply, Masayoshi Son might find himself overstretched. It was a risk that the shoot-for-the-stars billionaire was prepared to take.

Son, like that other Asian entrepreneurial master of the microchip era, Stan Shih of Acer in Taiwan, could take some comfort from the signs of growth around him. In 1995, world semiconductor sales passed US$150 billion; in late 1996 a Gallup survey found that telecommunications and information technology – prodigious consumers of microchips and software – made up the world's biggest industry, contributing US$1.5 trillion to annual global GDP.

The report said that the world's telecommunications market by itself would be worth US$650 billion in 2000. All that infrastructure meant that communicating would figure even larger in how societies use their time; reading a computer magazine online, downloading a video clip from the Net or just tweaking up the memory banks on the home PC to play the latest game should keep Masayoshi Son smiling all the way to the billionaires' bank.

And if any technophobes needed convincing about the revenue-generating potential of information technology, a trip to Las Vegas in November to attend Comdex, the computer trade show that Son's Softbank Corp now owns, would soon have them thinking about the many paths to fortune.

More than 215,000 visitors poured into Comdex 96, drawn by 10,000 new products and the imperative that this is the world's biggest display of computer hardware, software and peripherals – plus it is the networking event that everyone in the industry *must* attend. Son knows this, and charges accordingly; the smallest space for one of the 2200 exhibitors at Comdex in November 1996 went for US$45 a square foot for the five days of the event – much more than companies pay for annual office rent in New York City. All told, Son's Softbank raked in more than US$60 million in rent from exhibitors at the show – almost as much as the group's entire pre-tax profit for the previous six months.[12]

Comdex is where the industry meets, makes backroom deals, announces some new products, checks out the opposition's offerings for next season, and hears keynote speakers like Bill Gates of

Microsoft. Son's task will be to ensure that Comdex keeps its No. 1 title, in the face of competition from a host of new Internet-related shows and events in the United States.

While Son was counting the customers through the Comdex turnstiles in Las Vegas, a Japanese billionaire-in-waiting, Yoshitaro Iwasaki, was wrestling with the intricacies of another late twentieth-century bloomer, the tourism business.

This is a far, far different tale to Masayoshi Son's. It starts with Iwasaki's late grandfather 70 years ago in an obscure part of southern Japan...

Japanese dreamer and the resort down under

Sometimes when light from a tropical moon skips over the surface of Lake Ikeda in the southern Japanese island of Kyushu, the locals swear that a fast-moving object can be seen undulating its way across the water. Like Scotland's Nessie, this humped monster of the lake is as much a tourist marketing gimmick as a figment of fertile imaginations, but the thick, heavy eels that inhabit this 265 metre deep caldera lake are real enough to keep the swimmers at bay. When tourists are not on monster watch by Lake Ikeda, they can usually be found taking the waters in the hot springs resort created by Japan's billionaire Iwasaki family at nearby Ibusuki.

From the outside, the Ibusuki resort is an architectural excess of concrete in need of a paint job. But once inside, the resort dissolves into a ripe green explosion of tropical growth, where hot baths of strange shapes, sizes and secret scents emerge from among *faux* marble statues, and in the dim light, squads of visitors, naked save for a small towel across the loins, troop from one bath to the next in search of magic elixirs that will restore youthful vitality and potency.

Until a 1980 bomb blast at another tropical paradise 8000km away rocketed the Iwasaki name to prominence, for many years the Ibusuki resort at the southernmost tip of Kyushu was the only internationally known feature of the Iwasaki business empire. Indeed, despite its great wealth, the Iwasaki family was little known even in Japan, outside its home base of Kagoshima prefecture. Its fortune, built on timber, transport, tourism, real estate and heavy industry, rested almost entirely on the efforts of Yohachiro Iwasaki, founder of the Iwasaki Sangyo group and the man against whom that bomb was directed. Iwasaki, who died in December 1993 at the age of 91, was left fatherless at an early age. He had no formal education beyond primary school, but was smart enough to study accountancy at night while he worked in a liquor shop during the day.

Eventually, he quit to start his own business, buying and selling railroad sleepers. With access to timber in the rich forests of Kyushu, Iwasaki was able to make his first real money in the sleeper business as Japan embarked on its early twentieth-century industrialization. Then came the Great Kanto Earthquake that devastated Tokyo in September 1923, claiming 130,000 lives and ripping apart the city's transport system.

In the massive rebuilding process that followed, Iwasaki was able to consolidate his fortune through supplying sleepers to the railroad companies. In the 1930s, as the Japanese armed forces pushed into Manchuria, their need for sleepers to build their railroad enterprises turned more profits for Iwasaki, enabling him to buy up more timber leases and forestry land in southern Japan. That business pattern continued during the Second World War.

Unlike his son, Fukuzo [29], who heads the Iwasaki Sangyo group today, the dictatorial Yohachiro Iwasaki ran a one-man band. As the group expanded in the postwar years, Iwasaki senior decided everything and made every strategic move across 60 companies operating in sectors from timber to food to tourism.

But Iwasaki still had some mountains to climb: not content with his tourism operations in Japan, he wanted to build the world's best 'natural resort'. To do that, he needed land, and lots of it. On a visit to Australia in 1970, he found what he wanted – a large stretch of unused and virtually unwanted land on the Queensland coast near the sleepy little town of Yeppoon, 800km north of Brisbane. Iwasaki started acquiring the land in the early 1970s and, with the enthusiastic backing of the state government, began planning his resort to cater for the hundreds of thousands of Japanese honeymooners and other visitors he envisaged would flock to his coastal paradise.[13]

But the going was far from easy for the Japanese businessman, already then well into his seventies. For much of the next decade, the name Iwasaki was synonymous in parts of Australia with the ugly face of international capital. In Yeppoon, racism, conservatism and environmental concerns combined to create dangerous divisions between those supporting the US$100 million Iwasaki resort and those opposed to it. The local council was against the development, but was over-ridden by the Queensland state government when its controversial Premier, Sir Joh Bjelke-Petersen, pushed through special legislation that allowed the resort to bypass normal planning requirements.

Building work started in 1979, but then came the bomb blast in the early hours of Saturday morning, 29 November 1980, signifying that not everyone wanted the project to proceed. Just outside the main building, someone detonated six cases of gelignite packed into a bed of fertilizer soaked in diesel fuel. The blast, heard 30km away, caused no casualties but wrecked about three floors of work in progress. Eventually, a local man known to be hostile to the resort was charged, along with his young nephew, but both were acquitted by a jury. Even before the blast, there had been plenty of incidents; war veterans in Yeppoon protested about land being sold to a Japanese billionaire, and the town's war memorial carried a sign saying 'Welcome to Jappoon'.

But Iwasaki was unperturbed. He had the full support of the state's most powerful politician, he had 8500 hectares of coastal land – including 15km of beachfront – and he had the money to make it happen.

'Many men dream dreams, but there are few in the fortunate position to be able to finance them,' Iwasaki said soon after the bombing.[14] He slowly pushed on with the project, gradually winning over the local community until, by the time the resort opened for visitors in 1986, it was seen as a benefit to the town in terms of jobs and tourism income. At a ceremony to mark completion of the first stage in September 1984, Iwasaki was joined by Bjelke-Petersen – complete with a koala in one arm – who promptly promised to send four koalas to a zoo in Iwasaki's home prefecture of Kagoshima. The Bjelke-Petersen link, allied to Iwasaki's wealth and influence in Kagoshima, ensured that when the first batch of Australian koalas was sent to Japan in the mid-1980s – a hugely symbolic step at the time – Kagoshima's city zoo was one of the three destinations. In June 1989, Iwasaki staged Australia's most expensive birthday party at what he had by then named the Capricorn Iwasaki Resort, flying in 700 Japanese visitors plus assorted local politicians and business identities. In the years that followed, most of the visitors were from other parts of Australia, and the anticipated *tsunami* (tidal wave) of Japanese visitors that the citizens of Yeppoon feared would crash on their shoreline proved to be a much more manageable ripple.

Iwasaki declared himself very proud of the Capricorn resort, even though it continued to operate at a loss throughout the 1980s and has yet to reach the 'world's best natural resort' aspirations he held for it. Iwasaki died on 28 December 1993 at the age of 91, fittingly on the day the Japanese know as *shigotosame*, or the 'end of work' holiday. Two years later, the project he had dreamt about for more than two decades turned in its first profit.

But it seems unlikely that it will ever add hugely to the Iwasaki family's US$3.5 billion fortune; a Japanese executive of the resort's operating company offered the observation in 1996 that Capricorn was a project whose chief objective was to promote Australia–Japan friendship. 'So we will keep it forever, whether it is profitable or not,' he said. One measure of the family's feeling about the resort is the special arrangements it makes for Australian senior citizens; it has set aside 50 guest rooms where pensioners can stay at about a quarter of the normal rate.[15]

After Yohachiro Iwasaki's death in 1993, his son, Fukuzo, born in 1924, took over the family business and has since given it a gentler, more consensus-like face. Although Fukuzo had been president of Iwasaki Sangyo since 1981, his father held the chairmanship almost until his death and was the controlling force. A graduate of the prestigious Rikkyo University, Fukuzo restructured the group to provide a more modern, corporate approach. The one-man-band style was out, and board decisions relied on input from a team of professional executives.

A 14-handicap golfer who enjoys jogging, Fukuzo Iwasaki is also chairman of the Kagoshima chamber of commerce and industry and an energetic supporter of business and tourism in Kyushu. But all those years playing second fiddle to his long-lived father mean that he is now in his seventies. His own son and heir apparent, Yoshitaro, is vice-president of the group's hotel and resort businesses and is responsible for making a success of the family's newest project: a resort on the heavily forested island of Yakushima, a national park about 100km south of Ibusuki by ferry.

Be it the hot springs and secret bath essences of Ibusuki, the lush subtropical island of Yakushima, or the wide open Australian coastline near Yeppoon, the Iwasaki name and fortune has progressed a long way from the rugged loner who first bought and sold railway sleepers in the industrializing Japan of the early twentieth century. Now, the successors to Yohachiro Iwasaki seem destined to make their money from kindlier pursuits in a world where leisure, like information technology, is a fast-growing industry. But will tourism's growth be fast enough for Iwasaki's grandson Yoshitaro to match the spectacular success in computers that has thrust Masayoshi Son into the Japanese spotlight, or will the Iwasakis remain the unsung backwoods billionaires from the south?

That is merely one of the questions facing Yoshitaro Iwasaki, Masayoshi Son and the other young billionaires contemplating the future of their family enterprises as the twenty-first century draws near. Where will the growth be, and can they best preserve and expand the family fortune by going public or staying private? In a borderless world, are their interests best served by transparency or opacity? And does an international brand name, or the ability to tap capital globally, outweigh the value that can be drawn from a private conglomerate's trusted web of quiet connections?

Some of the billionaires intend to stay fiercely private, while others have already decided that the best strategy is to take parts of their companies public. Li Ka-Shing's restructuring of his four Hong-Kong-listed companies in early 1997 was, he says, designed to smooth the succession for his sons Victor and Richard. In effect, it tightened his grip on an empire with a total market capitalization of US$58 billion. In Indonesia, where the fear is that envy of the ethnic Chinese business community might once again spark violence, groups like Salim, Sinar Mas and Gajah Tunggal have sought insurance for their assets either through listing their flagships locally, or by repackaging some of the choicest pieces into listed companies in safe havens like Singapore, Hong Kong and New York. In the Philippines, Lucio Tan keeps most of his fortune tucked away from public view in his privately held beer and tobacco companies, leaving only his majority ownership of the struggling Philippines Airlines on the table. In contrast, Henry Sy and his daughter Teresita are continuing to list more and more pieces of their SM Prime empire.

Knocking on the door

Some of the billionaire babies are already named in the Top 100 section that follows, while some figure among the 20 Asian names listed overleaf, knocking on the door of billionaire status.

Knocking on the door
(Rank, Name, Country, Net Worth in $US)

1	**Yasuyuki Nambu**, Pasona, Japan	2.0 billion
2	**Ciputra**, Ciputra Group, Indonesia	1.0 billion
3	**Phornprapha family**, Siam Motors, Thailand	1.0 billion
4	**Vincent Lo**, Shui On, Hong Kong	1.0 billion
5	**Nina Wang**, Chinachem, Hong Kong	1.0 billion
6	**Tsui Tsin Tong**, New China Hong Kong Group, Hong Kong	1.0 billion
7	**Kartar Singh Thakral**, Thakral Group, Singapore	1.0 billion
8	**Charn Uswachoke**, Alphatec Group, Thailand	0.9 billion
9	**Soh Chee Wen**, Promet, Malaysia	0.9 billion
10	**Jose Go**, Ever-Gotesco Group, Philippines	0.8 billion
11	**William Gatchalian**, Gatchalian Group, Philippines	0.8 billion
12	**Patrick Wang**, Johnson Electric, Hong Kong	0.7 billion
13	**Larry Yung**, CITIC Pacific, Hong Kong	0.6 billion
14	**Rahul Bajaj**, Bajaj Auto, India	0.6 billion
15	**Modi brothers**, Modi Group, India	0.6 billion
16	**Goenka family**, RPG Enterprises, India	0.5 billion
17	**Ravi and Shashi Ruia**, Essar Group, India	0.5 billion
18	**Fadel Muhamad**, Bukaka Teknik Utama, Indonesia	0.5 billion
19	**Jose Concepcion III**, RFM Corp, Philippines	0.5 billion
20	**Aboitiz family**, Aboitiz Equity Ventures, Philippines	0.5 billion

Part II

The Wealth Club

Explanatory Note

A PART FROM PROFILING THE TOP 100 BILLIONAIRE FAMILIES IN ASIA, the material in Part II also shows the interlocking nature of much of the region's business. Certain companies are natural allies and joint-venture partners; they coalesce for large projects like the Fort Bonifacio development in Manila or the Suzhou 'new town' in China, then go their own way again. That can lead to hard choices for investors seeking to benefit from the high growth rates that have been Asia's norm for much of the past two decades. Listed companies connected to the billionaire families offer one route, but flexibility, a strong stomach, deep pockets and a long time horizon are prerequisites for would-be investors. The level of control exercised by the founding family is often the critical factor, and control does not necessarily correlate to the size of the shareholding. The usual advice is to get as close as possible to where the families put their money. Just how much money they have is a source of endless speculation and interest.

The background information and financial estimates that follow have been compiled from a variety of sources, including interviews, company annual reports, statements to stock exchanges, the Jardine Fleming Asia Pacific regional earnings guide, *The Estimates Directory*, the *MeesPierson Guide to Hong Kong Companies*, David Ch'ng's study *Overseas Chinese Entrepreneurs in East Asia* and the Australian Department of Foreign Affairs and Trade's study *Overseas Chinese Business Networks in Asia*.

Other publications from which material has been drawn include *Asia Inc*, *Asia 21*, *Asia Today*, *Asiamoney*, *Asian Business*,

Asiaweek, Bangkok Post, Business Day (Bangkok), *Business India, Business Times* (Singapore), *Business Tokyo, China Times* (Taipei), *CommonWealth* magazine (Taipei), *Economic & Business Review Indonesia, Far Eastern Economic Review, Forbes* magazine's annual billionaires' listing, *Fortune* magazine's annual Global 500 listing, *International Business Asia, Korean Economic Weekly, Malaysian Business, Nikkei Weekly, South China Morning Post, Straits Times Weekly, Thailand Times, The Asian Wall Street Journal, The Australian, The Australian Business Asia, The Nation* (Bangkok), *Vietnam Investment Review* and various books listed in the bibliography.

Market capitalizations of listed companies are as at January 1997, converted to US$ using the following exchange rates:

US$1 =	Australian $1.26	Chinese RMB8.26
	HK$7.7	Indian rupee 35.6
	Indonesian rupiah 2300	Japanese yen 110
	Korean won 840	Malaysian $2.5
	Philippine peso 26	Singapore $1.4
	NTaiwan $27	Thai baht 25
	UK £0.6	

Because of purchasing-power parity, only Japanese families with at least US$2 billion in net worth are included in the Top 100 listing. About 35 Japanese families are in the US$1–2 billion range.

Number of billionaires by country

Indonesia	15	Japan	7*
Malaysia	15	Korea	7
Hong Kong	13	Singapore	6
Thailand	13	India	3
Philippines	12	Brunei	1
Taiwan	8	*Total*	100

*Japan would dominate the list if the 35+ Japanese with net worth between US$1 and 2 billion were included.

Breakdown of billionaires by country
(with estimated net worth in US$ billion)

Brunei

1	The Sultan of Brunei and family	30.0

Hong Kong

1	Walter, Thomas and Raymond KWOK	13.5
2	LEE Shau-kee	11.0
3	LI Ka-shing and family	8.0
4	Michael D. KADOORIE and family	4.0
5	Peter WOO Kwong-ching and the Pao family	3.7
6	CHENG Yu-tung	2.5
7	Henry (Ying-tung) FOK	2.5
8	Stanley HO	2.3
9	LEE Hon Chiu	1.4
10	Gordon WU Yung-sheung	1.2
11	LO Ying Shek	1.1
12	Sir Run Run SHAW	1.0
13	TUNG Chee-hwa and family	1.0

India

1	Kumaramangalam BIRLA and famiily	2.0
2	Dhirubhai AMBANI and family	1.2
3	Ratan N. TATA	1.0

Indonesia

1	Rachman Halim and the WONOWIDJOJO family	7.7
2	SUHARTO family	6.3
3	LIEM Sioe Liong (Sudono Salim)	4.5
4	Eka Tjipta WIDJAJA (OEI Ek Tjhong)	3.7
5	PUTERA Sampoerna and family	2.3
6	PRAJOGO Pangestu	2.0
7	Djuhar SUTANTO	1.8
8	Sjamsul NURSALIM (Liem Tek Siong) and family	1.3
9	Mohamad Bob HASAN	1.2

10	Sukanto TANOTO and family	1.0
11	R. Budi HARTONO and family	1.0
12	Mochtar RIADY and family	1.0
13	William SOERYADJAYA and family	1.0
14	Hashim DJOJOHADIKUSUMO	1.0
15	Mu'min Ali GUNAWAN and family	1.0

Japan

1	Yoshiaki TSUTSUMI and family	11.5
2	Minoru and Akira MORI	6.5
3	Yasuo TAKEI and family	5.0
4	Masayoshi SON	4.7
5	Masatoshi ITO and family	3.8
6	Fukuzo IWASAKI and family	3.5
7	Masahito OTSUKA and family	3.0

Korea

1	CHUNG Ju Yung and family	6.2
2	SHIN Kyuk-ho (Takeo Shigemitsu)	4.5
3	LEE Kun Hee and family	4.0
4	KOO Cha-kyung and family	2.9
5	KIM Woo-choong	1.9
6	CHEY Jong-hyon and family	1.9
7	KIM Suk-won and family	1.3

Malaysia

1	LIM Goh Tong	5.2
2	Vincent TAN Chee Yioun	4.5
3	QUEK Leng Chan and family	4.0
4	Robert KUOK Hock Nien	3.5
5	TIONG Hiew King	2.5
6	Francis YEOH Sock Ping	2.2
7	TEH Hong Piow	1.8
8	HALIM Saad	1.7
9	YAW Teck Seng and family	1.6
10	T. Ananda KRISHNAN	1.4
11	RASHID Hussain	1.4

Malaysia (cont.)

12	TAJUDIN Ramli	1.2
13	KHOO Kay Peng	1.0
14	William CHENG Teng-jem	1.0
15	Estate of YAHAYA Ahmad*	1.0

Philippines

1	TAN Yu	3.0
2	Don Jaime Zobel de AYALA and family	2.8
3	George TY and family	2.8
4	Manuel VILLAR	2.4
5	Henry SY	1.9
6	Lucio TAN	1.7
7	Andrew GOTIANUN Sr and family	1.5
8	Eugenio (Geny) LOPEZ Jr	1.4
9	John GOKONGWEI	1.0
10	Alfonso T. YUCHENGCO	1.0
11	Eduardo COJUANGCO Jr and family	1.0
12	Andres SORIANO III	1.0

Singapore

1	KWEK Leng Beng and family	4.0
2	NG Teng-fong and family (also in Hong Kong)	3.5
3	KHOO Teck Puat	2.2
4	LEE Seng Wee	1.8
5	WEE Cho Yaw	1.5
6	ONG Beng Seng	1.0

Taiwan

1	TSAI Wan-lin and family	8.5
2	WANG Yung-ching and family	6.0
3	Eugene WU Tung-chin and family	5.0
4	HSU Yu-ziang	2.4
5	CHANG Yung-fa	2.1
6	KOO Chen-fu and family	1.5
7	CHEN Yu-hau	1.4
8	HUANG Shi-hui	1.3

Thailand

1	DHANIN Chearavanont and family	5.5
2	CHATRI Sophonpanich and family	3.0
3	Dr THAKSIN Shinawatra	2.4
4	BANYONG Lamsam and family	2.3
5	Dr CHAIJUDH Karnasuta and family	2.3
6	PIYA Bhirombakdi and family	1.7
7	BOONCHAI Bencharongkul and family	1.6
8	ADISAI Bodharamik	1.6
9	PRACHAI Leophairatana and family	1.5
10	KRIT Ratanarak and family	1.4
11	ANANT Asavabhokin	1.4
12	MONGKOL Kanjanapas and family	1.1
13	UDANE Tejapaibul and family	1.0

*Yahaya Ahmad and his wife died in a helicopter crash in March 1997. Their four children are heirs to the estate.

1 The Sultan of Brunei

Estimated net worth: *US$30 billion*
Owner: *Brunei Investment Agency*
Born: *15 July 1946, Bandar Seri Begawan*
Educated: *Brunei, Malaysia and Sandhurst Military College (UK), commissioned a captain in 1967*
Marital status: *Two wives, four sons, six daughters*
Hobbies: *Polo, flying*

WITH HIS OWN HELICOPTERS, BOEING 767 AND CHOICE OF 165 ROLLS-ROYCES, Bentleys, Aston Martins and other well-bred marques, His Majesty Sultan Haji Hassanal Bolkiah Mu'izzaddin Waddaulah is never short of personal transport. But then, his responsibilities are as numerous as his wealth is vast. For almost 30 years he has served as head of state, Prime Minister (and later also as Defence Minister and Finance Minister) of the sultanate of Brunei, the tiny independent nation which borders the Malaysian state of Sarawak on the island of Borneo.

Brunei, which regained full independence in 1984 after a long association with Britain, is a member of the Association of South East Asian Nations (ASEAN). It owes its status as one of the richest per capita nations in Asia to revenue from oil and liquefied natural gas, first discovered in the 1920s.

At least 40 per cent of Brunei's income is from oil and gas. The Sultan hopes to change that dependence by expanding the offshore investment base and by turning Brunei into a trade and tourism services hub by 2003.

In a sense, what the Sultan owns belongs also to the 300,000 citizens of Brunei, although few are able to enjoy life in the way the Sultan and other members of the royal family do. Once or twice a year Brunei's citizens can pay him a visit at home in the official residence, the Istana Nurul Iman, which is also Brunei's centre of administration. The Istana Nurul Iman, with 1788 rooms and two domes in 24-carat gold, is the biggest residential palace in the world.

The Sultan, born in 1946 at the Istana Darussalam (royal palace) in Brunei Town (now Bandar Seri Begawan), is the 29th of his line, which dates back to the fourteenth century. He is the eldest son of Sultan Haji Sir Muda Omar 'Ali Saifuddien III, who died in 1986. He became Crown Prince in 1961 and ascended the throne on 5 October 1967, following his father's abdication.

The Sultan is married to his cousin Her Majesty Paduka Seri Baginda Raja Isteri Pengiran Anaka Hajah Saleha (Queen Saleha) and Her Royal Highness Pengiran Isteri Hajah Mariam (Princess Mariam, a former air hostess with Royal Brunei Airlines).

Queen Saleha, whom he married in 1965 when he was 19, shares the Istana Nurul Iman with the Sultan. Princes Mariam, who became his second wife in 1981, has her own residence, the Istana Nurul Izza, about 25km away. Two of the Sultan's brothers hold or held high government positions – Prince Mohamad is Minister of Foreign Affairs and Prince Jefri was Minister of Finance until his resignation in February 1997 – and are involved in the royal family's extensive domestic and foreign investments.

Funding entertainment and education for his citizens, or the cost of the royal family's homes and lifestyle, is not difficult for the Sultan, thanks to oil and investment revenues. The Sultan's overseas investments, operated by the Brunei Investment Agency with advice from parties such as Citibank, Morgan Guaranty, Nomura, Daiwa, UBS and Singapore's Government Investment Corporation, are valued at about US$40 billion. They generate income of around US$2.5 billion a year.

WALTER KWOK

2 Walter, Thomas & Raymond KWOK, Hong Kong

Estimated net worth: *US$13.5 billion*
Chairman and vice-chairmen: *Sun Hung Kai Properties*
Born: *Walter Ping-sheung 1950, Thomas Ping-kwong 1951, Raymond Ping-leun 1952*
Educated: *Hong Kong, Britain, United States*
Marital status: *All three brothers are married*
Hobbies: *Boating*

THE KWOK BROTHERS OWN 45.6 PER CENT OF HONG KONG'S LARGEST PROPERTY group, Sun Hung Kai Properties, which was founded by their late father Kwok Tak-sing. Kwok senior, who died in 1990, came to Hong Kong from the neighbouring Chinese province of Guangzhou in 1946 and went into partnership with another property entrepreneur, Lee Shau-kee, to establish Sun Hung Kai Properties in 1963.

The three Kwok brothers were educated in the UK and the US. Walter, the eldest and family spokesman, trained as a civil engineer and is chairman and chief executive officer of the company. Thomas and Raymond both carry the title vice-chairman and managing director. Unlike their father, who worked seven days a week, the brothers work 'only' six days a week.

Like all of Hong Kong's richest families, the Kwoks have grown wealthy on the inexorable rise of property values, both residential and commercial. But, like their father before them, they brought an extra quality to the mix – a vision of where the best opportunities were to be found as circumstances changed, and the best partners to work with. Today, their Sun Hung Kai Properties group, which develops residential land mainly in Hong Kong's New Territories, is rated as one of the best-run and most dynamic entities in Hong Kong. Its average profit margin for development projects is a high 40 per cent, it controls Hong Kong's largest land bank (more than 4 million square metres) and, according to US investment bank Lehman Brothers, it will post annual earnings per share increases of 20 per cent in 1997–99.

Among its office developments on Hong Kong island, Sun Hung Kai Properties built the Central Plaza building at Wanchai, the tallest office block in Asia until its eclipse in 1996 by the 88 storeys of the Petronas Twin Towers in Kuala Lumpur.

Sun Hung Kai Properties also has a 47.5 per cent stake in a massive US$5 billion project covering the main station for the new airport railway line in Hong Kong. With Lee Shau-kee's Henderson Land and the Bank of China, the Kwoks aim to build an 85-storey office tower on top of the new Central station. The project, expected to take eight years to complete, is already generating controversy because of a design that could obscure sightlines to Hong Kong's Peak.

In early 1997 Sun Hung Kai Properties had a market capitalization of US$29.6 billion, making it the largest company on the Hong Kong Stock Exchange. Its profit figure for 1995–96 was US$1.43 billion, on revenue of $2.94 billion. Chairman Walter Kwok, announcing the 6.5 per cent profit rise, said that property sales continued to be the group's mainstay and predicted more growth ahead.

3 Yoshiaki TSUTSUMI, Japan

Estimated net worth: *US$11.5 billion*
President: *Seibu Railway*
Born: *29 May 1934, Shiga Prefecture*
Educated: *Waseda University*
Marital status: *Married*
Hobbies: *Baseball*

YOSHIAKI TSUTSUMI MAY STILL BE ASIA'S RICHEST INDIVIDUAL NON-ROYAL, WITH a fortune of US$11.5 billion, based mainly on the 48.7 per cent he is known to hold of listed Seibu Railway (market capitalization US$20 billion) through Kokudo Corp.

Tsutsumi heads the Seibu real-estate, railway, hotel and leisure industry empire developed in Japan by his father, Yasujiro (Pistol) Tsutsumi. Yoshiaki, the son of Yasujiro and his mistress Tsuneko, has an elder half-brother Seiji (son of Yasujiro's wife Misao). Their feud has been one of the great sagas of the Japanese corporate scene.

Charismatic and decisive, Yoshiaki Tsutsumi was widely regarded as the world's richest businessman during the late 1980s, although Japan's recession in the early 1990s sliced into that wealth. Yoshiaki owes his status partly to the fact that in 1964 he was favoured in his father's will at the expense of his elder half-brother Seiji. For the next 20 years the half-brothers generally kept their feud under wraps, until both their mothers died within days of each other in 1984.

While Seiji used his energy to develop the decrepit Seibu department store into the trendy, fashionable Seibu Saison chain of stores in the 1980s, Yoshiaki built up the vast railway and property group which his father created. Among Yoshiaki Tsutsumi's companies are Seibu Real Estate, the Prince Hotels chain, golf courses and the Kokudo Group. He also owns the Seibu Lions baseball team and is a former president of the Japan Olympic Committee. Half-brother Seiji also ventured into hotels, creating the ultra-exclusive Seiyo Hotel in Tokyo's Ginza, and then buying a controlling interest in the Inter-Continental Chain. But in 1991, Seiji stepped down as head of the Saison Group to write poetry under the pen name Tsuji. In March 1996, he returned as chairman and chief executive of Inter-Continental Hotels & Resorts, following the death of the incumbent, Sueaki Takaoka.

In an interview some years ago Yoshiaki was asked how he felt about working with his brother Seiji. His response was: 'We only work well together if the job is not very serious. Our individual business senses are quite different and we clash on every issue if the job is serious. This is not good, so we work apart and make free and full use of our individual talents.'

4 LEE Shau-kee, Hong Kong

Estimated net worth: *US$11 billion*
Chairman: *Henderson Land*
Born: *1928, Shun Tak county, Guangdong province, China*
Marital status: *Married, five children*

DEPENDING ON HOW THE STOCK MARKET IS FARING, LEE SHAU-KEE IS generally regarded as Hong Kong's richest individual (behind the three Kwok brothers). Dividends from his 68-per-cent-held flagship company, Henderson Land Development, added around US$350 million to his wealth in 1996, after the company turned in a net profit in 1995–96 of US$1.08 billion. Lee described it as a 'satisfactory' result.

The property and finance magnate arrived in Hong Kong from southern China in 1947, where his father was a banker. His first job in Hong Kong was as a dealer with a finance and foreign exchange company, and in 1956 he was one of a group of eight investors to found Eternal Enterprises. Among his co-shareholders was Kwok Tak-sing, with whom Lee worked closely to set up the Sun Hung Kai Properties group in 1963, to develop extensive real-estate interests in Hong Kong.

Today SHK Properties is the largest developer in Hong Kong. But Lee's flagship is Henderson Land, the company he set up on his own in 1976, while keeping his pivotal role in SHK Properties. In 1995, Lee Shau-kee bundled together his Chinese property interests in Beijing, Shanghai and Guangzhou and spun them off into Henderson China Holdings. It subsequently listed on the Hong Kong stock exchange at the end of March 1996.

Lee's other interests include substantial stakes in such blue-chip companies as Hong Kong & China Gas, Hong Kong Ferry (which runs services between Kowloon and Hong Kong and to the outlying islands), Miramar Hotel & Investment, and property investments in China, Singapore and North America. Every time a Hong Kong commuter boards a ferry to the islands or turns on the gas at home, a few more cents of profits trickle into

Lee Shau-kee's coffers.

Lee's greatest strength has been his ability to forge alliances with the other property and infrastructure developers in Hong Kong to bid for major new projects. The Kwok brothers' SHK Properties remains a favourite partner.

Lee's children work in his companies, with son Peter serving as vice-chairman of Henderson Land. Lee is an adviser to China on Hong Kong affairs. As a member of the Preparatory Committee and the Better Hong Kong Foundation, he hopes for a 'smooth transition' to Chinese rule from July 1997.

Henderson Land's market capitalization in early 1997 was US$16.2 billion.

5 TSAI Wan-lin and family, Taiwan

Estimated net worth: *US$8.5 billion*
Founder and honorary chairman:
Lin-Yuan Group; insurance, property and construction magnate
Born: *1925, Taiwan*
Marital status: *Two wives, four sons and three daughters*
Hobby: *Golf*

IN THE LOBBY OF THE CATHAY LIFE HEAD OFFICE ON FASHIONABLE JEN AI ROAD in downtown Taipei is a marvellously evocative artwork entitled *The Picturesque Dragon Cave*. It was not just the painting itself that took the fancy of Cathay Life founder and honorary chairman Tsai Wan-lin. What he admired most was the fearless spirit of determination that lay behind the work. In 1987, at the age of 80, Taipei artist Yang San-lang tied himself to a rope and edged his way down a cliff-face on Taiwan's northeast coast so he could paint that 'picturesque Dragon Cave'.

Tsai Wan-lin's own determination has enabled his family to become dominant players in Taiwan's construction, financial services and health industries over more than three decades. Tsai, who founded Cathay Life, the flagship of his Lin-Yuan Group, in September 1962, has built it into the biggest insurance company in the country and Taiwan's single largest private enterprise. Similarly, Cathay Construction, which Tsai established in September 1964, is the country's biggest construction business. Other members of the Lin-Yuan Group are Taiwan First Investment & Trust Co (founded in 1971 as the first of its type in the domestic market), San Ching Engineering Co and Cathay General Hospital.

The Tsai family owns 50 per cent of Cathay Life (market capitalization US$21.26 billion) and more than 30 per cent of Cathay Construction (market capitalization US$2.6 billion). Tsai Wan-lin is honorary chairman of the group, while his four sons are all involved in the business. No. 2 son Tsai Hong-tu is chairman of the flagship enterprise, Cathay Life, while No. 1 son Tsai Cheng-ta is executive director of Cathay Construction and one of three managing directors of Cathay Life. No. 3 son Tsai Cheng-yu runs Taiwan First Investment & Trust Corp, plus the Cathay General Hospital and other philanthropic foundations. No. 4 son Tsai Cheng-chiu is executive director of Tung Tai Insurance Co, set up in August 1993 to explore opportunities in the non-life market.

Tsai Wan-lin's brother, Tsai Wan-chun, helped popularize the concept of savings accounts in Taiwan, while another brother, Tsai Wan-tsai, runs the financial services company Foremost.

In 1995, the Taiwanese business magazine *Excellence* estimated Tsai Wan-lin's wealth at NT$160 billion and that of his brother Tsai Wan-tsai at NT$40 billion, or a total of around US$8 billion. Since then, Cathay Life has forged ahead, and with many of their business assets unlisted, the Tsai family's wealth may well be nearing or even exceeding the US$10 billion mark. But the rise of the Tsai family has not been without controversy. A nephew of Tsai Wan-lin was jailed in 1985 on fraud charges that led to the collapse of the savings and loan institution Tenth Credit Co-operative.

Tsai is viewed as a financial backer of Taiwan's main opposition party, the Democratic Progressive Party (DPP), yet maintains good relations with President Lee Teng-hui and the ruling Kuomingtang (KMT) party.

From the outset Tsai Wan-lin laid down some operational guidelines for his children in running Cathay Life and Cathay Construction. The first of these was to 'do business in a down-to-earth manner'. He also told them: 'The elements of success in an enterprise are honesty, diligence and circumspection.'

That philosophy was already evident when he set up Cathay Construction Co. His promise of no 'jerry-built' developments and explicit property rights (in a country where malpractice involving property rights is not unusual) struck the right chords with his clients. Cathay Construction was the first company in the building industry to list on the Taiwan stock exchange, and reported a net profit of US$45 million in 1995 on revenue of US$210 million.

Tsai also saw how the growth of consumerism would change the insurance scene. In August 1993, the Lin-Yuan group set up Tong Tai Insurance as a non-life insurance company, starting with motor vehicle, fire and marine. Today, more than 60 per cent of the business it writes is motor insurance. Tsai Wan-lin's youngest son is the managing director.

The Lin-Yuan Group set up the Cathay Life Charity Foundation in 1980 and has since distributed more than NT$300 million in social welfare projects, mainly to do with children and the disabled.

Cathay Life reported a net profit of almost US$400 million for 1995, and its market capitalization in early 1997 of just under US$20 billion accounted for around 8 per cent of the Taiwan Stock Exchange's total capitalization. With 4.7 million policy holders, Cathay Life claims a 45 per cent share of the Taiwanese life insurance market, but the company is gradually losing competitiveness.

Chairman Tsai Hong-tu said that competition in 1995 was 'unprecedentedly intense' with 30 players bidding for a market of only 21 million people. Taking a cue from his father's company motto of 'Seek to improve on all fronts, pursue every growth opportunity', Tsai Hong-tu cast his eye on a much bigger emerging market across the Taiwan Strait. In February 1996 he set up Cathay Life's own Mainland China Affairs Department to 'plan for future development'. Cathay Life is also the largest landlord in Taiwan with more than 600,000 square metres of land, conservatively valued at US$2 billion. It has 37,000 employees.

6 LI Ka-shing and family, Hong Kong

Estimated net worth: *US$8 billion*
Chairman: *Cheung Kong (Holdings) and Hutchison Whampoa*
Born: *1928, Chuizhou, Guangdong province, China*
Marital status: *Widowed, sons Victor Li Tzar-kuoi (born 1964) and Richard Li Tzar-kai (born 1966)*
Hobby: *Golf*

LI KA-SHING IS ONLY NO. 3 IN THE HONG KONG WEALTH STAKES BEHIND THE Kwok brothers and Lee Shau-kee, but the man termed Hong Kong's 'Superman' is the best known of the property tycoons. Very well connected in China, he is chairman of Cheung Kong (Holdings) and Hutchison Whampoa, which have extensive property, construction, container terminal, oil and communications interests. In July 1996, Li listed Cheung Kong Infrastructure, a new company containing his China assets – primarily power plants, toll roads and bridges in southern China – and then in January 1997 unveiled a major reorganization designed to streamline operations of his flagship, Cheung Kong (Holdings), which had a market capitalization of US$20.6 billion in early 1997. Cheung Kong will control about 50 per cent of Hutchison Whampoa, which in turn will own about 84 per cent of CKI and CKI will hold up to 50 per cent of Hongkong Electric, the power utility that supplies Hong Kong island.

Li left school at 14 when his father, a school teacher, died. He came to Hong Kong from south China's Chuizhou during the Japanese occupation in 1945 and began a plastics manufacturing business in 1951 that later became his flagship, Cheung Kong.

Over the next 25 years he gradually built Cheung Kong (which he listed in 1972) into a major property developer. Then in 1979, Li stunned the Hong Kong business world when he acquired a large share of Hutchison Whampoa from the Hongkong Bank – a sale that reflected the faith the banking giant had in Li's abilities and potential. In July 1993 Li presided over the sale of 63.6 per cent of Hong Kong-based satellite television broadcaster Star TV (then headed by his son Richard) to Rupert Murdoch's News Corporation for US$525 million. Richard later sold the remaining share to Murdoch for US$300 million in 1995.

By the mid-1990s Li's sights were set firmly on major property and infrastructure deals in Hong Kong and China, including the much-delayed Oriental Plaza project in Beijing, where his partners included Hong Kong chief executive designate and Orient Overseas shipping tycoon Chung Tee-hwa. Like his occasional business partner Robert Kuok, Li is the networker *par excellence*. He knows everyone in the Asian business scene and has very strong connections with the Chinese leadership in Beijing. Along with fellow property tycoons Lee Shau-kee and Cheng Yu-tung, he is a member of China's Preparatory Committee for Hong Kong. Apart from Robert Kuok, Lee Shau-kee and Cheng Yu-tung, his partners include Mochtar Riady's Lippo group, Gordon Wu's Hopewell Holdings and the Quek family's Guoco Group.

Sons Victor and Richard both attended Stanford University and now occupy key posts in the Li empire, with Victor regarded as the heir apparent. After the Star TV deal, Richard Li's privately held Pacific Century Group ventured into new business, including a satellite-based telephone service designed to help large companies bypass congested local networks in Asia. He also targeted infrastructure and financial services as a growth area.

7 Rachman Halim and the WONOWIDJOJO family, Indonesia

Estimated net worth: *US$7.7 billion*
President: *Gudang Garam*
Born: *1947, Java*
Educated: *Secondary school*

THE ETHNIC CHINESE WONOWIDJOJO FAMILY HAS DONE VERY WELL FROM Indonesia's continuing love affair with the cigarette. With more than 50 per cent of the Indonesian population under 24 years old and per capita cigarette consumption still very low at 2.5 sticks per day, the market is headed for growth rates of up to 20 per cent a year in the late 1990s.

Gudang Garam, which sold 84 billion cigarettes in 1995, is Indonesia's biggest cigarette company, accounting for about 45 per cent of the market for *kretek* (clove-flavoured) cigarettes through its two top brands, Surya and International. Its major rivals are Sampoerna and Djarum, which hold about 20 per cent and 15 per cent respectively of the urban cigarette market.

Gudang Garam was founded in 1958 by Tjoa Ing-hwie, whose family migrated to Indonesia from China's Fujian province in 1927 when he was four. Tjoa, who took the Indonesian name Surya Wononwidjojo, worked for a while with his father and then in a relative's tobacco company, before venturing into the cigarette business on his own with Gudang Garam. When he died in 1985, his eldest son, Rachman Halim (Tjoa To-hing), took over as president. Tjoa had two other sons and a daughter.

Today, Gudang Garam, ranked as Indonesia's 11th largest conglomerate by assets, is still 80 per cent held by members of the Wonowidjojo family. The company listed in August 1990 with an initial public offering of 57.6 million shares, and reported net profit for the year to December 1995 of US$158 million on sales of US$2.41 billion. Its market capitalization in early 1997 was US$8.3 billion.

8 Minoru and Akira MORI, Japan

Estimated net worth: *US$6.5 billion*
Owners: *Mori Group*
Born: *1935 and 1937*
Hobbies: *Go (Japanese chess), golf*

MINORU MORI

LATE IN 1996, MORI BUILDING PRESIDENT MINORU MORI DECLARED THAT THE bottom of Tokyo's commercial property market had almost been reached. With Tokyo office rents at a 10-year low, it was time for Minoru, 61, and his younger brother Akira, 59, to see some blue sky and to think about fresh developments to add to the 1.34 million square metres of office space which their family controls. The next big project for the Mori brothers is a US$3.2 billion transformation of 11 hectares in Tokyo's glitzy Roppongi entertainment area, where they will create a 'new age urban cultural centre' that includes a hotel and a 58-storey office block. The project should be completed by 2001.

Even with Tokyo's property blues of the past decade, the Mori brothers and their sister are the heirs to a fabulous real-estate empire created by their late father, Yasukichi Mori.

His brainchild was an office-space-renting agency called the Mori Building Company that today controls 89 high-rise buildings, mainly in the Minato ward of central Tokyo. More than 90 per cent of the Mori Group's income is from rent. Both the major companies, Mori Building and Mori Development, are unlisted but are worth an estimated US$6 billion. Construction company Taisei holds a 22.5 per cent stake in Mori Building, which had revenue in 1994 of about US$1.2 billion.

Recent developments include a move into the Chinese property market. In Shanghai, where the Moris operate under the name Forest Overseas Group (Mori means 'forest' in Japanese), the brothers are building a 460 metre skyscraper in the Pudong Development Zone. The 95-storey building, to be known as the World Financial Centre and designed by New York architects Kohn Pedersen Fox Associates, will be Asia's highest when it is completed in 2000. Other projects include a 46-storey building in Shanghai due to open in 1998 and a 24-storey building in Dalian, in the north of China.

9 SUHARTO *and family, Indonesia*

Estimated net worth: *US$6.3 billion plus (split among the family members)*
President: *Republic of Indonesia*
Born: *20 February 1921, near Jogjakarta, central Java*
Educated: *Military school*
Marital status: *Married in December 1947 to Madame Tien Siti Hartinah Suharto (born 23 August 1923 Solo, central Java, died 28 April 1996, aged 72). Six children: Siti Hardijanti Rukmana, Sigit Harjojudanto, Bambang Trihatmodjo, Siti Hedijanti Harijadi, Hutomo Mandala Putra, Siti Hutami Endang Adiningsih*
Hobbies: *Breeding cattle, golf*

SITI HARDIJANTI RUKMANA

EACH OF THE SIX SUHARTO CHILDREN HAS DEVELOPED A VARIETY OF BUSINESS interests, as follows.

Siti Hardijanti Rukmana, known popularly as Mbak (sister) Tutut, was born in 1949 and is the eldest child. She is married to businessman Indra Rukmana. Her listed company is tollroad operator Citra Marga Nusaphala Persada (CMNP), which owns and operates the 52km Jakarta A ring road and has a market capitalization of about US$310 million. She floated it in November 1994, raising US$145 million through an offer of 24.4 per cent of its shares. Her main company, begun in 1983, is Citra Lamtoro Gung Persada, of which she owns 35 per cent. Her husband holds 20 per cent, and sisters Titiek and Mamie (10 per cent) also have shares. Tutut also holds 17.5 per cent of Bank Central Asia, controlled by Liem Sioe Liong's Salim Group.

During the past decade, Tutut and her husband have developed interests in tollroad construction and operation, finance, oil, petrochemicals, agribusiness, television and banking. One of her most visible holdings is educational television station Televisi Pendidikan Indonesia.

Along with a proposed 56km Jakarta–Bandung tollroad and inter-city links across Jakarta (where traffic usage is growing at a rapid rate), Tutut also has a listed Manila tollroad operation, Citra Metro Manila, which should start making a contribution to revenue in 1998.

Among her business partners is the timber tycoon Prajogo Pangestu of Barito Pacific. Tutut has a stake in his US$400 million South Sumatra major pulp and paper project, and both are shareholders in Astra International, the large conglomerate which dominates the Indonesian auto industry as an assembler of Toyota vehicles.

Tutut's estimated net worth is US$2 billion.

Sigit Harjojudanto, born in 1951, is the eldest son and is married to Elsye Anneke Ratnawati. Their children include first son Ari Haryo Wibowo Sigit, 23, who shot to prominence in February 1996 when he tried, unsuccessfully, to impose a special levy on beer and alcohol sales in Bali. The move was overturned by the President – the first time Suharto had felt inclined to curb a family member's business greed. Still, Ari was unperturbed; following in the footsteps of his parents, aunts and uncles, his ARHA Group aims to be a major force in commodities, telecoms, tourism and manufacturing.

Once known as a gambler, Sigit was a relatively low-profile member of the family, involved in banking and plastics through his Hanurata Group, until the 1996 Astra play and the spectacular Bre-X gold fraud of 1997 brought him once again to prominence. He holds a 17.5 per cent stake in Liem Sioe Liong's Bank Central Asia and has a petrochemicals joint venture with British Petroleum, PT PENI. He also holds 40 per cent stake in Humpuss, the group he helped his younger brother, Tommy, establish.

Sigit and his father's confidant and golf partner, Mohamad Bob Hasan, each have a 10 per cent stake in PT Nusantara Ampera Bhakti (Nusamba), an investment company which is 80 per cent owned by three foundations controlled by Suharto.

Because of Tommy Suharto's lead role in the Timor national car project, Sigit's stake in Nusamba became the subject of much speculation when it was involved in a share-buying move on Astra International, Indonesia's largest car assembler. By the time the dust settled in late 1996, Sigit's partner Bob Hasan had put together an informal group controlling more than 50 per cent of Astra, made up of the *kretek* (clove) cigarette tycoon Putera Sampoerna, Liem Sioe Liong's son and Salim Group chief executive Anthony Salim, another timber tycoon, Prajogo Pangestu, and the chairman of Bank Danamon, Usman Admajaja.

If Astra was a big play, the second move in late 1996 was even more audacious and included some potential sibling rivalry: Sigit became involved in a goldmining deal in the Indonesian state of Kalimantan (part of the island of Borneo) with the junior Canadian miner, Bre-X Minerals. Busang, hyped by Bre-X as the biggest gold play ever seen in Indonesia, purportedly contained a reputed 71 million ounces of gold worth US$30 billion, with some boosters putting the figure at US$50 billion. But it was a monumental scam. Busang had been 'salted' and there was no gold. Initially, Calgary-based Bre-X thought that having Sigit as a US$40 million consultant and 10 per cent stakeholder might give it the muscle to get a smooth passage through Indonesia's bureaucracy. Not so; the Indonesian government insisted that tiny Bre-X work out an agreement with giant Canadian rival Barrick Gold, a proven miner with the ability to fund the US$1.5 billion needed to develop the supposed Busang deposit.

Indonesia wanted such a potentially valuable find developed and operated by a major player, rather than a junior miner like Bre-X. And if Bre-X had Sigit, then Barrick was able to call on its own heavy hitters – international stars like former Canadian prime minister Brian Mulroney and former US president George Bush and, domestically, Sigit's elder sister Tutut as a potential partner. For months, Jakarta was treated to the unedifying sight of two foreign goldminers, each with one of the Suharto children as a potential partner, squabbling about the find, with the Indonesian government increasing the pressure for them to work out an agreement. It looked like a win for Tutut was on the cards when it seemed that a deal on Busang was on the verge of completion, split 67.5 per cent for Barrick, 22.5 per cent for Bre-X and 10 per cent for the Indonesian government.

But then in February 1997 Sigit's partner in Nusamba, Mohamad Bob Hasan, played his trump card. Even as another large Canadian miner, Placer Dome, was seeking to tempt Bre-X into a joint venture, Hasan signed up an old mining mate, James 'Jim Bob' Moffett, chairman of US giant Freeport McMoRan Copper and Gold, to fund, construct and operate the Busang mine. Moffett was already on good terms with Suharto through Freeport's operation of the Grasberg copper and gold mine in Irian Jaya, which poured billions into the government's tax coffers. Hasan brokered a new Busang deal which left Bre-X with 45 per cent, Freeport with 15 per cent, 30 per cent for two companies 50 per cent owned by Hasan and Sigit (through Nusamba) and 10 per cent for the Indonesian government. Only when Freeport ordered its own due diligence on the deposit and Bre-X chief geologist Michael de Guzman apparently took his life in a helicopter fall did the Busang fraud unwind. The full story is yet to unfold.

Sigit's estimated net worth is US$450 million.

Bambang Trihatmodjo, born in 1953, is the second son and married to Siti Halimah. Bambang is well known internationally – a consequence of investment roadshows in the United States and Europe when he took his holding company, Bimantara Citra, public in 1995. That initial public offering of 200 million shares raised US$115 million.

Bambang set up Bimantara in 1981 and today has more than 100 subsidiaries in the group, with interests in broadcasting and telecommunications, the automotive and oil industries, and infrastructure, finance, electronics and entertainment.

Bimantara, which reported a net profit of around US$48 million in 1995 on revenue of around US$320 million, ranks in the top 12 companies on the Jakarta stock exchange by market capitalization (about US$1.4 billion in early 1997).

Bimantara's auto interests include a 20,000-unit assembly line which began producing Hyundai cars in July 1996. A much larger 100,000-unit assembly line is due for completion in 1998 in a deal with Hyundai that could involve an investment of up to US$700 million. Bimantara's Cakra sedan will compete with the Timor of younger brother Tommy's Humpuss group.

Bambang's major assets in Bimantara include the 45-per-cent-held telecommunications subsidiary Satelindo (in which Deutsche Telekom holds a 25 per cent stake, bought from Bambang for almost US$600 million in 1994), domestic private television station RCTI and a pay-TV network. Bambang holds 10 per cent of Pasifik Satelit Nusantara (PSN), which operates Indonesia's Palapa B satellites and plans to start a pan-Asia digital mobile-phone service.

Bambang benefited hugely from government concessions after starting Bimantara in 1981 with friends Rosano Barack, Muhamad Tachril and ex-Citibanker Peter Gontha. He holds 41.1 per cent of Bimantara. Brother-in-law Indra Rukmana (Tutut's husband) holds a small share and is group chairman.

In the power-generation industry, Bimantara has a stake in Paiton Two, the private power plant being built by US partners General Electric and Edison Mission Energy. Bambang also holds a controlling stake in Indonesia's largest textile maker, Kanindo, with the former Salim Group executive Johannes Kotjo.

Another partner is Henry Pribadi, who shares a stake in the controversial West Java petrochemical complex PT Chandra Asri with Bambang and timber tycoon Prajogo Pangestu. Indonesia is giving special tariff protection to Chandra Asri.

Bambang's estimated net worth is US$3 billion.

Siti Hedijanti Harijadi, popularly known as Titiek, was born in 1959 and is the second daughter. Her husband, Major-General Prabowo Subianto, commands the élite Kopassus special forces regiment. They have one son. Prabowo, who is hailed in some quarters as a potential successor to Suharto for the presidency, studied in Switzerland, the United States and Britain before joining the Indonesian armed forces.

With elder sister Tutut, Titiek started the Datam Group in the 1980s. Today her main company is Maharani Paramita, which has property, telecommunications, finance and forestry interests.

She is also a business partner of Prabowo's elder brother Hashim Djojohadikusumo, chairman of Semen Cibinong. They control Batu Hitam Perkasa, which has 15 per cent of the US$2 billion Paiton power project in Java.

Titiek, who heads the Indonesian Arts Foundation and the national Table Tennis Association, has an estimated net worth of US$200 million.

Hutomo Mandala Putra, known as Tommy, was born in 1962 and is the third and youngest son. He married civil engineering graduate Ardhia 'Tata' Pramesti Regita Cahyani, 22, in April 1997. Tommy started the Humpuss group in 1984, which covers about 70 companies in fields such as aviation (through a controlling stake in Sempati Air, Indonesia's second international carrier after state-owned Garuda), agribusiness, tollroad construction, oil, gas, commodities, manufacturing, media, petrochemicals and timber. Humpuss earns much of its revenue from oil-shipment contracts with Pertamina, the state oil and gas corporation.

Tommy was seldom far from the news in 1996 after his company PT Timor Putra Nasional (TPN) formed a joint venture with South Korea's Kia Motors to produce the controversial Timor 'national car'. On 27 February 1996, a day after Tommy and Kia announced their US$1 billion joint venture PT Kia-Timor Motor (held 30 per cent by Kia, 70 per cent by TPN) to assemble a sedan and a utility vehicle based on two Kia models, Tommy's father, Suharto, announced that the venture would have 'pioneer' status.

This special status, free of import duties and a luxury tax, meant that the venture would gain a tax break of up to US$1 billion and a substantial price advantage over other carmakers in the Indonesian market such as Astra and Indomobil. Japanese automakers, heavy investors in Indonesia, immediately complained and threatened to take their case to the World Trade Organisation. Another to complain was Tommy's elder brother Bambang, whose own carmaking ambitions (also with a Korean partner, Hyundai) were dealt a severe blow by the favoured treatment for the Timor project.

But the Kia–TPN plan proved slow to move, with no start on the West Java production facility in sight and the joint venture forced to import fully built cars from Kia. The new ownership at Astra, with the possibility that it could have a role in Indonesia's national car programme, added a further note of uncertainty for Tommy.

The Humpuss Group has estimated assets of around US$400 million. It is held 60 per cent by Tommy and 40 per cent by his elder brother Sigit. Tommy is also head of the Clove Marketing Board, which has a monopoly on the sale and distribution of cloves, used in the manufacture of Indonesia's distinctive *kretek* cigarettes. Tommy's business partners include Mohamad Bob Hasan, who holds 20 per cent of Sempati Air.

Tommy's estimated net worth is US$600 million.

Siti Hutami Endang Adiningsih, known as Mamie or Mimiek, was born in 1964 and is the third daughter and youngest child. She is married to Pratikto Prayitno Singgih. They have one son. Her companies are involved in plantations, warehousing, transport and a land-reclamation project near Jakarta. She also holds various stakes in her elder sisters' and brothers' ventures, and is a director of the Mekarsari Fruit Garden, a project outside Jakarta started by her late mother.

Her estimated net worth is US$100 million.

10 CHUNG Ju Yung and family, Korea

Estimated net worth: *US$6.2 billion*
Founder: *Hyundai Group*
Born: *November 1915, Asan, North Korea*
Educated: *Local school until age 15*
Marital status: *Married Byun Joong-suk in 1938, seven sons (first and fourth deceased), one daughter. Sons are Mong Koo, Mong Kun, Mong Hun, Mong Joon, Mong Yun*

BORN INTO A RICE-FARMING FAMILY IN THE SMALL VILLAGE OF ASAN IN WHAT IS now North Korea, Chung Ju Yung spent more than 40 years at the helm of Korea's mightiest conglomerate, the Hyundai Business Group.

In his book *There Are Difficulties, But No Failures*, Chung Ju Yung described himself as 'merely a rich labourer who, through his labour, produces commodities'. As a teenager, Chung left home to seek his fortune, working as a labourer in the North Korean city of Wonsan and later on the Inchon docks, near Seoul. He became a delivery boy, worked in a rice mill where he gained enough business knowledge to open his own rice store in Seoul, then moved into the car-repair business. This was the first step to a permanent business presence; after Korea was liberated from Japanese rule in 1945, Chung established the Hyundai (which means 'modern') Auto

Repair Co. From this, he moved into the construction industry and benefited hugely from large government contracts as Korea modernized its infrastructure, building roads, dams, bridges and power stations. By the 1970s, Hyundai had ventured into shipbuilding and motor vehicles, and later into electronics and energy.

Chung, now group honorary chairman, was forced to step aside from the reins of power at Hyundai after a disastrous run-in with South Korean President Kim Young-sam. The Kim administration harassed Hyundai with tax audits because Chung ran against him in the 1992 elections. This culminated in a court decision in July 1994, when Chung, then 78, was given a three-year suspended sentence for spending more than US$65 million of Hyundai company money on his unsuccessful 1992 presidential bid.

In 1989 Chung Ju Yung was the first South Korean business leader to visit North Korea. His avowed aim is to build a tourist resort where he was born at Asan, just north of the demilitarized zone (DMZ). Chung was also keen to enter the energy business in North Korea, and hoped to build a pipeline via North Korea to transport natural gas from Russia and oil from China to South Korea. But his application to visit North Korea in January 1996 was refused by the Seoul government.

Chung, now in his eighties, has four brothers and one sister. Of these, Chung Se Yung, born 1928 and educated at Korea University, Seoul, is the other major participant in the Hyundai Group that Chung founded in 1947, serving as chairman from 1987 until the end of 1995. But it was Chung Ju Yung's son, Chung Mong Koo, then 58, who took over as chairman at the beginning of 1996 and followed his father's aggressive style, with a call for 'value management'. Mong Koo, whose elder brother died in a car crash some years ago, was previously chairman of Hyundai Precision & Industry Co. His younger brother, Mong Hun, became group vice-chairman.

Chung Se Yung's only son, Oxford-educated Chung Mong Kyu, 34, was promoted from vice-president to the key post of chairman of Hyundai Motor Co, putting Hyundai Motor and other auto-related parts of the group under the control of Se Yung and his family. Chung Mong Kyu, who holds a master's degree in politics, philosophy and economics, is the youngest of the new-generation heads of Hyundai divisions.

In the intensely tough car wars that swept across Korea in the mid-1990s, Chung warned that only the best automakers would survive the onslaught of international competition as Korea's own market opened up to outsiders. 'The best approach … is to give customers the maximum satisfaction,' Chung said.

In his inaugural speech in January 1996, Chung Mong Koo said that Hyundai would actively pursue steel production, with the construction of a blast furnace. This activity, a long-held dream of his father's, would put Hyundai in competition with one of its major suppliers, Pohang Iron & Steel Co (Posco), which is one-third state controlled. Hyundai expects to need 5 million tonnes of steel a year by 2000 to support its carmaking, shipbuilding, construction, engineering and electronics activities. But the Korean government has so far declined to approve Chung's plan.

In 1995, Hyundai held on to its position as the leading conglomerate in Korea, with total assets of US$55 billion, ahead of the Samsung Group with US$51 billion. But Samsung is gaining fast, and is soon likely to eclipse Hyundai. In revenue, Samsung leapt ahead in 1995, with sales of US$78.7 billion, compared to Hyundai's US$73.8 billion.

11 WANG *Yung-ching and family, Taiwan*

Estimated net worth: *US$6 billion*
Chairman: *Formosa Plastics Group*
Public offices: *Chairman, Ming-chi Institute of Technology*
Born: *18 January 1917, Taipei*
Marital status: *Married, 10 children (two sons, eight daughters)*
Hobby: *Jogging*

WANG YUNG-CHING IS TAIWAN'S MOST POWERFUL INDUSTRIALIST AND founder in 1954 of the Formosa Plastics Group (FPG), a petrochemicals conglomerate of more than 20 companies which includes Nan Ya Plastics, Formosa Chemical & Fibre and Formosa Taffeta.

Wang's emergence as one of the richest businessmen in Asia, sitting at the head of a conglomerate with annual revenues of more than US$10 billion, is a classic rags-to-riches tale in which hard work and frugality triumph. He summed up his philosophy in a message to shareholders in 1996: 'We believe that under the sun there is no easy task, nor an impossible mission.'

Wang, the son of a poor tea merchant in Taipei, made his first money tending a neighbour's cattle at the age of 9. He started his first business at age 16, running a rice shop. Corporate legend has it that he was 13 before he got his first pair of shoes. During the 1940s, when the Japanese still occupied

Taiwan, Wang expanded from rice milling into timber, building up a nest egg that helped put him on the first wave of Taiwan's postwar industrial surge.

With a development loan from the United States government, Wang established Formosa Plastics in 1954 and set up a small plant to make polyvinyl chloride (PVC). He followed that with a second company, Nan Ya Plastics, and gradually built the Formosa Plastics Group into Taiwan's biggest conglomerate and private employer, and the world's largest producer of PVC.

Wang's most important project is of immense scale and has been delayed by environmental objections since he first formulated it in the early 1990s. On the west coast of central Taiwan, Wang is building a US$10 billion petro-chemical complex, known as the Sixth Naphtha Cracker, at the Mailiau and Hai Fong industrial zone in Yunlin county. The complex, which also involves a 2400 megawatt power plant, the reclamation of 2600 hectares of land from the sea and the building of a harbour to handle 200,000-tonne tankers, is regarded as the world's largest private investment project. When the Mailiau harbour is completed, it will be only 200km from coastal ports in China's Fujian provinc. Direct shipping links between Taiwan and the mainland were suspended in 1949 but resumed hesitantly in April 1997.

Wang, who has already built five plants in the United States and one in Indonesia, has another major development on the books – a US$3 billion project to build a series of six coal-fired power stations in Fujian. But pressure from the Taipei government about the speed and scale of investments in China by Taiwanese business interests prompted Wang to run this project through a foreign subsidiary.

Wang's son Winston, 45, was senior vice-president of Nan Ya Plastics and heir apparent until a fall from grace in late 1994 (over a romance with a college student) put his status in the family at risk. He remains in his father's black books. A daughter, Margaret, is also a Nan Ya vice-president, while Wang's younger brother Yang Yung-tsai plays a key role as president of Formosa Chemical & Fibre. Other family members are prominent shareholders throughout the FPG companies; Wang's daughter Charlene, for example, is president of First International Computer (which she runs with her husband Chieng Ming), while another daughter, Cher, runs California-based Everex Systems.

Electronics is seen as a new growth area for the group, with Wang declaring in 1996 that FPG needed to increase its investment in capital-intensive high-tech electronics. Nan Ya Plastics is leading FPG's charge into this new business, with its own wafer-fabrication plant and a joint venture with Japan's Komatsu Electronic Metals to produce silicon wafers.

Wang also told shareholders that the group should never stop its corporate task of 'business rationalization' to enhance competitiveness. 'It is my belief that this is the only approach to business survival and development,' he said.

Further down the track lie investments in the mobile-phone business in Taiwan, and the mass production of two-seat electric cars – both through the investment arm of FPG, Asia Pacific Investment Corp.

In 1995, the group overtook the Lin-Yuan conglomerate of the Tsai family to become Taiwan's most profitable business group, reporting total net profit of US$1.6 billion on revenue of US$13.6 billion. That was more than enough to buy the chairman a pair of shoes for his favourite form of relaxation: jogging.

12 DHANIN
Chearavanont and family, Thailand

Estimated net worth: *US$5.5 billion*
Chairman and CEO: *Charoen Pokphand Group. Parliamentary senator 1992–96*
Born: *April 1939, Bangkok*
Educated: *Schools in Thailand and China, Hong Kong Commercial College (1956) and the National Defence College, Bangkok*
Marital status: *Married to Thavee Watanalikhit, three sons and two daughters*
Hobby: *Homing pigeons*

UNDER DHANIN'S LEADERSHIP, FIRST AS GENERAL MANAGER IN 1964 AND then as president since 1969, Thailand's giant Charoen Pokphand group has expanded to have interests in more than 20 countries. From its humble beginnings as a seed store started in 1921 by Dhanin's father and uncle (who were Chinese immigrants from Shantou), the CP Group now employs 35,000 people through more than 250 companies that have a combined annual revenue of around US$7.5 billion.

Dhanin has taken the company from agribusiness into areas such as store franchises, property and land development, petrochemicals, motor vehicles, beer and telecommunications, including a stake in Hong-Kong-based APT Satellite Co and a high-profile joint venture in Bangkok's telephone business with US partner Nynex. This venture, TelecomAsia, has grown into one of the largest listed companies on the Stock Exchange of Thailand, with a market capitalization of more than US$7 billion. The group's 29 per cent stake is valued at US$2.06 billion.

While the newer projects grab the spotlight, the cornerstone of the CP Group's activities remains agribusiness. The Chearavanont family has taken a special interest in chicken raising and fish farming, the latter project earning it commendation from Thailand's King Bhumipol Adulyadej.

Dhanin was appointed an adviser on Hong Kong affairs for China in 1993, and his Hong-Kong-based holding company (run by elder brother Sumet Jiaravanon) controls most of the group's China investments. Besides agribusiness operations and a very successful motorcycle manufacturing plant, these include a joint-venture brewery in Shanghai, service stations in Guangdong province and a planned shopping centre in Guangzhou.

Dhanin's philosophy reflects his family's modest origins: 'To succeed, talent … is only half the equation. One needs to work hard, to be patient.' That hard work over the last 75 years has helped create a family fortune that is the largest in Thailand. Dhanin's eldest son Supakij is chairman of the group's cable-television outlet UTV, while second son Narong is vice-president of Ek Chai Distribution Co and third son Supachai is a director at TelecomAsia.

13 LIM Goh Tong, Malaysia

Estimated net worth: *US$5.2 billion*
Chairman: *Genting Bhd*
Born: *1918, in Anwei, Fujian province, China*
Marital status: *Married, six children*

LIM, WHO MIGRATED TO MALAYSIA FROM CHINA'S FUJIAN PROVINCE, IS founder and chairman of Genting Bhd, the Malaysian conglomerate with interests in gaming and leisure. He started with one casino licence in the 1970s and has built up an empire that dominates the Malaysian gaming scene. With an estimated net worth of US$5.2 billion, he is regarded as Malaysia's richest man.

Along with 40-per-cent-held Genting Bhd, the Lim family controls Kien Huat Realty, 58-per-cent-held Resorts World, plantations unit Asiatic Development (held 64 per cent by the family), Genting Highland Casino and Genting International, which will take delivery of two new 75,000-tonne cruise ships in 1998–99. The ships, costing US$350 million each, will carry 2800 passengers and spearhead Lim's move into the Asian cruise market.

Lim carved out a resort centre in the Genting Highlands north of Kuala Lumpur more than 20 years ago. There he has developed South-East Asia's biggest casino, along with golf courses, hotels and theme parks. His Resorts World continues to add to its 4000 hotel rooms to cater for a growing market, even in a country whose dominant religion, Islam, frowns on gambling. But operations at the hilltop resort suffered a temporary setback in June 1995 when a landslide on its 25km main access road killed 20 people.

Apart from gambling, resorts and cruises, Lim is an investor in a power plant, paper mill and property development. About 20km north of the southern Malaysian city of Johor Bahru, Lim has a stake in a massive new development for a city at Kulai. He also controls palm-oil plantations, and made money in iron mining and construction in the early days of his business endeavours. In China, Lim has a palm-oil bulking installation plant in Guangdong, and a 45 per cent interest in an oil and gas exploration concession in Indonesia's Irian Jaya with British Gas Exploration.

Lim's sons Lim Kok Thay (managing director) and Lim Chee Wah are involved in the management of Genting, which regularly tops the Malaysian list in the *Far Eastern Economic Review*'s annual survey of Asia's leading companies. Genting reported a 1996 profit of around US$230 million. Its market capitalization in early 1997 was just under US$5 billion, while that for Resorts World was US$5.7 billion. This makes it the biggest gaming company in Malaysia, well ahead of lottery companies Magnum Corp, Berjaya Sports Toto and Tanjong.

14 Eugene WU Tung-chin and family, Taiwan

Estimated net worth: *US$5 billion*
Chairman: *Shin Kong Group*
Born: *1944*
Marital status: *Married*

EUGENE WU TUNG-CHIN, CHAIRMAN OF TAIWAN'S SHIN KONG GROUP, TAKES A special pride in the rose-coloured 51-storey Shin Kong Life Tower that dominates the Taipei city skyline. The 244 metre building, designed by Japanese architect Kaku Morin, rises near Taipei's central railway station and quickly became the Taiwan capital's best-known landmark after its completion in December 1993. But it was a long time coming – Wu and three other potential business partners first started planning the project in 1981. In 1985, when the original partnership foundered, Shin Kong reached agreement on the development with the Asiaworld International Group (run by Filipino-Chinese developer Tan Yu), which built its own 27-storey department store on its half of the original site. The observation tower on the 46th floor mixes historical scenes of old Taipei with photos of Eugene Wu and son Benson hosting a variety of distinguished visitors to the building.

Eugene Wu Tung-chin took over the Shin Kong group in October 1976, following the death of his father and group founder, Wu Hou-shih, from a heart attack. Wu has three brothers; one, Wu Tung-liang, is president of Shin Kong Synthetic Fibre and chairman of Taishin International Bank.

While Shin Kong Life ranks second behind Cathay Life in Taiwan's insurance market, it is still one of the country's biggest enterprises and flagship of the Wu family. The group's other interests are in construction, energy (through Great Taipei Gas Co), synthetic fibres (through Shin Kong Synthetic Fibre and Shin Kong Spinning Co) and retailing through its joint venture with the Japanese department store Mitsukoshi, which occupies the first 12 floors of the Shin Kong Life building. The group has a stake in Taiwan Securities and an interest in 36th-ranked Taishin International Bank. In the non-life area, the group controls Shin Kong Fire & Marine Insurance Co, of which Anthony T.S. Wu is chairman.

Shin Kong Life, which went public in December 1993, had a market capitalization in early 1997 of US$6.4 billion, ranking it Taiwan's second biggest life insurance company behind Cathay Life. Its 1995 sales of US$3.86 billion gave it a pre-tax profit of US$210 million. Eugene Wu has set a group sales target of US$7.5 billion by 2000.

15 Yasuo TAKEI and family, Japan

Estimated net worth: *US$5 billion*
Founder: *Takefuji Corp*
Born: *1930*

W HEN SHARES OF TAKEFUJI CORP OPENED ON JAPAN'S OVER-THE-COUNTER (OTC) market on 30 August 1996, the market valued the consumer finance company at almost US$10 billion. And with the company predicting that its 1997 pre-tax profits would leap past US$1.1 billion, it was easy to understand the love affair with Takefuji.

Shareholders had rushed for the initial public offering of 5 million shares – the biggest IPO in the history of the Japanese OTC market. By the time it went public, Takefuji accounted for more than 6 per cent of the OTC market by value.

It was a far cry from three decades earlier, when *pachinko* (Japanese pinball) parlour employee Yasuo Takei founded Takefuji. Over the years, the demand for unsecured credit skyrocketed as Japanese consumers went on a spending spree, with interest rates reaching prodigious levels in the 1980s and 1990s.

Takefuji generated huge profits from these consumer loans in the early 1990s, charging up to 29 per cent for unsecured loans. Yasuo Takei, who stepped down as president in June 1995, to be replaced by Takanori Sakamoto, saw his company go public in 1966 and emerged with a family holding worth an estimated US$5 billion.

Takefuji stock opened more than 5 per cent above the 9690 yen price for its initial public offering, and continued to be regarded as a growth company in Japan's financial services sector. By early 1997, the Tokyo stock market in general had eased down, but the company was still valued at US$8.7 billion and Takefuji predicted that its 1997 profit would top 125 billion yen (US$1.16 billion). The company had revenue of US$2.24 billion in the year to March 1996 for a pre-tax profit of more than US$1 billion and a net profit of US$436 million.

16 Masayoshi SON, Japan

Estimated net worth: *US$4.7 billion*
Founder and president: *Softbank Corporation*
Born: *1957, Japan*
Educated: *University of California, Berkeley*
Marital status: *Married to Masami Son, two daughters*
Hobby: *Golf*

IN THE WORLD OF MASAYOSHI SON, ETHNIC KOREAN PRESIDENT OF TOKYO-BASED Softbank Corporation, superlatives abound. Since 1994, he has paid top dollar in double-quick time to become one of the biggest players in the computer and multimedia industry. Now he presides over the world's largest publisher of computer magazines, the world's biggest supplier of memory-board products, and the world's biggest organizer of computer trade shows and exhibitions.

Son, born to Korean parents in Japan, left for the United States while still a teenager, worked his way through college in California and began to see the business possibilities of the information technology revolution. He returned to Japan, fiddled around with some electronic devices and in 1981 set up Softbank to handle software distribution. The first 10 years of Son's business career were less than overwhelming, but by the early 1990s Softbank had reached critical mass. Its software sales began to rise, and Son was ready for his massive expansion plans.

Son took Softbank public in 1994 with an IPO that raised US$600 million plus – enough money to pay for the computer trade show business Comdex. Son's purchase of Ziff-Davis Publishing Co for US$2.1 billion in 1995 fuelled ambitions that seem to rival those of Microsoft founder Bill Gates in their global scope. The group includes market-leading titles such as *PC Magazine* and *PC Week*. In June 1996, he stunned Japan's staid broadcasting world when, in partnership with Rupert Murdoch, head of News Corporation, he took a 22 per cent stake in Japanese television station TV Asahi. That move was designed to tap in to a stream of Japanese-language content for the 150 satellite channels that Son and Murdoch will beam into the Japanese market from 1998 onwards, as part of their JSkyB joint venture. In March 1997 Son and Murdoch sold their TV Asahi stake back to the Asahi group, then two months later welcomed Sony and the powerful Fuji TV network as 20 per cent partners and content providers in JSkyB.

Son, ever the evangelist of the computer world, predicted that his 1997 group sales would reach more than US$3 billion. In early 1997, his 61.4 per cent stake in Softbank was worth around US$3.6 billion, more than double its value when he went public in July 1994.

17 SHIN Kyuk-ho (Takeo Shigemitsu), Korea

Estimated net worth: *US$4.5 billion*
Chairman: *Lotte Group*
Born: *October 1922, Ulsan, Korea*
Educated: *Waseda University, Japan*
Marital status: *Twice married., one daughter and two sons*
Hobbies: *Baseball, golf*

CANDY KING SHIN KYUK-HO RUNS A KOREAN AND JAPANESE FOOD AND beverage conglomerate which takes its name, Lotte, from Charlotte, heroine of a Goethe novel, *The Sorrow of Young Werther*. Shin's companies are also involved in wholesale distribution, tourism, construction, petrochemicals, heavy industries, hotels, department stores, theme parks and two baseball teams – the Lotte Giants in Korea and the Lotte Marines in Japan. With 24 affiliates and 35,000 employees, the Lotte group aims to reach sales of US$35 billion by 2000. Shin is looking to genetic engineering and biotechnology for future breakthroughs in food development.

Born into a peasant family in Korea's South Kyongsan province, Shin sailed for Japan in 1941 at the age of 19. He paid his way through Tokyo's prestigious Waseda University (where he studied chemistry) by selling newspapers on the streets, before finding a postwar niche in Japan as a trader of black-market commodities like soap and chewing gum. During the 1950s and 1960s, Shin built a business in Japan as a maker of gum and chocolate. Using Japan as a base (where he is known as Takeo Shigemitsu), he returned to Korea and founded the Lotte Confectionery Co in 1967 to make gum, chocolate and candy, and then expanded into beverages like cider, fruit drinks and soft drinks through his Lotte Chilsung Beverage Co.

Shin pioneered the Korean fastfood industry with the Lotteria chain of restaurants, a concept which he took to China. He now owns gum and chocolate factories in Korea and Japan, plus baseball teams in both countries. He also has extensive real-estate holdings in Seoul and Tokyo. His Hotel Lotte in downtown Seoul and the mammoth indoor leisure centre, hotel and shopping mall known as Lotte World are two of the Lotte Group's signature developments. The latter, built for a reported US$1 billion in 1989, draws 5 million visitors a year.

Shin's daughter by his first marriage, Shin Yong Ja, is vice-chairman of Lotte Shipping. Two sons by his second marriage, Shin Dong Joo and Shin Tong Hyuk, work in Japan.

18 LIEM Sioe Liong (Sudono Salim), Indonesia

Estimated net worth: *US$4.5 billion*
Chairman: *Salim Group*
Born: *1917, Fuqing, Fujian province, South China*
Marital status: *Married, three sons, Andree, Anthony, Albert Halim,*
 daughter Macani. Two brothers, Liem Sioe Hie (elder) and Liem Sioe
 Kong (younger)

FUJIAN-BORN LIEM SIOE LIONG, ALSO KNOWN BY HIS INDONESIAN NAME, Sudono Salim, is Indonesia's richest man and founder of the Salim Group, the nation's largest conglomerate.

With more than 300 companies, 135,000 employees and annual revenue of around US$10 billion, the Salim Group is among the most powerful and diverse business entities in Asia. Its interests span food and beverages, cooking oil, cement and other building materials, motor vehicles, commodity trading, property, chemicals, pharmaceuticals, textiles, financial services, distribution, media and telecommunications.

Listed companies include Indocement and Indofood in Jakarta, First Pacific in Hong Kong, Metro Pacific in Manila, Berli Jucker in Bangkok and United Industrial Corp in Singapore.

Liem arrived in Central Java from China in 1938 to work with his elder brother in an uncle's peanut-oil shop in Kudus. With his savings, he started his first business, selling coffee powder, during the Second World War.

Liem moved from Central Java to Jakarta in 1952 where he set up a small bank, PT Bank Windu Kentjana, the forerunner of what became Bank

Central Asia. In the mid-1970s, with the help of banker Mochtar Riady, head of the Lippo Group, Liem built BCA into Indonesia's largest private bank.

In the 1960s Liem had established the companies that were to lay the foundations for the Salim Group: PT Bogasari Flour Mill, which eventually became the world's largest wheat-buying company, and PT Mega, which imported cloves under an exclusive concession from the government. That was followed in 1973 by PT Indocement, the nation's largest cement maker.

In addition to his close links with Suharto, dating from an acquaintance in the 1950s, Liem's business partners include several Suharto family members. Suharto's cousin, Sudwikatmono, is president director and a major shareholder in Indofood and Indocement, while Suharto's younger half-brother, Probosutedjo, is a partner in the clove-import business.

Liem's youngest son and heir apparent, Anthony Salim, is close to Suharto's second son, Bambang Trihatmodjo. Educated in Singapore and London, Anthony is the Salim Group's public face in the English-speaking world. He heads the main Indonesian holding company, Salim Economic Development Corporation, and is group president and chief executive officer. His elder brother, Andree, is group vice-chairman, while Liem retains the chairmanship.

Besides his Suharto family connections, Liem's partners include a string of native Fujianese businessmen, including Djuhar Sutanto and his cousin Henry Pribadi; banking ally Mochtar Riady of the Lippo Group; Eka Tjipta Widjaja (Oei Ek Tjhong) who heads Indonesia's second largest conglomerate, the Sinar Mas Group, and like Liem was born in Fujian province; Prajogo Pangestu of Barito Group, who looked after Liem's timber interests; and Ibrahim Risjad (one of the original 'Liem investors' from Aceh in northern Sumatra).

19 Vincent TAN Chee Yioun, Malaysia

Estimated net worth: *US$4.5 billion*
Chairman: *Berjaya Group*
Born: *1952, Johor, Malaysia*
Educated: *Johor secondary school*

V INCENT TAN, WHOSE FAMILY'S ANCESTRAL HOME IS CHINA'S FUJIAN PROVINCE, started his working life in Malaysia as a junior clerk at Malayan Bank.

After hours, he sold insurance and was so good at it that he quit the bank to go full time with AIA (American International Assurance). His first big break came in 1981 when he won the McDonald's franchise for Malaysia.

Today, after a roller-coaster business career, he is an associate of the Malaysian political élite and a major force in the gaming, leisure, healthcare and telecommunications sectors. Tan built his empire on gambling enterprises and astute deal making. He controls the diversified Berjaya group which includes listed Berjaya Industrial and Berjaya Sports Toto, the company he formed after acquiring the state-owned Sports Toto betting agency in 1985. In early 1997 Berjaya Sports had a market capitalization of US$2.8 billion, while Berjaya Group was valued at more than US$670 million.

Tan, an aggressive investor over the years in such Malaysian stocks as Singer, Magnum Corp and Malayan United Industries (MUI), is described as the antithesis of older, conservative ethnic Chinese businessmen like Robert Kuok and Khoo Kay Peng. In 1995 he took a 20 per cent stake in Singapore-listed Parkway Holdings as part of his plan to move into the regional healthcare business. He followed that by buying a half share of Australian pathology group Gribbles, with the aim of creating 100 pathology laboratories in South-East Asia.

Tan heads a group of developers embarking on a US$4 billion project in Kuala Lumpur known as the Linear City – at 12km the world's longest building, straddling the Klang River which flows through the city. The project, involving office space, apartments, shopping malls, a theme park and a mass transit system called the Peoplemover, is going ahead with the support of the Prime Minister, Dr Mahathir.

Tan is also keen to get connected in the multimedia world. The vehicle is his private company Mutiara Telecommunications, which operates Malaysia's largest mobile-communications network with around 13,000 subscribers.

20 LEE Kun Hee and family, Korea

Estimated net worth: *US$4 billion*
Chairman: *Samsung Group*
Born: *1942*
Educated: *Waseda University (Japan) and George Washington University (US)*
Hobbies: *Films, animal welfare*

MEMBERSHIP OF THE PRESTIGIOUS INTERNATIONAL OLYMPIC COMMITTEE, announced at the 1996 Atlanta Olympic Games, helped balance the opprobrium of a bribery conviction for one of South Korea's richest men, Samsung chairman Lee Kun Hee. Lee, a schoolboy wrestler and long-time supporter of Korea's Olympic teams, was one of eight leading business executives indicted in December 1995 on bribery charges related to former president Roh Tae Woo. In August 1996, he was given a two-year suspended sentence.

Lee's father, the late Lee Byung-chul, founded Samsung in 1938. But when it came time in 1987 to pass on the reins of the conglomerate, he chose third son Lee Kun Hee rather than his eldest son Lee Meng Hee (with whom he did not get on).

Until then, Lee Kun Hee had had little to do with running the Samsung group, but his elevation to the top slot changed that. He set about turning Samsung into Korea's leading conglomerate, with a target of surpassing arch rival Hyundai's sales figures (achieved in 1995). With a focus on semiconductors, Samsung Electronics became the world's largest producer of DRAM computer chips and opened factories around the world.

Along with sponsorship of sports (Samsung paid US$9 million to secure the top sponsor's spot for the 1998 Asian Games in Bangkok), Lee is an avid movie fan, with a library of 6000 titles at home. In 1995 he made an unsuccessful bid to tie up with Hollywood production house DreamWorks SKG, only to see it go to his nephew and niece, 'Jay' Lee Jae Hyun and 'Mikey' Lee Mee Kyong, a few months later. Their vehicle was one-time food maker Cheil Jedang, which had been the heart of the Samsung empire until 1993.

Lee is also an animal lover, and keeps about 300 dogs in kennels outside Seoul.

In 1995, the record-breaking performance of the group's listed flagship Samsung Electronics helped swell the Lee family's fortune to around US$4 billion, with Lee Kun Hee picking up a US$16 million dividend cheque. Net profit for Korea's biggest electronics maker rose 165 per cent to more than US$3 billion, on sales of US$20 billion.

Lee has embarked on expansion plans to lift revenue for the group's 24 companies above US$100 billion. These include investment decisions designed to take advantage of emerging market opportunities in Asia and South America and to consolidate Samsung's stake in high-value markets such as Europe and North America.

21 Michael D. KADOORIE and family, Hong Kong

Estimated net worth: *US$4 billion*
Chairman: *China Light & Power, Hongkong and Shanghai Hotels*
Born: *1941*
Hobby: *Flying helicopters*

MICHAEL KADOORIE IS THE SON OF THE LATE LORD (LAWRENCE) KADOORIE OF Kowloon, who died in 1993, aged 94. Lord Kadoorie and his brother Sir Horace were the sons of Sir Elly Kadoorie, who arrived on the China coast in the 1880s. The Kadoories, originally from Iraq, settled in Shanghai (where both Lawrence and Horace were educated) and over the next few decades established key footholds in Shanghai's textile industries and in Hong Kong, where they set up China Light & Power in 1901.

In 1962 the Kadoorie brothers were awarded the Ramon Magsaysay award, Asia's equivalent of the Nobel prize.

Today Michael Kadoorie heads one of the best-known dynasties in the region. That fame comes mainly through the family's association with Hong Kong's most prestigious hotel, The Peninsula, usually known as 'The Pen', the recipient of a US$200 million facelift and 30-storey extension in 1994. The family controls Hong Kong & Shanghai Hotels, which in addition to the Peninsula Hotel runs the Kowloon Hotel in Hong Kong, plus other Asian properties such as the Peninsula Manila and a 40 per cent stake in the Bangkok Peninsula, due for completion in 1997. It also has a 20 per cent stake in the Palace Hotel in Beijing. The company, which had a market capitalization in early 1997 of just over US$2 billion, turned in a net profit in 1995 of US$84 million on revenue of just over US$300 million. Its other Hong Kong interests include the Peak tramway and luxury residential developments.

Not all the Kadoorie family's assets are in Asia. It owns an apartment building in Manhattan and the New York Peninsula, and has a minority stake in the Beverly Hills Peninsula in Los Angeles. The company is involved in a controversial bid to build a Peninsula Hotel in Sydney on Australia's most valuable site, adjoining the Opera House.

China Light & Power is now Hong Kong's largest power utility with a market capitalization of US$8.6 billion in early 1997. After CITIC Pacific agreed to pay US$2.1 billion for 20 per cent of the company in January 1997, the Kadoorie family's stake fell to 26.6 per cent. China Light turned in a profit of US$627 million in the year to September 1996. Its 25 per cent stake in the Daya Bay nuclear power station in China's adjoining Guangdong province is seen as evidence that the Kadoories have good relations with the mainland.

22 KWEK Leng Beng and family, Singapore

Estimated net worth: *US$4 billion*
Chairman: *City Developments, Hong Leong Group (Singapore), CDL Hotels. Singapore Businessman of the Year 1996*
Born: *1942, Singapore*
Hobby: *Cars*

FERRARI-DRIVING KWEK LENG BENG IS THE SON OF THE LATE KWEK HONG PNG, the eldest of four Hokkien Chinese brothers (the others were Hong Khai, Hong Lye and Hong Leong) who arrived in Singapore from Fujian province in 1928. Hong Png, who was 16 at the time, worked in a relative's store until he had enough money to begin his own trading company in 1941, which he named Hong Leong after his youngest brother. The brothers worked together until the 1960s, when Hong Lye moved to Malaysia to build up the Hong Leong Group's activities there. Hong Lye's son Quek Leng Chan (see next listing) now heads the Malaysian operation.

Under Hong Png, who died in 1994 at the age of 82, Hong Leong (Singapore) diversified from trading into property development, setting up City Developments Ltd (CDL) to operate in the residential, industrial and retail sectors. By the time he retired in 1984 and handed over the reins to his eldest son Leng Beng, the group was on its way to becoming a major property and financial services company.

Today, City Developments Ltd dominates the listed Singapore real-estate companies. Its market capitalization of US$6.8 billion is more than twice that of nearest rivals DBS Land and Singapore Land. CDL in turn controls Hong-Kong-listed CDL Hotels International, the vehicle which Kwek set up in

1989 to use in an ambitious expansion into the international hotel business. By the end of 1996, Kwek controlled 56 hotels in 11 countries, including such trophy sites as the Plaza in New York (bought from Donald Trump, in partnership with the Saudi billionaire Prince Al Waleed), the Gloucester and Britannia in London, the Nikko in Hong Kong, the Manila Plaza, the Grand Hyatt in Taipei and the Hyatt Regency in Sydney's Kings Cross.

He also held 16 properties in Britain, Germany and France via his takeover of Britain's Copthorne Group in 1995 and 23 in New Zealand (acquired in 1992 and 1993). Other hotels are in Singapore, Malaysia and China, where Kwek is building a chain of budget hotels.

Kwek Leng Beng's younger brother, Kwek Leng Joo, who is managing director of City Developments, was president of the Singapore Chinese Chamber of Commerce and Industry, 1993–97. When he was elected in February 1993 at the age of 39, he was the youngest president in the chamber's history, and vowed to shake-up the factionalized 'clan' system (based on Chinese dialects such as Hokkien, Teochiu and Cantonese) which he said was hampering the chamber's activities and prestige.

23 QUEK Leng Chan and family, Malaysia

Estimated net worth: *US$4 billion*
Chairman: *Hong Leong Group (Malaysia), Guoco Group (Hong Kong)*
Born: *1941, Singapore*

QUEK LENG CHAN HEADS THE MALAYSIAN ARM OF THE FAMILY KNOWN IN Singapore as the Kweks. Quek's father, Kwek Hong Lye, who died in July 1996 at the age of 81, was the last of four Chinese brothers who founded the Hong Leong Group, which became one of the largest and most diversified conglomerates in Singapore and Malaysia. The Hong Leong empire eventually split into two branches, with Quek Leng Chan becoming head of Malaysia in 1973 and his cousin Kwek Leng Beng (the son of Kwek Hong Png) running the Singapore arm (see previous listing).

The four Kwek brothers – Hong Png (who died in 1994), Hong Khai, Hong Lye and Hong Leong – arrived in Singapore from China's Fujian province in 1928. The eldest, Hong Png, was 16 at the time. After working in a relative's store, he began his trading company in 1941, which he named Hong Leong after his youngest brother. The brothers worked together until the 1960s, when Hong Lye moved to Malaysia to build up the group's activities there in trading, eventually diversifying into other areas such as property, manufacturing, construction, motorcycle assembly, finance, banking and insurance, and publishing.

Quek's Hong Leong Company (Malaysia) has 13 listed companies including such heavyweights as Hong Leong Bank (market capitalization US$1.3 billion), Hong Leong Credit, Hong Leong Industries, Nanyang Press and Hume Industries (market capitalization US$1.28 billion). The Malaysian arm has also been active offshore, with investments in Hong Kong (where its Guoco Group has stakes in China, Philippines and Singapore).

With a 72 per cent stake, Guoco controls fourth-ranked Dao Heng Bank in Hong Kong (assets US$10.5 billion) and First Capital Corp in Singapore. In 1996 Quek, in partnership with Liem Sioe Liong and Singapore investors, bought into the New Zealand company Brierley Investments Limited (BIL) through privately held Delham Investments. The BIL stake, which Delham will move to listed Malaysian cement company Malex, took on increased significance in late 1996 when BIL bought 20 per cent of the Fairfax newspaper empire in Australia.

Although relations between the Malaysian Queks and the Singapore Kweks have sometimes been strained, the families continue to have cross-holdings in each other's companies.

Until his death, Kwek Hong Lye remained a director of the Singapore family flagship, City Developments. His nephew, Kwek Leng Beng, heads the Singapore operations.

24 Masatoshi ITO and family, Japan

Estimated net worth: *US$3.8 billion*
Honorary chairman: *Ito-Yokado Group*
Born: *1924, Japan*

MASATOSHI ITO AND HIS FAMILY OWE THEIR FORTUNE TO A SIGNIFICANT 15 PER cent stake in the giant Japanese retail group, Ito-Yokado, parent of the Seven-Eleven Japan convenience store chain. Ito-Yokado, founded by Ito in 1958, picked up the 7-Eleven franchise for Japan in 1973, and ran it so well that almost two decades later it was able to rescue the US 7-Eleven chain from bankruptcy, through buying a 70 per cent stake in the parent company, Southland. Ito-Yokado, which listed in 1972 and had a market capitalization in early 1997 of US$19 billion, has almost 16,000 employees. Besides Seven-Eleven Japan, its other subsidiaries include Denny's Japan, Daikuma and York Mart.

With 1996 group sales of US$27.5 billion, Ito-Yokado ranks second among Japanese retailers. Only Daei has higher revenue, but Ito-Yokado wrings out more profit from concentrating its stores in the wealthiest parts of Japan: the Tokyo area and neighbouring Kanagawa prefecture. Location is not the whole story; the retailer keeps its distribution costs down by not being too geographically diverse, and it uses state-of-the-art electronic monitoring for stock control and to give it a clear picture of customers' buying tastes.

Ito-Yokado changed its conservative image in the 1990s, expanding into more upmarket outlets and forging a reputation as the most aggressive innovator in Japanese retailing. It planned to open six new outlets in 1997. The big profit contributor continues to be Seven-Eleven Japan, which generated more than US$500 million for the group in the year to February 1996. In 1991, Ito-Yokado and Seven-Eleven Japan paid around US$430 million for 70 per cent of Southland, the parent company of the 7-Eleven chain in the United States.

But founder Masatoshi Ito suffered an embarrassing setback in October 1992, when he was forced to resign as president of Ito-Yokado to take responsibility for alleged payments by his staff to *yakuza* gangsters so that shareholder meetings would run smoothly. He became an adviser to the board but now spends little time on the group's affairs.

With the title of honorary chairman, Ito holds a direct 2 per cent stake in Ito-Yokado and another 13 per cent through Ito Kogyo. At the time of his resignation, he handed over the reins to his successor as president, Toshifumi Suzuki, and these days concentrates on good works in education and cultural fields. Suzuki has taken the group into other international ventures with Wal-Mart of the US and the European-based retailer Metro.

25 Eka Tjipta WIDJAJA (OEI Ek Tjhong), Indonesia

Estimated net worth: *US$3.7 billion*
Chairman: *Sinar Mas Group*
Born: *1922, Fujian province, south China*
Marital status: *Married, son Oei Hong Leong runs China/Hong Kong operations, another son Indra heads Indonesian operations*

Eka Tjipta Widjaja is the founder of the Sinar Mas ('Golden Light') Group, Indonesia's second largest conglomerate with annual revenue of around US$5 billion and assets of US$9 billion. Sinar Mas is a dominant player in South-East Asia's pulp and paper industry through 86-per-cent-owned Asia Pulp & Paper Company. APP, which is listed in Singapore, reported 1995 sales of US$1.9 billion and net profit of US$220 million. It controls Jakarta-listed pulp and paper subsidiaries Tjiwi Kimia and Indah Kiat.

Sinar Mas also is active in plantations, cooking oil, chemicals, property development (Duta Pertiwi), banking (Bank Internasional Indonesia), finance and consumer products, and hotels (the Grand Hyatt, Jakarta). Its listed Sinar Mas Multiartha, which began trading on the Jakarta stock exchange in July 1995, is the holding company for the group's financial interests, including its 51 per cent stake in Bank Internasional Indonesia. BII is Indonesia's biggest listed bank, with a market capitalization of US$1.5 billion.

The son of a Sulawesi shopkeeper, Eka Tjipta Widjaja came to Indonesia at the age of seven. While in his twenties, in the Second World War, he became a copra trader, then moved into the palm-oil business before venturing into timber and paper in the 1970s. In the 1980s Eka was a partner in a cooking-oil venture with Liem Sioe Liong, head of the Salim Group, Indonesia's largest conglomerate. Today, Sinar Mas is the largest manufacturer of pulp and paper in South-East Asia, via its Asia Pulp & Paper. In late 1996 it moved to acquire the troubled Singapore-listed Amcol Holdings, possibly as a prelude to moving more of its businesses out of Indonesia. The Sinar Mas Group now has numerous joint ventures with offshore companies in the food industry and in financial services.

Sinar Mas is also active in China, with family investments managed by Eka's son Oei Hong Leong, who spent his teenage years in China but is now based in Hong Kong. Oei's China Strategic Holdings controls more than 30 state-owned enterprises in China (including beer and tyre-making operations), and at the beginning of 1995 acquired a stake in the prestigious Hong Kong daily newspaper, *Ming Pao Daily News*. Oei was appointed chairman in place of Ming Pao's controlling shareholder Yu Pun-hoi, forced out for failing to disclose a 15-year-old criminal record in Canada.

Another of Eka's sons, Indra Widjaja, is president of Bank Internasional Indonesia (BII). Sinar Mas has a number of joint ventures with Australia's Lend Lease in financial services and property management.

In late 1996, Sinar Mas started production at its first Indian paper plant in Pune. With India having more than 16 per cent of the world's population but only 1 per cent of paper consumption, Sinar Mas is betting that its US$100 million investment will turn in big dividends.

26 Peter WOO Kwong-ching and the Pao family, Hong Kong

Estimated net worth: *US$3.7 billion*
Former chairman: *Wheelock & Co, and Wharf (Holdings)*
Public offices: *Chairman of the Hong Kong hospital authority*
Born: *5 September 1946, Shanghai*
Educated: *University of Cincinnati, Columbia University*
Marital status: *Married to Betty, daughter of the late Sir Y.K. Pao*

PETER WOO STEPPED DOWN IN SEPTEMBER 1996 AS HONORARY CHAIRMAN OF the Wheelock & Co conglomerate to make his bid for the job of Hong Kong's Chief Executive under Chinese rule. Woo's campaign, although skilfully conducted, could make no real impact on the man who was always going to win, shipping tycoon Chung Tee-hwa. Woo picked up only 36 votes out of 400 in the December poll, while Chung cantered home with 320.

Through family trusts, Woo controls property developer Wheelock, which in turn has 50 per cent of Wharf (Holdings). Wharf's interests include cable television, the Star Ferry, the cross-harbour tunnel, trams and infrastructure developments through its Modern Terminals subsidiary.

Woo, a former banker, is the son-in-law of one of Hong Kong's most successful tycoons, the late Sir Y.K. Pao, who established the Worldwide

Shipping company in 1955 and built it into one of the world's biggest ship-ping lines. Woo first studied architecture before deciding that he wanted to be a banker.

He joined the Chase Manhattan Bank for a few years, but then went to work for his father-in-law at Worldwide and took the business into new ven-tures beyond shipping and property. When Sir Y.K. Pao died in 1991, Woo became chairman of the holding company, World International, which was later renamed Wheelock & Co. He was the driving force behind the growth and diversification of Wharf (including its ambitious infrastructure plans centred on Wuhan in China), but retired as Wharf's chairman in 1994 and from Wheelock in 1995, at the age of 49.

Woo and the Pao family are estimated to be worth US$3.7 billion through their 60 per cent stake in Wheelock & Co, and the associated Wharf interests which include Omni hotels worldwide and a mobile-phone network that is under development in Hong Kong. Wheelock had a market capitalization in early 1997 of US$5.8 billion and a net profit in 1995–96 of US$318 million. Wharf's market capitalization was US$11.5 billion; it reported a net profit in 1995 of US$473 million on revenue of US$880 million.

27 NG Teng-fong and family, Singapore & Hong Kong

Estimated net worth: *US$3.5 billion*
Chairman: *Far East Organisation (Singapore), son Robert is chairman of*
*   *Sino Land (Hong Kong)*
Born: *1928, China*
Marital status: *Married to Tan Kim Choo, son Robert Ng Chee-siong*

NG IS SINGAPORE'S RICHEST MAN, WITH A FAMILY FORTUNE ESTIMATED AT US$3.5 billion. He founded Far East Organisation, the second-largest landowner in Singapore (after the Singapore government), and also has interests in China, Malaysia, Hong Kong and Taiwan. His privately held Far East controls 68 per cent of Singapore real-estate developer Orchard Parade Holdings. OPH owns and operates the Orchard Parade Hotel and the Albert Court boutique hotel in Singapore, and has a stake in the landmark US$300 million Raffles Square project in Shanghai, a retail block and 46-storey office tower due for completion in 2000.

Ng's son Robert Ng Chee-siong, 44, has taken over as head of Sino Land and Tsim Sha Tsui Properties, the two major Hong Kong operations of the group. A third company, Sino Hotels, was spun off in 1996 to consolidate the group's hotel investments. Sino Land has become known as Hong Kong's most aggressive developer, and turned in a profit of US$372 million in the year to June 1995. Its market capitalization in early 1997 was more than US$3.3 billion.

Sino Land became part of Hong Kong's blue-chip Hang Seng index from February 1995 and was an aggressive property player during bidding in 1996 for projects involving the new Chek Lap Kok airport in Hong Kong and its associated infrastructure, such as the mass rapid transit station developments.

Another Sino Land venture is the Gold Coast hotel, marina and high-rise residential development at Tsai Yuen in the New Territories, opposite the new airport site. In 1996, Ng told readers of *Apple Daily*, the Chinese-language newspaper founded in 1995 by maverick publisher Jimmy Lai, that demand for real estate would never falter, meaning that property prices could not help but rise. 'Hong Kong will never collapse,' he declared.

In late 1995, Ng won a fierce bidding war for control of Singapore food and beverage company Yeo Hiap Seng, in competition with a group of investors led by Quek Leng Chan, head of the Malaysian arm of the Hong Leong group. Ng paid more than US$290 million to take control of YHS and aims to make it a major beverage manufacturer in China. YHS also controls the Pepsi franchise in Singapore.

28 Robert KUOK (Kuok Hock Nien), Malaysia

Estimated net worth: *US$3.5 billion*
Chairman: *Kerry Group and Kuok Brothers*
Born: *October 1923, Johor Bahru, Malaysia*
Educated: *Johor Bahru schools, Raffles College, Singapore*
Marital status: *Married, five children*

ROBERT KUOK, ALSO KNOWN AS KUOK HOCK NIEN, HAS TRADED IN SUGAR, rice, flour, palm oil, timber and other commodities for half a century. He is regarded as Asia's consummate deal maker and one of the five most important ethnic Chinese businessmen in the world. In recent years Kuok has diversified into residential and commercial property, hotels, media investments, retailing, shipping, building materials and financial services.

Kuok was born in Johor Bahru, Malaysia, in October 1923, the youngest of three sons. His father arrived in Malaysia from Fujian in 1911 and established himself as a commodity trader in Johor Bahru, across the causeway from Singapore. Kuok went to school in Johor, before enrolling at Raffles College in Singapore in mid-1941. His studies there were interrupted by the Second World War. After the war he followed his father into commodities and in later years became known as Malaysia's 'sugar king', controlling around 10 per cent of the world's sugar trade. His Malaysian company, Kuok Brothers, dealing in sugar, rice and flour, became the basis for his fortune.

After spending time in London in the 1950s, Kuok returned to Malaysia to set up his first sugar refinery in a joint venture with the Federal Land Development Authority. Perlis Plantations, established in 1968, provided home-grown sugar cane for him in the 1970s, along with raw sugar from Thailand, Indonesia, Cuba and Australia.

In 1974 he established Kerry Trading Co in Hong Kong, where his Kerry Group controls interests that range from media to hotels. Through Kerry Media, Kuok is chairman and 34.9 per cent owner of the highly profitable newspaper publisher, South China Morning Post Holdings. His frequent business partner and fellow Malaysian Chinese entrepreneur, Khoo Kay Peng, owns 22.15 per cent of SCMP.

In June 1996, after a four-month tussle with Shaw Brothers, controlled by Hong Kong movie tycoon Sir Run Run Shaw, Kuok's SCMP took over TVE Holdings, a property, publishing and entertainment group, for about US$150 million. A month later, in July 1996, Kuok put about 20 of his China and Hong Kong properties into Kerry Properties and floated 15 per cent of it on the Hong Kong Stock Exchange.

Of Kuok's five children, sons Beau Kuok (Kuok Khoon Chen) and Kuok Khoon Ean run the Shangri-la hotel chain, although the chairman is Kuok associate Richard Liu Tai-fung. There are Shangri-la Hotels in Bangkok, Beijing, Fiji, Jakarta, Hong Kong (Kowloon and Central), Kuala Lumpur, Manila (Makati and Edsa), Mactan, Penang, Shanghai, Singapore and Vancouver. In China, Shangri-la Asia has 13 hotels (nine of the luxury Shangri-la brand and four the cheaper Traders brand) either completed or due to be completed between 1998 and 2002.

His eldest brother Philip runs the Malaysian and Singapore operations, while Robert Kuok concentrates on China, Hong Kong and other parts of Asia.

Kuok holds an 18 per cent stake in CITIC Pacific, the Hong Kong arm of the China International Trust and Investment Corporation, and his son Beau is a member of the Better Hong Kong Foundation, set up in late 1995 to bolster investor confidence in Hong Kong.

Kuok, although born in Malaysia, is a Fuzhou Hokkien, a sub-dialect group whose members settled in large numbers in Malaysia early in the twentieth century. Kuok is a leading member of the International Association of Fuzhous and serves on its international executive committee.

29 Fukuzo IWASAKI and family, Japan

Estimated net worth: *US$3.5 billion*
Chairman: *Iwasaki Sangyo*
Born: *1924*
Educated: *Rikkyo University, Japan*
Marital status: *Married, son (Yoshitaro), three daughters*
Hobbies: *Jogging, golf (off a handicap of 14)*

FUKUZO IWASAKI INHERITED THE FAMILY BUSINESS FROM HIS HARD-DRIVING entrepreneurial father, the late Yohachiro Iwasaki, who died in 1993 at the age of 93. Iwasaki senior, a legendary corporate figure in his home base of Kagoshima prefecture on the southern Japanese island of Kyushu, had little formal education but was able to create Iwasaki Sangyo, a major conglomerate with more than 60 companies. He started in timber, then moved into real estate, hotels and resorts and related transportation services. Other interests included food processing and distribution.

Iwasaki Sangyo is an investor in tourist developments in Kyushu and in Australia, where its Capricorn resort on the east coast, about 750km north of Brisbane, has had a chequered career. At one stage, a bomb blast by opponents of the Capricorn development seemed likely to spell its demise, but it opened in May 1986 after a seven-year construction period.

In Kyushu, the Iwasaki resort in the tiny town of Ibusuki is famed for its staggering variety of heated pools, each with its own shape and secret ingredient in the water. The company's latest resort is on the island of Yakushima, a national park about 100km south of Ibusuki by ferry.

Fukuzo Iwasaki, who is also chairman of the Kagoshima chamber of commerce and industry, became president of the family company in 1981 but his father remained chairman almost until his death in 1993. Fukuzo's son and heir apparent, Yoshitaro, is vice-president of the group's hotel and resort businesses.

30 CHATRI Sophonpanich and family, Thailand

Estimated net worth: *US$3 billion*
Chairman: *Bangkok Bank*
Born: *1934*
Marital status: *Married, seven children, eldest son Chartsiri (born May 1959) is heir apparent*

THE WEALTHY SOPHONPANICH CLAN REMAINS BANGKOK'S PREMIER BANKING family, with a history of more than half a century in the industry. Its patriarch, Chatri Sophonpanich, is the second son of the late Chin Sophonpanich, the man who co-founded Bangkok Bank in December 1944 with a group of ethnic Chinese traders and government officials. Chatri serves as chairman, while his eldest son, Chartsiri ('Tony'), was appointed president in December 1994 and is being groomed to take over from his father.

Until his death in January 1988 at the age of 78, Chin Sophonpanich was regarded as the most important ethnic Chinese business figure anywhere in the world. He was born in Thon Buri, across the Chao Phraya river from central Bangkok in November 1910, and went to the Chinese port city of Shantou (Swatow) in China at the age of 5, where he stayed until he was 17. When he returned to Thailand he became a rice trader, then ran a small-goods store. By 1931 he was back in China again with his parents, where he married and had two sons, Robin Chan (who runs the family's Hong Kong business operations, including Asia Financial Holdings and the Commercial Bank of Hong Kong) and Chatri Sophonpanich.

Returning to Thailand, he married again in 1936 and had five children: Charn, Chote, Chai, Chodchoy and Choedchu. The Second World War brought new opportunities; Thai and Chinese businesses needed money from a bank that would look favourably on local entrepreneurs. They also wanted a mechanism that would allow them to remit money back to their families in Shantou. Chin saw the need and, with some associates, helped found the Bangkok Bank. He served on its board, then as *comprador* (chief organizer and fixer) and became president in 1952.

Through the turbulent years of the 1950s, Chin tried to keep on good terms with the Thai business, political and military élites, but found it politic to spend the years 1957–63 in profitable exile in Hong Kong. He returned to Bangkok in 1963 and began building up the family's holding in the bank. In 1973 he took over as the bank's executive chairman from Field Marshall Prapass Charusathira and served until his retirement in 1984, aged 74, when he was made honorary chairman.

Today, under Chin's son Chatri, the Bangkok Bank is the biggest and most profitable in South-East Asia, with impeccable financial credentials and a 1996 profit figure of US$800 million. Its 22 offshore branches include one in Shantou and the Sophonpanich family still holds about a one-third share of the bank. Although other banks have risen to challenge its status, Bangkok Bank remains the *pla buek* or giant catfish of the Thai corporate scene. Market capitalization in early 1997 stood at US$7.7 billion.

Chartsiri, grandson of the founder, is US educated with master's degrees in management and chemical engineering from Massachusetts Institute of Technology. He worked with Citibank in its New York office from 1984–85, before joining Bangkok Bank in 1986. Chin's other sons by his second marriage work either in the bank or in related companies.

31 Masahito OTSUKA and family, Japan

Estimated net worth: *US$3 billion*
Adviser: *Otsuka Pharmaceutical*
Born: *1916, Naruto City, Shikoku, Japan*

THE EVOCATIVELY NAMED HEALTH DRINK POCARI SWEAT HAS BEEN A MARKET leader in Japan almost since its introduction in 1980, with annual sales topping US$1 billion a year. Pocari Sweat is the brainchild of Japan's innovative Otsuka family, controllers of one of the largest pharmaceutical, health drinks and consumer health products groups in Japan. Other big sellers in the group's line-up are the Oronine ointment range and Mucosta, a treatment for gastric ulcers.

Masahito Otsuka, who stepped down as group chairman of the Otsuka family's pharmaceutical business in 1987 but remains a board member and adviser, is the eldest son of the group's late founder, Busaburo Otsuka. Masahito's eldest son Akihiko has been president since 1976 and in the past two decades has taken Otsuka Pharmaceutical to an international market, with 19 overseas factories in 10 countries. It also has subsidiaries and joint ventures in another seven countries.

But it was Masahito, who took over the management of Otsuka Pharmaceutical from his father in 1947, who built it into a huge, unlisted conglomerate with 67 companies, 21,000 workers and an annual revenue of US$8 billion.

Masahito switched the company's focus from producing raw materials for intravenous solutions to producing the more profitable IV solutions themselves. Today it holds about 40 per cent of the Japanese market for IV solutions. Pharmaceutical products account for about 40 per cent of the Otsuka group's revenue, with health drinks and foodstuffs accounting for the remainder.

Family members hold about 25 per cent of the group, which includes Taiho Pharmaceutical, a leading maker of anti-cancer drugs. Masahito Otsuka remains the chief shareholder and has declined to see any of the group companies go public.

32 TAN Yu, Philippines

Estimated net worth: *US$3 billion*
Chairman: *Fuga Internationale Group*
Born: *1935, Bicol region of Luzon, Philippines*
Marital status: *Married, eldest daughter Emilia, eldest son Elton*

TAN YU, BORN INTO A COPRA-TRADING FAMILY IN THE PHILIPPINES, HAS BUILT UP a textile, retailing, hotel and property-development operation which extends to China and the United States. But Taiwan is the major focus, where his flagship is Asia Trust & Investment Corp, and his other interests include the Asiaworld Department Store and the Asiaworld Hotel in Taipei, and

Asiaworld Investment Corp.

In the Philippines, he and his brother Jesus expanded the family's Luzon-based copra-trading business into textiles, eventually forming a link with the Taiwan-based Tuntex conglomerate headed by Chen Yu-hau. Tuntex has a stake in Tan Yu's biggest property development in the Philippines, the 10,000 hectare island of Fuga, off the Luzon coast. On Fuga and a smaller, adjacent island named Barit, Tan Yu hopes to build a tropical paradise that will attract international tourists and an economic zone that will lure foreign investors. But the islands, 45 minutes by air from Manila, lack any infrastructure and will require billions of dollars to develop. Tan Yu has said that more than US$5 billion will be ploughed into the Fuga development between 1997 and 2000.

Tan Yu has hotel and property interests in China, mainly in Fujian province. In the United States he has banking and real-estate interests in California, Nevada and Texas, including a sizeable land bank outside Houston. His eldest son, Elton Tan See, runs the family's hotels in Taiwan, while daughter Tan Bien-Bien, known in the Philippines as Emilia Roxas, runs the main company, Asia Internationale Group.

33 KOO Cha-kyung and family, Korea

Estimated net worth: *US$2.9 billion*
Former chairman: *LG Group*
Born: *1924*
Marital status: *Married, eldest son Koo Bon-moo, born 1945*

L G GROUP, THE KOREAN CONGLOMERATE ONCE KNOWN AS LUCKY-GOLDSTAR, passed a major transition point in February 1995, when it became the first of the big Korean *chaebol* to appoint a third-generation leader. Stepping down in favour of his eldest son, Koo Bon-moo, was 71-year-old Koo Cha-kyung, who had guided Lucky Goldstar for much of the previous 20 years. He in turn had taken over from his father, Koo In-hwoi, who founded the group in 1947 with a factory that turned out soap, facial cream and toothpaste.

When Koo Bon-moo moved into the top chair at the age of 50 (coinciding with the name change to LG), he had already spent 20 years as understudy to his father. In that time, the LG group had grown to annual revenues of US$64 billion, ranking it third behind Hyundai and Samsung. But Koo Bon-moo was aware that LG had once been ahead of both Hyundai and Samsung. He was eager to push on with plans that would ensure the LG group's survival in a world where Korea no longer automatically enjoyed a cost advantage in key fields such as electronics and petrochemicals. He gave his management team a tough new goal: Jump 2005, which calls for the LG group to regain its spot as Korea's No. 1 conglomerate by 2005 and reach revenues of US$385 billion.

In November 1995, Koo paid $350 million for a 58 per cent stake in the US television manufacturer Zenith Electronics. The objective was not just to gain access to the US market, but to help LG understand American business culture in preparation for the internationalization that Koo believes is vital for the company's future. He followed up the US acquisition with an announcement in mid-1996 of the single largest overseas investment by a Korean company – a US$2.6 billion semiconductor and electronics complex in Newport, Wales. The plant, scheduled to open in 2002, represents the largest foreign investment yet seen in Europe.

At the same time, Koo had his eyes on two other major markets – China and Latin America. He earmarked US$10 billion in investment for China by 2005, and US$5 billion for Latin America. He figures that the payoff, mainly from electronics and consumer goods like soap and toothpaste, will run into many billions of dollars.

Koo Bon-moo (whose hobbies are golf and bird watching) and the other members of the Koo family share a fortune of around US$2.9 billion. In early 1997, the listed LG Electronics had a market capitalization of US$1.49 billion after the share price more than halved from a January 1996 high of 33,200 won to around 14,000 won.

34 Don Jaime Zobel de AYALA and family, Philippines

Estimated net worth: *US$2.8 billion*
Chairman: *Ayala Corp*
Born: *1934*
Educated: *Philippines, Spain, United States*
Marital status: *Married to Bea, sons Jaime Augusto and Fernando*
Hobbies: *Photography, scuba diving*

OUTSIDE OF JAPAN AND KOREA, THE AYALA FAMILY OF THE PHILIPPINES IS ONE of the few non-Chinese clans that rank among Asia's super-rich. Founded in 1834 by Spanish settler Don Antonio de Ayala, the Ayala group has grown into a conglomerate with annual revenues of US$1 billion on the strength of its trade in sugar, coffee plantations, other agribusiness, financial services, property development, telecommunications and aviation.

A huge land bank in the Makati area of Metro Manila has been central to the Ayala group's fortunes, with sales from its development generating as much as 60 per cent of annual revenue. Its flagship holding company, Ayala Corp, posted a 1996 net profit of US$236 million. It had a market capitalization of around US$6 billion in early 1997, but this was exceeded by its property arm, Ayala Land Inc (ALI), with a market capitalization of US$6.6 billion. Other key companies in the group include 43-per-cent-owned Bank of the Philippines Islands, 75-per-cent-owned Pure Foods Corp and 38-per-cent-owned Globe Telecom, where its major partner is Singapore Telecom.

After studying abroad to be an architect, current Ayala clan patriarch Don Jaime Zobel de Ayala joined the company in 1958 and spent more than 20 years in various posts before replacing his cousin, Enrique Zobel, as president in 1983. These were difficult times; family feuding over the sale of shares in San Miguel Corporation had led to Zobel's resignation, and the Philippines was racked by the turmoil that followed the assassination of opposition leader Benigno Aquino in August 1983. The Ayalas opposed then President Marcos and his cronies and survived to tell the tale. With Don Jaime at the helm, the Ayala group's fortunes rose in the late 1980s, then surged in the early 1990s as property, banking, agribusiness and financial services began to deliver big profits.

After 36 years with the Philippines' most noble house, Don Jaime stepped down as president in December 1994 in favour of his Harvard-educated son, Jaime Augusto Zobel de Ayala II, known simply as 'JAZA'. Jaime Augusto's younger brother, Fernando, also a Harvard graduate, is senior vice-president and handles the group's overseas operations. JAZA, 38, has identified telecommunications and financial services as big growth areas for the future, along with property.

35 George TY and family, Philippines

Estimated net worth: *US$2.8 billion*
Chairman: *Metropolitan Bank & Trust*
Born: *1933, Fujian province, China*
Marital status: *Married to Mary Uy Ty, eldest son Arthur*
Hobby: *Art collecting*

GEORGE TY SIAO KIAN AND HIS FAMILY HOLD A 65 PER CENT INTEREST IN Metropolitan Bank and Trust Co (known as Metrobank), which is the Philippines' largest bank ranked by assets and profits, and the largest over-all financial conglomerate in the country.

The key members of the Metrobank conglomerate are 54-per-cent-held Philippine Savings Bank (now the country's second largest savings bank), First Metro Investments, merchant bank Sumigin Metro, International Bank of California, Unibancard Corp and 35-per-cent-held Toyota Motor Philippines.

Ty, born in China's Fujian province, began his business career in food-stuffs, establishing the Wellington Flour Mills in the mid-1950s. With money from his successful flour-milling venture, he set up Metrobank in 1962 with some associates, and determined to target the ethnic Chinese business community.

The bank's progress was steady enough for the first two decades, but then a burst of spectacular growth in the mid-1990s lifted Metrobank out of the ruck and allowed it to overtake Philippines National Bank and Bank of the Philippine Islands for the top spot. Ty's focus on the Chinese business middle market, allied with the Philippines' strong economic recovery under President Fidel Ramos and an expanded branch network, won him annual growth of 25 per cent. By 1996 Metrobank had more than 430 branches, including offices in China, Hong Kong, Taiwan, Japan and the United States.

In early 1997, Metrobank had more than 5600 employees, assets of US$6.7 billion, a 1996 profit of US$190 million and a market capitalization of US$4.5 billion. The Ty family's stake in the bank, through a direct 21 per cent shareholding and through the unlisted companies Federal Homes and Tytana Corp, was worth US$2.8 billion.

36 TIONG Hiew King, Malaysia

Estimated net worth: *US$2.5 billion*
Chairman: *Rimbunan Hijau Group*
Born: *1935*

TIONG HIEW KING IS CHAIRMAN OF RIMBUNAN HIJAU GROUP, A MALAYSIAN timber concern which has extensive logging concessions in Papua New Guinea and tree plantations in New Zealand. Its annual revenue is around US$1 billion. The Tiong family's listed entity, Jaya Tiasa Holdings Bhd, is a plywood company with two mills in Sarawak. In 1996 Tiong proposed turning it into a vertically integrated timber company through the purchase of logging concession licences that other Tiong family companies held in Sarawak. Tiong's other timber interests include timber-processing plants in China.

Tiong has extensive media interests in the region. In October 1995, he increased his stake from 10 per cent to 46 per cent in Ming Pao Enterprise Corp, publisher of Hong Kong's leading Chinese-language newspaper, the *Ming Pao Daily*. Tiong also operates a Chinese daily, the *Sing Chew Jit Poh* in Malaysia, and the *National*, an English-language daily in Port Moresby, Papua New Guinea. He has stakes in finance and shipping companies and is also head of the Malaysian chapter of the International Society of Fuzhous and a member of the executive committee of the Federation of Hokkien Associations of Malaysia.

Tiong's headquarters are in Sibu, Sarawak, home of most of Malaysia's Fuzhous, who originate from China's Fujian province.

37 CHENG Yu-tung, Hong Kong

Estimated net worth: *US$2.5 billion*
Chairman: *New World Development*
Born: *1925, Shunde, Guangdong province, China*
Marital status: *Married, two sons Henry Cheng Kar-shun and Peter Cheng Kar-shing*
Hobby: *Golf*

CHENG YU-TUNG, THE FOUNDER AND CHAIRMAN OF THE NEW WORLD Development property group, had every reason to be pleased with his company's 1995–96 result: net profit of more than US$500 million and more lucrative spinoffs on the way. For Cheng, born in Guangdong province in 1925, it was a moment to savour after the family's early years of hardship. Cheng moved to Macau in 1939 to work in a goldshop, then on to Hong Kong at the war's end to run his uncle's jewellery store, Chow Tai Fook Jewellery. The postwar years were difficult in Hong Kong, but the family business survived. Cheng eventually bought the jewellery business, prospered and moved into real estate, surviving the riots that shook Hong Kong during the spillover of the Cultural Revolution in 1967.

Cheng has been a significant investor in China since the 1989 Tiananmen Square massacre, with close to US$2 billion invested there in infrastructure, low-cost housing and property development. Other interests include management of New World hotels in the Chinese cities of Guangzhou, Shanghai, Beijing, Harbin and Shenyang, and Ramada hotels in Wuhan and Qingdao. Cheng is one of the tycoons most concerned to see that Hong Kong's business reputation does not suffer too much from the July 1997 transition to Chinese sovereignty.

Accordingly, Cheng was more than happy to join a score of Hong Kong business leaders in late 1995 who chipped in HK$5 million (US$650,000) apiece to fund the Better Hong Kong Foundation, a body designed to send out positive messages about Hong Kong. Cheng's elder son, Henry Cheng Kar-shun, 49, is chairman of the foundation's advisory council and chief spokesman.

Henry Cheng is putting both the family's money and his own reputation on the line in China. But he has not lost sight of where the record profits are coming from: 'Hong Kong property is, and will continue to be, the core activity of New World Development,' he said at the November 1996 announcement of the previous year's results.

Henry is also chairman of New World Infrastructure, which listed on the Hong Kong stock exchange in October 1995 after being spun off from the core company. It develops toll roads, bridges, power plants and other infrastructure in China and Hong Kong. Named by one analyst as the 'best infrastructure stock in Hong Kong', it had a market capitalization of US$2.1 billion in January 1997, while that for New World Development was US$12.3 billion. The Cheng family holds a 37 per cent stake in New World Development through Chow Tai Fook Enterprises.

---

38 Henry (Ying-tung) FOK, Hong Kong

Estimated net worth: *US$2.5 billion*
Director: *STDM*
Born: *1923, Hong Kong*
Marital status: *Married, two sons, Timothy and Ian*

HENRY Y.T. FOK IS THE HONG KONG BUSINESSMAN KNOWN FOR HIS CLOSE TIES to China and for being one of the first big investors there. He is a partner with gambling magnate Stanley Ho in Sociedade de Turismo e Diversoes de Macau (STDM), the company which controls all of the Macau gambling operations; he helped Ho get the exclusive licence in 1962 that has since been the basis of the latter's fortune. Fok is also a shareholder in Ho's main Hong-Kong-listed company, Shun Tak Holdings, which runs the high-speed ferry service between Hong Kong and Macau and which also has investments in property development, hotels, restaurants and air-cargo services.

Fok is best known for organizing a US$120 million rescue operation to save the Orient Overseas shipping line of the Tung family in 1985. At the time, there was speculation that the funds had come from China, which did not want to see the family of shipping tycoon C.Y. Tung suffer a business failure.

Tung's son, Tung Chee Hwa, who stepped down as chairman of Orient Overseas (International) in October 1996 when he announced his ultimately successful candidacy for the post of first Chief Executive of Hong Kong from July 1997, acknowledged that Chinese money was behind the rescue. Fok was an influential figure in the run-up to the 1997 handover of Hong Kong to Chinese rule. He and another leading Hong Kong tycoon, Li Ka-shing, were strong supporters of Tung as the first Chief Executive.

Fok has been a long-time friend of the Chinese leadership, dating back to the Korean War of the 1950s when he is said to have smuggled medicine into China. He made his fortune as an early investor in Hong Kong real estate and then funded Ho's Macau gambling operation, beginning in 1962.

Fok and his two sons, Timothy and Ian, run the family's investments from an office in the Bank of China building, the distinctive tower designed by I.M. Pei that rises above the Central business district, a short distance from the Hongkong Bank's headquarters.

39 HSU Yu-ziang, Taiwan

Estimated net worth: *US$2.4 billion*
Honorary chairman: *Far Eastern Group*
Born: *1924, Shanghai*
Marital status: *Married, eldest son Douglas is now executive chairman*

WHEN THE CHINESE COMMUNISTS UNDER MAO ZEDONG TOOK CONTROL OF China in 1949, most of the capitalists who ran the great textile mills of Shanghai fled either south to Hong Kong or across the strait to Taiwan. One who took the Taiwan option was Hsu Yu-ziang, whose family had started a knitting mill in Shanghai in 1942 that was to become the foundation of the Far Eastern Group.

Benefiting from Taiwan's early industrialization phase, Hsu gradually built up a range of textile and garment interests, before expanding later into retailing, cement, construction, petrochemicals, transport and financial services. His eldest son, Douglas Tong (D.T.) Hsu, is now chairman and president of the flagship company, Far Eastern Textile Ltd. He is also president of the International Textile Manufacturers Federation and made a historic visit to Shanghai and Beijing in September 1993 to look at investment prospects on the mainland.

The Far Eastern group is Taiwan's fifth largest conglomerate, with more than 25 companies, 20,000 employees and annual revenue of more than US$3 billion. The major listed enterprises are Far Eastern Textile, Far Eastern Department Stores, Asia Cement, Oriental Union Chemical, Far Eastern International Bank and Far Eastern Plaza Hotel. Other companies are Far Eastern Enterprise, Ju Ming Shipping Co and Oriental Securities.

Far Eastern Textile is Taiwan's biggest textile exporter and ranked as the nation's 17th largest industrial company in 1995, with revenue of US$1.26 billion and profit of US$98 million. It employs more than 7400 people and had a market capitalization in early 1997 of more than US$2 billion.

Asia Cement, with 1360 employees, revenue of US$545 million and profit of US$132 million, ranked 51st on the industrial list by revenue, but 15th by profitability. Far Eastern Department Stores, with 2400 employees, ranked 20th among non-industrials, with revenue of US$641 million and profit of US$18 million. The group's Far Eastern International Bank, established only in 1992, is ranked 50th among financial institutions, but is gaining ground rapidly, with a 38 per cent sales growth in 1995. Total group net profit for the first half of 1996 was just over US$100 million.

Today the Hsu family owns 40 per cent of Far Eastern Textile, and stakes of 30 per cent and 40 per cent in Far East Department Stores and Asia Cement. The family has been keen to diversify into new growth areas and in September 1996 the Far Eastern group announced that it would seek a licence to operate a cellular-phone service in Taiwan, in partnership with AT&T of the United States.

40 Dr THAKSIN Shinawatra, Thailand

Estimated net worth: *US$2.4 billion*

Founder and chairman: *Shinawatra Group until October 1994*

Public offices: *Foreign Minister of Thailand, 1994–95; Deputy Prime Minister, 1995–96*

Born: *July 1949, Chiang Mai, northern Thailand.*

Educated: *Police Cadet School, Thailand and in the US, with a master's in criminal justice and public administration, Eastern Kentucky University, and a doctorate in criminal justice, Sam Houston State University, Texas*

Marital status: *Married to Potjaman Shinawatra, three children*

Hobbies: *Golf, collecting pipes*

THAKSIN SHINAWATRA, ONE OF THAILAND'S WEALTHIEST INDIVIDUALS, WAS chairman of his Shinawatra Computer & Communications Group until October 1994 when he stepped down to become Foreign Minister in the

Cabinet of Thailand's Prime Minister Chuan Leekpai. To mark his venture into politics, Thaksin cut his stake in the flagship Shinawatra Computer & Communications to just under 70 million shares, or less than 50 per cent, and relinquished all executive roles. His wife, Potjaman, took over as company president.

In the July 1995 elections which saw Banharn Silpa-archa come to power, Thaksin was appointed Deputy Prime Minister, but he resigned when he pulled his Palang Dharma Party out of the coalition in May 1996. He did not contest the November 1996 elections which led to General Chavalit Yongchaiyudh forming a new coalition.

Thaksin, a member of a well-connected Sino-Thai family based in Chiang Mai, established the Shinawatra company in 1983 after he resigned from the Thai police force with the rank of lieutenant colonel. Although he started off running a cinema and selling movies, he soon moved into computers – a legacy of his experience in charge of the police computer centre that left him well placed to take advantage of opportunities in computers and communications, one of Thailand's most dynamic growth sectors in the 1980s and 1990s.

Initially his company served as an agent for IBM, but his big break came in 1986 when he won a 20-year mobile-phone concession through his Shinawatra subsidiary, Advanced Information Service. In 1990 he picked up a licence to run a domestic satellite service, which led to Thaksin's launch of two satellites (Thaicom 1 and 2) in a joint venture with Singapore Telecom.

Since Thaksin listed Shinawatra on the Stock Exchange of Thailand in August 1990, the group has expanded into telecommunications, broadcasting, including data services, cable TV, mobile telephones, digital paging systems and satellite systems. There are now four listed companies: Shinawatra Computer & Communications, 56-per-cent-owned Advanced Information Service, Shinawatra Satellite and pay-TV operator International Broadcasting Corp. The group reported a 1995 profit of US$165 million.

41 Manuel VILLAR, Philippines

Estimated net worth: *US$2.4 billion*
Chairman and chief executive: *C&P Homes*
Born: *1950, Manila*
Educated: *University of the Philippines, Manila*
Marital status: *Married to Cynthia Villar*

CONGRESSMAN MANUEL VILLAR AND HIS WIFE CYNTHIA CONTROL THE LISTED company C&P Homes, a developer of low-income housing that has proved immensely popular with both its customers and investors. Foreign investors snapped up more than 60 per cent of the 566 million shares on offer in June 1995 when Villar took the company to the market with an initial public offering of 20 per cent of the stock for about US$320 million.

Villar aspires to be the world's biggest builder of homes. For the past 20 years, he has focused on the low-income bracket in the Philippines, where a house costs from US$8000 to $25,000. Now he is starting to raise his sights as demand for bigger houses flows from a growing middle class.

With his wife Cynthia, Villar still holds 80 per cent of C&P Homes – a stake worth about US$1.6 billion on the company's market capitalization of US$2.1 billion in early 1997. Along with a billion-dollar land bank in the Metro Manila area, this has rapidly propelled the Villar family to the top ranks of the Philippines rich list.

Villar's rise is the tale of a Manila boy made good. One of eight children, he delivered shrimps as a youngster, studied for an accounting degree at the University of the Philippines and later joined SGV, one of the nation's top accountancy practices. But eager to make his mark as an entrepreneur, he got into the building game in his mid-twenties and started the forerunner of C&P Homes. By focusing on housing for low-income earners and providing all the paperwork needed to get a government loan, Villar's company soon found its market niche.

Villar, re-elected to the House of Representatives in May 1995 as Congressman for suburban Las Piñas, believes that there is little likelihood of the company being hurt in a cyclical downturn in the property market. In 1995, Villar told *Asiaweek* magazine that he wanted to set an example to Filipino entrepreneurs. 'A lot of our people believe that Filipinos by nature can't make it in business, that only the Chinese have the capability. I have shown that it can be done,' he said.

42 Stanley HO, Macau and Hong Kong

Estimated net worth: *US$2.3 billion*
Chairman: *Shun Tak Holdings and Sociedade de Turismo e Diversoes de Macau (STDM)*
Born: *1921, Hong Kong*
Educated: *Hong Kong University*
Marital status: *Married, with four daughters*
Hobbies: *Ballroom dancing*

D R STANLEY HO IS AN ACCOMPLISHED BALLROOM DANCER, RACONTEUR, gambling magnate, property owner and the man who single-handedly transformed Macau from a sleepy little backwater into the biggest gambling operation in Asia. In the process, he amassed a US$2.3 billion family fortune from his share of the gaming tables, race track, dog track and a string of astute investments in hotels, restaurants, other real estate, air cargo and the busy Hong Kong–Macau passenger route that his fleet of 20 high-speed jet-foils and catamarans serves.

He also had a few brushes with the Red Guards, gangsters, the Chinese communist leaders across the border and, more recently, the anti-fraud units of the Hong Kong police. None of this deters the urbane Stanley Ho from his chief mission: to run the best and most profitable gambling operation in Asia.

Ho, born into a wealthy Hong Kong family in 1921, encountered poverty early in life when his father and his uncles went broke speculating on shares. His father left Hong Kong for Vietnam and Ho struggled through his teens in straitened circumstances. He won a scholarship and was three years into a science degree at Hong Kong University when war intervened.

Destitute, he headed for Macau, where he got a job with the Macau Cooperative Company. His command of Japanese marked him for higher office, and for the next few years he lived through interesting times as he travelled by boat to China on commodity-buying missions. Pirates in these waters were not unknown, but Ho's luck, courage and business acumen brought him a new round of wealth that eventually funded an import–export business in Hong Kong after the war.

In 1962, Stanley Ho, supported by his friend Henry Fok, had the chance to bid for Macau's first gambling franchise, expected to go to the well-connected Fu family. But Ho's generous bid upstaged the opposition and, with a monopoly that runs until 2001, the man dubbed 'the Casino King' has made Macau's tables hum to the sound of free-spending visitors from Hong Kong. More than just casinos, Ho supplied the infrastructure as well – replacing the old steamers that took four hours on the Hong Kong–Macau run with high-speed ferries, dredging the harbour, building hotels (including the garish, gangsterish but commercially magnificent Lisboa), a bridge, ferry terminal and getting the Macau airport project underway.

Ho's Macau company, STDM, is the territory's largest employer and has annual revenue of an estimated US$2 billion. Ho's share of this is reputed to be US$500 million, while 30 per cent – or US$600 million – goes in taxes. He and his family own around 36 per cent of Hong-Kong-listed Shun Tak Holdings, which had a market capitalization in early 1997 of just under US$1 billion. Shun Tak in turn has a 5 per cent stake in STDM.

The size of Ho's own direct stake in STDM is unknown. Ho's fellow directors at Shun Tak Holdings include New World tycoon Cheng Yu-tung, Ho's sister Winnie Ho Yuen Ki and daughters Pansy and Daisy.

43 BANYONG *Lamsam and family, Thailand*

Estimated net worth: *US$2.3 billion*
Chairman: *Thai Farmers Bank, Sansiri Pcl*
Born: *4 May 1933*
Educated: *University of New Mexico, Institute of Bankers (London), Harvard Business School*

THE LAMSAM FAMILY CONTROLS THAILAND'S THIRD LARGEST BANK, THAI Farmers Bank, which was founded by Choti Lamsam, grandfather of current chief executive Banthoon Lamsam, in June 1945.

Banthoon, born in January 1953 and educated at Princeton University and Harvard, was appointed president in 1992 by his late father Bancha, a few months before he died. Banyong Lamsam, Bancha's brother, succeeded him as chairman, a role he maintains today.

In its early days the bank specialized in taking banking services to remote areas, sending its staff to make calls on temples and houses. Choti Lamsam's sons, Bancha and Banyong, further expanded the bank in the

1960s and Bancha's son Banthoon has in turn presided over growth to the point where the bank in 1996 had more than 470 domestic branches and 15 overseas branches and offices.

The Lamsams are of Hakka ancestry and originally from China's Guangdong province. They moved to Thailand in the nineteenth century to trade in timber and rice and established a trading firm known as Loxley in 1925.

Today, along with its controlling stake in Thai Farmers Bank, the Lamsam family has extensive interests in financial services and insurance through Phatra Insurance, Muang Thai Life Insurance, Thai Investment & Securities and Phatra Thanakit. The head of this branch of the family business is Photipong Lamsam. The family is active in real estate through its Siripinyo Group, in telecommunications and trading via listed Loxley plc, and in joint ventures involving independent power plants.

The Lamsam family is also active in agribusiness, particularly pineapple growing and canning through Siam Food Products and Dole (Thailand).

In June 1994, the Lamsams joined forces with the Chutrakul family's San Samran Group to form listed Sansiri Pcl as a property-development, research and management company. Its chairman is Banyong Lamsam. Its main properties include the Siripinyo office building, the Baan Sansiri residential complex in the Bangkok CBD and Baan Kaimuk, a condominium development at the beach resort of Hua Hin.

Thai Farmers Bank earned around US$460 million in 1995 and reported that construction of the new headquarters building which it opened in 1996 had slowed growth to about 11 per cent on the previous year. Its market capitalization in early 1997 was US$4 billion.

44 Dr CHAIJUDH *Karnasuta and family,* Thailand

Estimated net worth: *US$2.3 billion*
Chairman: *Italian-Thai Development and Oriental Hotel*
Born: *1920*
Marital status: *Married, son Premchai is president*
Hobby: *Wine making*

DR CHAIJUDH KARNASUTA SPENT A LIFETIME BUILDING HIS ITALIAN-THAI Development company into Thailand's leading construction group, then stepped back in 1991 to concentrate on his newfound love – making wine at his vineyard in the northeastern Thai province of Loei.

Chaijudh's Château de Loei Chenin Blanc, grown from French vine stock, is not yet a household name in Thailand, but the 1995 harvest was the start of something that Chaijudh believes has massive potential. With Bangkok's middle class embracing wine as the new drink of choice, Chaijudh thinks he is on to a winner. Not that the developer-turned-wine-maker needs the money – his family's net worth, including a massive stake in Italian-Thai Development, is around US$2.3 billion.

Chaijudh, a medical doctor who founded Italian-Thai Development with Italian engineer Giorgio Berlingieri in 1954, took the company public 40 years later in August 1994, with an initial public offering of 25 million shares that raised about US$175 million. Ital-Thai, which is involved in most of Thailand's largest building projects including the Tanayong elevated railway in Bangkok, lifted profits to around US$64 million in 1995, on revenue of US$663 million. Italian-Thai Development's market capitalization in early 1997 was around US$1.65 billion, making it by far the largest listed construction company in Thailand. The Karnasuta family holds around 83 per cent. Chaijudh remains chairman, while his son Premchai is president.

Italian-Thai Development is a partner with Bangkok Bank and Malaysia's Hong Leong Group in the US$1 billion Centennial City, a 750 hectare land-reclamation project along Manila Bay that envisages office space, residential subdivisions and a golf course. Other offshore projects include a proposed hydropower plant in Burma.

In August 1996 an investment group headed by Italian-Thai

Development won one of three new commercial banking licences to be issued by the Thai government.

45 PUTERA *Sampoerna and family, Indonesia*

Estimated net worth: *US$2.3 billion*
President-director: *PT Hanjaya Mandala Sampoerna*
Born: *1948, Indonesia*
Educated: *University of Houston, US*
Marital status: *Married to Katie Chow, four children, eldest son Jonathan*

THE AROMA OF CLOVE-FLAVOURED *KRETEK* CIGARETTES IS AMONG THE FIRST distinctive smells to greet the senses in Indonesia. And with rising incomes among Indonesia's 200 million citizens pushing up spending on consumer items, that sweet smell is not likely to go away. Indonesia's massive cigarette market is steaming ahead at an annual growth rate of 20 per cent, fuelled by heavy advertising budgets and comprehensive market segmentation.

Among the major beneficiaries of this is 'kretek king' Putera Sampoerna, whose listed PT Hanjaya Mandala Sampoerna has about 20 per cent of the urban market, behind industry giant Gudang Garam (held by the Wonowidjojo family) with around 45 per cent. Sampoerna, which also has plants in Malaysia, Vietnam, Burma and the Philippines, produces a range of cigarette types to tackle Gudang Garam and the other heavyweight maker, Djarum, held by Budi Hartono and family. Sampoerna's hand-rolled Dji Sam Soe clove cigarette brand is the market leader in the premium segment, as is its A-Mild in the low-tar market segment.

Like most of the ethnic Chinese families who have risen to prominence in Indonesian commerce, the Sampoerna family hails from China's Fujian province. Putera's grandfather, Liem Seeng Tee, arrived in Surabaya (where Sampoerna's factories are still located) in 1913 and began making clove cigarettes. Later the family expanded into palm oil and rubber plantations. Further diversification into residential development followed. In 1986, Putera became president-director (chief executive) of Sampoerna, taking over from his father. He proceeded to expand the product range and introduced a completely new low-tar, low-nicotine clove cigarette, the A-Mild, in 1989.

The Sampoerna family now holds just over 55 per cent of HM Sampoerna, with Putera owning 5.3 per cent directly. The company reported a profit of US$167 million for 1996 and had a market capitalization in early 1997 of US$4.8 billion.

In 1996, the Sampoerna family began a further diversification away from the clove cigarette market, first through offshore expansion by the acquisition of Singapore-listed telecommunications equipment company Transmarco, and then in September 1996 through the surprise US$260 million purchase of a 12.6 per cent stake in PT Astra International, Indonesia's largest car assembler. Eventually Putera built his stake to 15 per cent and formed an informal alliance with fellow Astra investors Bob Hasan, Anthony Salim, Prajogo Pangestu and Bank Danamon to steer Astra on a 'more focused' track.

46 *Francis* YEOH *Sock Ping, Malaysia*

Estimated net worth: *US$2.2 billion*
Managing director: *YTL Corp*
Born: *1954*
Educated: *Kingston College, UK*
Marital status: *Married, three daughters, two sons*

'INFRASTRUCTURE IS BEST PROVIDED BY THE PRIVATE SECTOR' IS THE OPERATING credo for Francis Yeoh Sock Ping, whose company YTL Corp became Malaysia's first private power producer with the completion in 1995 of two gas-fired plants.

It was a bold move by YTL from general construction into the complex world of infrastructure, where the financial package is as important as the technical capability. But Francis Yeoh, ever the visionary, found the necessary US$1 billion in funds locally, then teamed up with Germany's Siemens to build the plants (total capacity 1200 megawatts) in record time.

Fortunately, Francis Yeoh had years of business experience before his 1992 decision to become an independent power producer. He was just 24 when his father, Yeoh Tiong Lay, decided it was time for his son to run the family's construction company. That was in 1978, when infrastructure projects such as dams, highways and bridges were still being funded through the Malaysian government or multilateral agencies such as the Asian Development Bank.

The forerunner of YTL was started as a construction firm in 1955 by Francis Yeoh's grandfather, Yeoh Cheng Liam, who left China's Fujian province for Malaysia during the Second World War. Cheng Liam's son, Tiong Lay, built up the business in the 1960s and 1970s, before handing it over to Francis in 1978. Tiong Lay remains chairman of the company, while Francis's six brothers and sisters have various corporate roles.

YTL now operates in five main fields: construction; property development; hotels and resorts; energy; and manufacturing. YTL controls the luxury Singapore–Bangkok train service, the Eastern and Oriental Express, which in turn has a number of boutique hotels in the region.

The Yeoh family controls about 48 per cent of YTL, which listed on the Kuala Lumpur stock exchange in 1985 and in Tokyo in February 1995. Its market capitalization in Kuala Lumpur was US$3.15 billion in early 1997. Another of the family's listed holdings is the ready-mix concrete company Buildcon.

47 KHOO Teck Puat, Singapore

Estimated net worth: *US$2.2 billion*
Founder: *Malayan Banking Corp*
Born: *1917*
Marital status: *Married, son Khoo Kim Hai, daughter Elizabeth*

KHOO TECK PUAT, WHOSE ANCESTRAL HOME IS CHINA'S FUJIAN PROVINCE, IS A major shareholder in two banks and the owner of extensive real-estate and hotel interests in Singapore, Malaysia, Britain and Australia. Khoo's first job was as a clerk in Singapore with the Lee family's Oversea-Chinese Banking Corp (OCBC). In 1959, at the age of 43 and by then deputy general manager of OCBC, Khoo left for Kuala Lumpur to set up his own bank, Malayan Banking Corp.

Today, Malayan Banking is Malaysia's biggest bank by assets (US$32.2 billion) and its most profitable, with net income in 1995–96 of US$430 million. The bank has more than 150 branches in Malaysia and 20 in Singapore, plus branches in Hong Kong, London and New York. But Malayan Banking's outlook wasn't always so rosy. The early 1960s were a struggle, with the result that Khoo Teck Puat was forced out of an executive role. He suffered a further setback in 1986 when his 98-per-cent-owned National Bank of Brunei closed.

In recent years, Khoo has based himself in Singapore, where he owns 82 per cent of listed Goodwood Park Hotel (market capitalization US$1.25 billion). The Goodwood Park group also operates the York Hotel and Ladyhill Hotel in Singapore, and in June 1995 bought the Royal Garden Hotel in London for about US$105 million from Rank Organisation plc. Khoo also has a controlling stake in Hotel Malaysia Ltd (which owns the Boulevard Hotel) and investment company Central Properties.

Khoo's single biggest asset is his 14.9 per cent stake in London-listed Standard Chartered Bank, worth about US$1.6 billion, based on the bank's market capitalization of US$10.9 billion. The bank made a profit of more than US$700 million in 1995.

---

48 CHANG *Yung-fa, Taiwan*

Estimated net worth: *US$2.1 billion*
Chairman: *Evergreen Group*
Born: *6 October 1927, Keelung*
Educated: *Taipei Commercial High School*
Marital status: *Married, three sons*

CHANG YUNG-FA, BORN THE SON OF A SHIP'S CARPENTER IN THE NORTHERN Taiwan port city of Keelung, was destined for a life involving the sea. After working with his father in the boat-repair business, he joined a Japanese shipping company in 1945 as a clerk and eventually graduated to command of ships on the Taiwan–Japan run.

In 1968, at the age of 40, he founded the Evergreen transport group with a single second-hand freighter. Over the next two decades he developed Evergreen into the world's largest container-shipping operation (a status lost in the 1990s), pioneering the use of satellite communications and launching a round-the-world freight service.

Evergreen has the largest share of both the trans-Pacific and round-the-world markets. Evergreen also runs trucks, freight terminals, container factories, a credit company, travel and hospitality services and, since 1991, EVA Airways.

Chang's eldest son, Chang Kuo-hua, is vice-chairman and president of Evergreen Marine, while second son Chang Kuo-ming handles the group's computerization needs and third son Chang Kuo-cheng heads EVA Airways and Evergreen Plaza Hotels. The family holds 57 per cent of the flagship company, Evergreen Marine, and has an estimated net worth of US$2.1 billion.

In October 1996 Chang announced that he would buy eight new container ships from Japan's Mitsubishi Heavy Industries for about US$600 million. This would lift Evergreen Marine's fleet to 108 vessels by 1998. Chang's aim is to increase numbers to 116 ships with a combined capacity of 300,000 TEUs (20-foot equivalent units) by 1999 so that he can regain the title of the world's largest container shipper. EVA Airways, now Taiwan's second largest airline behind China Airlines, also has expansion plans, aiming to boost its fleet from 28 aircraft in 1996 to 38 by the end of 1997.

Evergreen Marine, which had a market capitalization of US$3.3 billion in early 1997, reported sales in 1995 of US$1.16 billion and a net profit of US$117 million. EVA Airways, after four years of start-up losses, turned in its first profit in 1995: US$7 million on sales of US$1.06 billion.

49 PRAJOGO Pangestu, Indonesia

Estimated net worth: *US$2 billion*
Chairman: *Barito Pacific*
Born: *1945, West Kalimantan*
Marital status: *Married, two sons, one daughter*

Timber tycoon Prajogo Pangestu (Chinese name Pang Jun Pen) enjoyed a meteoric rise to prominence in Indonesia's business world of the 1980s and 1990s, when 'First Family' connections were the order of the day. In a series of politically powerful moves, he teamed up with various members of the Suharto family and their business associates to create a conglomerate that by 1995 ranked second only to Liem Sioe Liong's Salim Group in assets. But his star waned a little in 1996–97 as the market turned sour on his listed flagship, Barito Pacific.

Prajogo Pangestu is the son of a Chinese rubber farmer. He founded his Barito Pacific timber and plywood-processing company in the late 1970s and built an empire that grew to encompass more than 5 million hectares of timber concessions. This 'Lord of the Forest' also targeted timber concessions in Papua New Guinea and diversified into petrochemicals with Suharto's second son, Bambang Trihatmodjo, and into pulp and paper with Suharto's eldest daughter, Siti Hardijanti Rukmana (Tutut).

In 1995, Prajogo's Barito Pacific Group, with interests in timber, pulp and paper, agribusiness, banking, chemicals and property, had assets of US$6.3 billion. This was still well behind the US$10.6 billion of the Salim Group, but it put Prajogo comfortably in front of Eka Tjipta Widjaja's Sinar Mas Group which had hitherto been regarded as the No. 2 conglomerate. Prajogo also held a strategic 10.7 per cent stake in Indonesia's leading auto assembler, Astra International, which he rescued from financial oblivion in 1993 after the founding Soeryadjaya family stumbled and lost control. Prajogo, who is vice-chairman of Astra, led a group of investors who poured funds into the troubled company and turned it around. Today Astra, which is also active in electronics, finance and agribusiness, has assets of US$2.3 billion and is Indonesia's sixth-ranked conglomerate. Prajogo joined forces with Suharto golfing buddy Mohamad Bob Hasan, cigarette tycoon Putera Sampoerna, Anthony Salim and Bank Danamon in late 1996 to stiffen Astra's performance and give its automotive operations more focus.

Prajogo's various other well-connected business partners include Suharto's cousin Sudwikatmono and Henry Pribadi of the Napan Group.

Tutut has a stake in his US$400 million South Sumatra pulp and paper project, and is a shareholder with him in Astra International. Bambang Trihatmodjo and Henry Pribadi's Napan Group are shareholders with Prajogo in the controversial West Java petrochemical complex PT Chandra Asri. In a move that evoked criticism from ASEAN neighbours, Indonesia gave special tariff protection to Chandra Asri against imports of propylene.

Despite a downturn in Barito Pacific's status on the Jakarta stock exchange which saw its market capitalization plunge to US$860 million in early 1997, Prajogo Pangestu's net worth is around US$2 billion.

50 *Kumaramangalam* BIRLA *and family, India*

Estimated net worth: *US$2 billion*
Chairman: *Birla Group, which controls Hindalco Industries, Grasim Industries*
Born: *1968*
Educated: *London Business School*

When Aditya Vikram Birla, the chairman of the Calcutta-based Birla Group, died suddenly in the United States on 1 October 1995, his son Kumaramangalam, then 27, was thrust into the spotlight.

Aditya Birla, born in November 1944 and educated at Calcutta's St Xavier's College and MIT, Boston, had taken over the century-old Birla family firm in 1983 and embarked on an extensive but careful diversification programme. Until his untimely death at the age of 51, Aditya had presided over more than 20 companies – including such blue chips as Hindalco Industries, Grasim Industries, Indian Rayon and Indo-Gulf Fertilisers – that produced textiles, yarn, engineering goods, aluminium ingots, chemicals, cement and plywood.

Fortunately Kumaramangalam, a London Business School graduate better known as Kumar, had been well trained to take over eventually from his father, but it was an exacting task nonetheless, running a US$4 billion a year business empire that extended from India to the Philippines to Egypt.

His father had chosen his industries well – or, rather, his greatgrandfather had. When Aditya Birla's grandfather G.D. Birla died in 1983 after ruling the family empire for 60 years, Aditya and his father Basant Birla had inherited the bulk of the firm's best assets.

Early in his career, Aditya Birla set about expanding the group internationally, opening companies in Indonesia, Malaysia, the Philippines and Thailand. 'Babu', as he was known, preferred to take a long-term view of industry. A conservative businessman, he closely monitored the daily running of his companies. The main strengths that he left as a legacy to his son Kumaramangalam and daughter Basavadatta were good project management and very tight cost control.

Kumar, who chairs all the key companies in the Birla Group, has worked hard to bring the estranged factions of the Birla clan together, after a split in 1987. He has also continued his father's push into telecommunications through a tie-up with US-based AT&T in the Indian domestic market.

51 KIM Woo-choong, Korea

Estimated net worth: *US$1.9 billion*
Founder and chairman: *Daewoo Group*
Born: *19 December 1936, Taegu, Korea*
Educated: *Kyunggi High School, Seoul; BA Economics Yonsei University 1960. Honorary doctorates from Yonsei University, Korea University, George Washington University, University of South Carolina and Russian Economic Academy*
Marital status: *Married, two sons (one an architect, the other a professional golfer)*
Hobbies: *Movies and Paduk (the Korean name for the chess-like game better known as Go in Japanese)*

THE REPUTATION OF DAEWOO FOUNDER KIM WOO-CHOONG, SOMETIMES described as South Korea's most admired business leader, took a tumble in August 1996 when he was one of nine corporate heads convicted of bribing former South Korean president Roh Tae-woo. Kim received a two-year jail sentence (as did two others), while the remaining six, including Samsung founder Lee Kun-hee, received suspended sentences. Fortunately, Kim's sentence was suspended by an appeal court a few months later. That left the charismatic Kim free to keep up his energetic schedule of visits to investment sites in Eastern Europe, China, Vietnam, India and Central Asia.

It was not Kim's first brush with the law in the rough-and-tumble Korean business world. In 1994, he received a suspended sentence for bribing a former trade minister in return for contracts to build nuclear power plants.

But Kim, chain-smoking author of the classic appeal to Korea's youth, *It's a Big World and There's Lots to Be Done* (translated into English under the title *Every Street Is Paved With Gold*), did not falter, even though his Daewoo conglomerate is regarded as the weakest of the big four. He was punting on eventual big returns from his mammoth investments in the Eastern European automotive industry, where his preparedness to get in early has earned him top place at the table. While much of Daewoo's automotive technology is old fashioned, it is still appropriate for big emerging markets like China, India and Eastern Europe. This is the low-cost ace in Daewoo's global ambitions.

Kim, a graduate from Yonsei University, set up his own business, Daewoo Industrial Co, as a small textile company in 1967. From just five employees, over the next three decades he grew Daewoo into a global empire of 100,000 employees and 1996 sales of US$65 billion in textiles, electronics, motor vehicles and shipbuilding. By 2000, Kim's strategy calls for the group's total sales to reach US$134 billion – in keeping with the Korean meaning of Daewoo, 'great universe', and a long way from his teenage days selling newspapers.

52 Henry SY, Philippines

Estimated net worth: *US$1.9 billion*
Chairman: *SM Prime Holdings*
Born: *1925, Fujian province, China*
Educated: *Far Eastern University, Manila*
Marital status: *Married to Felicidad Tan, two daughters, four sons*
Hobby: *Cooking*

HENRY SY IS THE PHILIPPINES' RETAIL KING. IT IS A POSITION REACHED FROM A simple strategy: build a shopping mall, pack it with entertainment like cinemas, video games and restaurants, and the shoppers will come. It has been a winning formula, with Sy acknowledged as the pioneer of megamalls. He built his first, SM City, in 1985 in Metro Manila's suburban Quezon City and followed with three more in Metro Manila and one in Cebu City, in the central Philippines.

The story of Henry Sy, whose Chinese name is Si Tsi Xing, starts in China's Fujian province, where he was born in Long Hu Hong Xi in 1925. While still in his teens, Sy migrated with his parents to the Philippines, where his family opened a small drygoods store in the Quiapo commercial district of Manila. Sy studied at Far Eastern University in Manila and worked after hours buying and selling shoes as a middleman for shoe stores. In 1948 he opened his first shoe store and through the 1950s was able to set up a string of similar stores, finally forming Shoemart in 1960.

From shoes, Sy ventured into department stores and then into the bigger arena of shopping malls. By the end of 1996, his retail SM chain numbered nine department stores and five malls, including the massive SM Megamall in Metro Manila's Mandaluyong city.

Along with his retail interests, Sy is active in banking and financial services, through his Banco de Oro, plus stakes in China Banking and Far East Bank & Trust. In an unusual move for an ethnic Chinese businessman, Sy has listed two of his operations, SM Prime and SM Fund, on the Philippines stock exchange. The rest of his empire is covered under the family's wholly owned holding company, SM Investments Corp (SMIC).

Henry Sy's eldest daughter, Teresita Sy-Coson, is heir apparent to the family fortune. She handled SM Prime's first international roadshow in late 1996, making presentations to investors in Europe, and is president of Shoemart Inc and Banco de Oro. The other children also work in the various businesses, which today range from shoes and shopping malls to banking and financial services, investment, real estate, tourism and entertainment.

In early 1997, SM Prime had a market capitalization of US$2.6 billion. The Sy family holds 83 per cent.

53 CHEY Jong-hyon and family, Korea

Estimated net worth: *US$1.9 billion*

Chairman: *Sunkyong Group, and head of the Federation of Korean Industries, Korea's largest business organization*

Born: *1930*

Educated: *University of Wisconsin (chemical engineering) and University of Chicago (master's in economics)*

Marital status: *Married, son is married to the daughter of disgraced former South Korean president Roh Tae-woo*

SUNKYONG, WHICH RANKED NO. 5 AMONG THE KOREAN CONGLOMERATES WITH assets of US$17.7 billion in 1995 and revenue of US$21.2 billion, started life in 1953 as a small textile company. From 50 employees at the outset, it grew to a vertically integrated conglomerate with 22,500 employees worldwide, embracing the motto 'from fibre to petroleum' to describe its range of businesses. These extend from textiles to polyester film and magnetic media, to petroleum, construction, engineering, energy, telecoms and financial services.

After studying in the United States, Chey Jong-hyon returned to Korea in 1962 to help his elder brother and Sunkyong founder, Chey Jong-kun, with the business. When his brother died in 1973, Chey took over and set about expanding the group. Initially, he built Sunkyong's textile interests into Korea's biggest maker of polyester, before moving into oil refining in the 1980s through the acquisition of state-run Korea Oil Co, which became Yukong Ltd.

Like most of the Korean *chaebol* leaders, Chey has had his share of critics over examples of perceived government patronage. In 1992 Sunkyong was forced to give up a licence for Korea's second mobile-phone service after a public outcry. At the time, Chey denied any special deals with the Roh administration, asserting that Sunkyong won the bid on its financial and technological merits. Subsequently, in 1994 Chey took a controlling stake in Korea Mobile Telecom, the former state-owned entity which had a monopoly on mobile services. That made it Asia's largest cellular-phone company and it was not until mid-1996 that a US–Korean consortium, Shinsegi Telecom, was able to challenge Chey's dominant position in the Korean mobile market.

In November 1995, at the height of the inquiry into how Korean business leaders helped Roh Tae-woo build up a massive US$650 million slush fund, Chey spoke out in his capacity as chairman of the Federation of Korean Industries. He said: 'On behalf of the whole business community, I want to deliver a sincere apology for the past's undesirable connections between politicians and businessmen.'

54 TEH Hong Piow, Malaysia

Estimated net worth: *US$1.8 billion*
Founder and president: *Public Bank, Malaysia; chairman, JCG Holdings, Hong Kong*
Born: *1931, Singapore*

TEH HONG PIOW OWNS ABOUT 40 PER CENT OF PUBLIC BANK, MALAYSIA'S third largest bank in terms of assets (US$13 billion) and one of the big four commercial banks. With founder Teh as president and chief executive, Public Bank takes a highly conservative approach to lending, with the country's lowest ratio of loans to deposits. It turned in a profit of US$222 million in 1996, to rank third behind Malayan Banking and Bank Bumiputra Malaysia.

With a market capitalization in late 1996 of US$3.18 billion, Teh's 40 per cent stake was worth about US$1.27 billion.

After a clerical career first at the Lee family's Oversea-Chinese Banking Corp (OCBC) in Singapore and later with Malayan Banking in Kuala Lumpur, Teh started Public Bank in 1966. Over the next three decades, he built it into one of Malaysia's most stable and profitable banks, with his trademark conservatism manifesting itself in a very low incidence of non-performing loans.

Yet for all Teh's domestic caution, he has taken the bank into such risky financial markets as Vietnam and Cambodia as part of an extensive Asian expansion strategy. In Vietnam, the bank has 50 per cent of VID Public Bank, while in Cambodia it has 90 per cent of Cambodian Public Bank. In Hong Kong, Teh is chairman of JCG Holdings, a listed investment company controlled 55 per cent by Public Bank, with a market capitalization of US$640 million in late 1996. JCG's main subsidiary is JCG Finance Co, which takes deposits, makes loans, issues credit cards and runs a retail stockbroking service through its 34 branches in Hong Kong. Teh has said that Public Bank is looking at expanding into Thailand, Indonesia and the Philippines, and upgrading its offices in Myanmar and China. In 1993, Public Bank bought a 55 per cent stake in a Malaysian mutual fund.

Although Public Bank is seen as very much Teh's creation, his children do not work there and the question of a successor is uncertain. Teh also controls an insurance company, London & Pacific.

55 LEE Seng Wee, Singapore

Estimated net worth: *US$1.8 billion*
Chairman: *Oversea-Chinese Banking Corporation (OCBC)*
Born: *1925, Singapore*

LEE SENG WEE, CHAIRMAN OF THE EXECUTIVE COMMITTEE OF THE OVERSEA-Chinese Banking Corporation, is the son of Lee Kong-chian, who founded the Lee Rubber Company in 1931 and a string of other companies that eventually became the Lee Group. They included Lee Produce, Lee Sawmill and Lee Pineapple Factory.

Lee Kong-chian was born in China's Fujian province in 1894 and trained as a civil engineer. In 1918 he joined the Tan Kah Kee Rubber Co in Singapore and later married one of the founder's daughters. He began his own rubber company in the 1930s and gradually built it into a major corporation, with large rubber plantations and land holdings in Malaysia's Johor state and Singapore. Today, along with banking, food processing and plantations, the Lee Group has interests in insurance, brewing and trading.

The Lee family is the largest shareholder in the Oversea-Chinese Banking Corporation (OCBC), through a direct 9 per cent stake and 5.5 per cent through the major insurance firm Great Eastern Life, which has cross-holdings with OCBC. Ranked by assets, the conservatively managed bank is the second largest in Singapore, behind DBS Bank, with assets of US$32 billion and a 1995 profit of US$429 million. It has more than 50 branches in Singapore and another 60 offshore, mainly in Hong Kong and China.

By market capitalization of US$8.8 billion in early 1997, OCBC ranks first among the big four Singapore banks, well ahead of United Overseas Bank (US$6.8 billion) and DBS Bank (US$6 billion).

56 Djuhar SUTANTO, Indonesia

Estimated net worth: *US$1.8 billion*
Investor: *Salim Group*
Born: *1920 in Fuqing, Fujian province, China*
Marital status: *Married, eldest son Teddy Djuhar*

DJUHAR SUTANTO, ALSO KNOWN AS LIEM OEN KIAN, IS ONE OF THE 'LIEM investors' behind the Salim Group controlled by Indonesia's richest man, Liem Sioe Liong (whose Indonesian name is Sudono Salim). Sutanto, who is a distant relative of Liem's, joined with him in 1969 to set up PT Bogasari Flour Mill and again in 1973 to set up PT Indocement. Bogasari, the world's largest wheat buyer and instant-noodle maker, is a key part of the Salim empire, which spans 300 companies and has an annual revenue of around US$10 billion. In an asset shuffle in early 1995, listed Indocement (by then the region's largest cement producer) sold Bogasari to another of the

Salim group's main listed vehicles, PT Indofood.

Sutanto, like Liem, hails originally from China's Fujian province and has been a key business partner since the pair first arrived in Central Java. Their two sons, respectively Teddy Djuhar and Anthony Salim, are continuing the family ties by working together on projects. Sutanto and Teddy Djuhar hold stakes of around 18 per cent in the Salim Group's Hong-Kong-listed company, First Pacific, which had a market capitalization of US$3.8 billion in late 1996. Both are directors of First Pacific. They are also thought to hold similar-sized stakes in Indocement and Indofood, which had market capitalizations of US$1.7 billion and US$3 billion respectively in late 1996.

In a 1994 listing of Indonesia's largest individual taxpayers, Djuhar Sutanto ranked second, behind Liem Sioe Liong, while Teddy Djuhar ranked sixth.

57 PIYA Bhirombakdi and family, Thailand

Estimated net worth: *US$1.7 billion*
Chairman: *Boon Rawd Brewery*
Born: *1942, Thailand*

WHEN IT COMES TO BEER IN THAILAND, ALMOST EVERYONE REACHES FOR A Singha, the brand that has made a fortune for the Bhirombakdi family and its privately held company, Boon Rawd Brewery Co. Even with competition from imported brews such as Carlsberg and Heineken, Singha has 85 per cent of the market – largely because the name has been around for more than 60 years and the Bhirombakdi family – now led by Piya, a third-generation family member – has a lock on a national distribution chain.

In 1996, Santi Bhirombakdi, executive vice-president and grandson of Boon Rawd founder Phya Bhirombakdi, estimated that the company had lost about six percentage points to foreign beers in the previous three years, but said that the competition helped grow the market by 20 per cent a year. Boon Rawd expected to sell 640 million litres of Singha beer, worth US$2 billion, out of a total beer market of 750 million litres in 1996.

Boon Rawd, established in 1933, began handling Japan's Suntory brand of whisky in 1996 as part of a diversification move that it hopes will lead to

Suntory selling Singha beer in Japan. But there is still plenty of upside for the Bhirombakdi family just in selling beer in Thailand: per capita consumption is only 12 litres a year, less than a tenth the figure for Germany. And as long as newcomers like Carlsberg and Heineken keep spending big money to promote beer consumption, the Bhirombakdi family is happy to lose a few points of market share.

58 Lucio TAN, Philippines

Estimated net worth: *US$1.7 billion*
Chairman: *Philippine Airlines, Fortune Tobacco, Asia Brewery, Allied Bank*
Born: *1934 in Xiamen, China*
Educated: *Cebu City, the Philippines*
Marital status: *Married, son Michael is heir apparent*

BEER, TOBACCO, BANKING, PROPERTY, AN AIRLINE – THESE ARE JUST THE MOST visible pieces of the empire that Lucio Tan has built in the Philippines, Hong Kong and North America in the past three decades. Apart from Philippine Airlines, none of his companies is listed and Tan likes to keep it that way. No stranger to controversy on his way to great wealth, Tan sees no reason to go public if he can avoid it.

For many years Tan was regarded as the wealthiest ethnic Chinese in the Philippines until it appeared that banking tycoon George Ty had surged past him in the mid-1990s. Then again, Lucio and his brothers may have other assets that are not in the public eye. Eton Properties in Hong Kong, for example, has blue-chip office, hotel, retail and residential property in Causeway Bay, Wanchai, Kowloon Bay and on the Peak. Other sites held by Tan are in nearby Shenzhen and Guangzhou.

Tan, born in Xiamen, in China's Fujian province, moved to Cebu with his parents while still a boy, labouring away at different jobs until he found himself in a cigarette factory. Using the knowledge he gained there, he began his corporate career in the Philippines when he set up his Fortune Tobacco Corp in 1966. In the next three decades, despite his love of privacy, his name was never far from the headlines. He was regarded as a crony of the late Ferdinand Marcos, and was alleged to have won tax concessions in return for campaign funds during the Marcos era. In the 1980s and 1990s, he faced a flurry of courtroom jousts – first with Corazon Aquino's government over whether his companies were secretly held for the Marcos family, and later with the Fidel Ramos administration over allegations of tax evasion by Fortune Tobacco.

Through it all, Lucio Tan and his brothers kept on taking care of business, building Fortune Tobacco Corp into the country's major cigarette producer, with a two-thirds share of the domestic market, acquiring General Banking & Trust in 1977 and renaming it Allied Banking Corp, and establishing Asia Brewery to tackle front-running San Miguel Corp in beer. Today Asia Brewery, run by Tan's brother Harry, has about 20 per cent of the US$1 billion beer market, plus it is heavily involved in breweries on the Chinese mainland.

In September 1996, Tan finally won the prize he had been seeking since 1992 – control of Philippine Airlines. The four-year battle culminated in victory when stockholders formally agreed to double the ailing airline's capital to 10 billion pesos (about US$380 million), leaving Tan with 57 per cent.

Tan had started with an undisclosed stake of 40 per cent in PR Holdings – the company that successfully bid for control of Philippine Airlines when it was privatized in March 1992. Tan increased his stake in PR Holdings to just over 50 per cent in February 1993, precipitating a bitter battle with other shareholders (including the Ayala family) that dragged on until the Supreme Court and the Securities and Exchange Commission resolved it in Tan's favour in May 1996. When it was all over, Tan announced a US$4 billion re-equipment plan designed to restore the airline to profitability, then abruptly cancelled the plan in November 1996 when pilots won salary increases. Getting PAL into the black may be the toughest challenge yet for the man from Xiamen.

59 HALIM Saad, Malaysia

Estimated net worth: *US$1.7 billion*
Chairman and chief executive: *Renong Group*
Born: *20 October 1953*
Educated: *New Zealand, with Bachelor of Commerce and Administration from Victoria University, Wellington*
Marital status: *Married, three children. Application for divorce from wife Norani Zolkifli rejected by Islamic court in May 1997*

HALIM SAAD, A FORMER ACCOUNTANT WHO IS LINKED TO MALAYSIA'S RULING United Malays National Organisation and is a protégé of the formidable UMNO treasurer and ex-finance minister Daim Zainuddin, controls the Renong Group. This listed conglomerate is now one of the heavyweights on the Kuala Lumpur stock exchange, with a market capitalization of US$3.8 billion in early 1997.

Renong, which was once a London-listed tin-dredging company, blossomed under Halim Saad and now includes 13 listed subsidiaries, mainly in infrastructure and development. Its advance into Malaysia's blue-chip league began in 1990, when the group emerged as the owner of a number of former UMNO-controlled companies. This was after a Malaysian court declared UMNO illegal in 1988 and its assets were turned over to the official assignee. Halim's connections were the key; since the early 1980s he had prospered under the business tutelage of Daim Zainuddin, who had been put in charge of UMNO's business interests by Malaysian Prime Minister Dr Mahathir Mohamad.

The group's many infrastructure successes in the 1990s include the construction and operation of Malaysia's 845km US$3 billion North–South Highway by listed subsidiary United Engineers Malaysia (UEM). Other big projects are a share of a new US$900 million bridge with Singapore, and a US$400 million contract to build a sports complex in Kuala Lumpur for the 1998 Commonwealth Games. Part of the Renong group is listed Time Engineering; its subsidiary, Time Telecommunications, has a licence to operate payphone and mobile services and hopes to win a bigger share of the expanding Malaysian telecoms market.

Halim Saad's attempted divorce from wife Norani Zolkifli in 1996–97, with its black magic allegations and the claim by Norani's lawyers that

Halim had assets of more than US$2 billion, enthralled onlookers. Halim engineered his wife's removal from the company's board in March 1996, but she retained an indirect interest through a 28.34 per cent Renong stake that was in her husband's name. Separately, Halim held another 5 per cent of Renong through a family trust. That total 33 per cent Renong stake was worth more than US$1.25 million in early 1997.

The Renong group reported a profit of US$163 million in 1995–96 on revenue of US$440 million.

60 YAW Teck Seng and family, Malaysia

Estimated net worth: *US$1.6 billion*
Chairman: *Samling Corp*
Marital status: *Married, son Yaw Chee Ming runs the company*

THE YAW FAMILY CONTROLS PLYWOOD PLANTS AND EXTENSIVE TIMBER concessions in the Malaysian state of Sarawak through privately held Samling Plywood, which employs around 3000 workers in four plywood-manufacturing plants. The family's listed vehicle in Kuala Lumpur is Glenealy Plantations (Malaya), rated one of the fastest growing stocks in Asia. The Yaw family acquired the company in 1995 as a backdoor listing.

Glenealy has a 20-year timber concession covering 1.2 million acres of land at Lawas in Sarawak with an estimated loggable volume of 8.14 million cubic metres – the largest concession in the state. At Kapit, also in Sarawak, it controls a 15-year concession over 418,000 acres with an estimated loggable volume of 3.6 million cubic metres.

This is held via listed Lingui Developments in which Samling Corp is the major shareholder, with a stake of around 30 per cent. Together, Lingui and Glenealy are regarded as having very favourable prospects because of their reafforestation plans and downstream wood processing. Lingui Developments, which had a market capitalization of just under US$1 billion in late 1996, also manufactures rubber retreads for tyres.

Yaw Teck Seng, one of numerous ethnic Chinese businessmen involved in the Sarawak and Sabah timber trade, began Samling 30 years ago. He passed the day-to-day running of the company to his son Yaw Chee Ming in the late 1980s, but remains chairman. Besides Malaysia, the company is active in Cambodia and proposes to target Asia's growing need for fibreboard with a new plant in Sarawak.

Yaw is also keen to develop the oil and gas sectors from his base in Miri, Sarawak.

---

61 BOONCHAI *Bencharongkul and family, Thailand*

Estimated net worth: *US$1.6 billion*
Chairman: *United Communication (UCOM)*
Born: *1944*
Educated: *Northern Illinois University, Motorola University*
Hobbies: *Art, collecting cars*

IN THE MID-1990S, THE EXPLOSION OF THE TELECOMMUNICATIONS BROADCASTING industries created a whole new array of billionaires in Thailand. Among the most prominent was Boonchai Bencharongkul, who with his brothers Somchai and Wanna had set up United Communication (UCOM) more than a decade earlier.

Boonchai, whose shareholding in UCOM is worth US$1.6 billion, began a swag of ventures in the mid-1990s, including a stake in Motorola's Iridium global satellite project. This involves the launch of 66 low-orbiting satellites – one reason that UCOM began funding a study of a possible satellite launch site at Gunn Point, near Darwin in Australia's north. Space Transportation Systems Ltd, the Australia-based consortium 50 per cent owned by UCOM, aims to reach agreement with Russian rocket maker Krunichev to use its new Proton-M rocket to launch satellites from the Darwin site.

UCOM, which had a 1995 profit of US$110 million, holds 72 per cent of Total Access Communication, the mobile-phone subsidiary that goes head to head with arch rival Thaksin Shinawatra's Advanced Info Service for Bangkok's burgeoning cellular market. Total Access reported a net profit of US$106 million in 1996 and is gaining ground on Advanced Info, with a much faster rate of subscriber growth.

But Boonchai and Thaksin face increased competition from another well-funded participant – TelecomAsia, controlled by Thailand's richest family, the Chearavanont clan. TelecomAsia won the right in 1996 to operate a new limited mobile-phone service, the personal handiphone system (PHS).

Boonchai, whose family also has interests in property, is betting that UCOM's stake in the Motorola-led Iridium satellite project will give the company regional dominance in the battle for global cellular-phone services.

62 ADISAI Bodharamik, Thailand

Estimated net worth: *US$1.6 billion*
Founder and chief executive: *Jasmine International, chairman Thai*
   Telephone & Telecommunications
Born: *1940*
Educated: *University of Maryland, US*

THAILAND'S THIRD TELECOMMUNICATIONS BILLIONAIRE, DR ADISAI Bodharamik, is founder and chief executive of listed Jasmine International, and also chairman, chief executive and a significant shareholder in listed Thai Telephone & Telecommunications.

Adisai began Jasmine in 1982 as an engineering company, but expanded into telecommunications in the late 1980s to the point where the company now runs a domestic satellite network, a mobile radio service, and is installing underwater fibre-optic cables for the Telephone Organisation of Thailand in the Gulf of Thailand under a 20-year concession. In the mid-1990s it began diversifying into the energy sector through its involvement in a hydropower project in Laos.

One of its biggest regional ventures is as a partner in Asia Cellular Satellite System, which is due to launch its first satellite in 1999. This project, which joins Jasmine with PT Pasifik Satelit Nusantara of Indonesia (a company part owned by President Suharto's second son, Bambang Trihatmodjo) and Philippine Long Distance Telephone, will compete regionally with the Motorola-led Iridium system in which Adisai's domestic competitor Boonchai Bencharongkul has a stake through his United Communication (UCOM).

Jasmine's other offshore joint ventures include a mobile-phone service in the Indian centres of Andhra Pradesh, Karnataka and Punjab, and pager services in the Philippines and Nepal.

For Adisai, potentially the most lucrative operation is likely to be 20-per-cent-owned Thai Telephone & Telecommunication, a company he helped found and which he chairs. In September 1996, TT&T completed installation of 1.5 million phone lines in Thailand's information-hungry rural areas. It sold the first million lines during 1996 and expected to sell the remainder during 1997. Jasmine, which listed in July 1994 and is held 67 per cent by Adisai, reported a relatively modest profit of US$54 million in 1995. In early 1997, the company had a market capitalization of US$514 million.

63 Andrew GOTIANUN Sr and family, Philippines

Estimated net worth: *US$1.5 billion*
Founder and chairman: *Filinvest Group*
Born: *1927*
Marital status: *Married to Mercedes Gotianun. Son-in-law, Joseph Yap, is senior vice-president of Filinvest*
Hobby: *Golf*

A NDREW GOTIANUN AND HIS FAMILY CONTROL THE PHILIPPINES' SEVENTH largest listed company, Filinvest Development Corp (FDC), which in turn holds 70 per cent of property developer Filinvest Land. The two listed companies, which had respective market capitalizations of US$1.8 billion and US$1.2 billion in early 1997, are among the biggest real-estate companies in the Philippines, exceeded only by the Ayala family's giant Ayala Land Inc.

Gotianun, who started in business in 1955 by financing used cars, moved into other areas of consumer financing in the 1960s, and in 1970 started the Family Savings Bank. By the time the family divested it 14 years later, it had grown into the largest savings bank in the Philippines as the Insular Bank of Asia & America. Gotianun, who left the Philippines from 1983–86, during the last years of the Marcos era, was still able to use the money to buy property in Manila and today has a land bank of around 2100 hectares. His Filinvest Land dominates residential subdivisions for Manila's middle class. The Gotianuns also control a new commercial bank, the East-West Banking Corp, one of more than 130 Filipino-owned banks.

The Gotianun family started in real estate in 1967 and incorporated FDC in 1973. From residential subdivisions, the company extended into housing in 1990. In 1992 Filinvest Land won a bid to join with the government in developing the Alabang Stock Farm, giving Gotianun a lock on one of the Philippines' biggest property plays. The Alabang deal covers a 244 hectare site 15km from Makati between Metro Manila and the rapidly industrializing Calabarzon area to the south. On the site, Filinvest Land will build its 'Corporate City', which includes a US$115 million, 20 hectare shopping mall called Festival Supermall.

While Gotianun describes Filinvest Corporate City (80 per cent owned by FDC) as the company's largest project to date, Filinvest also stands to gain an important revenue stream from its 16 per cent stake in the massive Fort Bonifacio Global City project. This development is turning a former military camp in the heart of Manila into prime commercial and residential property. Leader of the Fort Bonifacio consortium is Metro Pacific, controlled by Indonesian tycoon Liem Sioe Liong's Salim Group. Along with Gotianun, ethnic Chinese tycoon Lucio Tan has a stake. Both also have 17 per cent shares with four other business leaders in the Asia Emerging Dragon Corp, formed at the invitation of President Fidel Ramos to take part in infrastructure projects.

64 WEE Cho Yaw, Singapore

Estimated net worth: *US$1.5 billion*
Chairman: *United Overseas Bank*
Born: *1929, Quemoy island, Taiwan*
Educated: *Chung Cheng High School, Singapore*
Marital status: *Married, three sons, two daughters*

WEE CHO YAW IS CHAIRMAN AND CHIEF EXECUTIVE OF SINGAPORE'S MOST profitable bank, United Overseas Bank, which turned in a profit of US$447 million in 1995. Wee and his family hold around 20 per cent of the bank, which had a market capitalization in early 1997 of US$6.8 billion. UOB was founded in 1935 as the United Chinese Bank by a group of business people that included Wee's father, Fujian-born Wee Kheng Chiang, a wealthy Sarawak businessman who moved to Singapore in 1930.

Wee Cho Yaw, Wee Kheng Chiang's fourth son, started his working life as a commodity trader, dealing in rubber and pepper at Kheng Leong Co, a company controlled by his father. In 1960, at the age of 31, he was appointed managing director of the United Chinese Bank. UCB then catered mainly to the Hokkien-speaking Fujian business community in Singapore, but a period of rapid expansion in the 1960s saw it extend its reach into the wider Singapore community and change its name to the United Overseas Bank (UOB) in 1965.

In 1974 Wee Kheng Chiang stepped down and was succeeded as chairman by his son Wee Cho Yaw, who has been at the helm for more than two decades and has presided over the bank's growth to 120 branches. In turn, Cho Yaw's eldest son Wee Ee Cheong, currently UOB deputy president, is expected to succeed him as chief executive. Wee's other children also serve as executives in various parts of the Wee family empire, which includes an interest in the Haw Par group, the bank's hotel and property company United Overseas Land (UOL), and United Industrial Corp (UIC), a company controlled by the head of Indonesia's Salim group, Liem Sioe Liong.

UOB, which, with assets of $28.7 billion, is Singapore's third largest bank behind DBS Bank and OCBC, also controls Chung Khiaw Bank and Industrial and Commercial Bank, rated seventh and eighth among Singapore's top ten banks.

65 KOO Chen-fu and family, Taiwan

Estimated net worth: *US$1.5 billion*
Patriarch: *the Koos Group, honorary chairman Chinatrust Commercial Bank, chairman Taiwan Cement*
Born: *1917, Taiwan*
Marital status: *Married, five children*

ALTHOUGH 79-YEAR-OLD KOO CHEN-FU IS PATRIARCH OF THE KOOS GROUP, IT is his aggressive nephew Dr Jeffrey Leng-song (L.S.) Koo who is the highly visible face of the group in the 1990s. Known as 'Mr Taiwan' for his prominence in international affairs, 63-year-old Jeffrey Koo is chairman and chief executive officer of the group's flagship, Chinatrust Commercial Bank.

'Modesty leads to harmony; honesty builds credibility' is the corporate philosophy of the Koos Group, derived from the two primary characters in its name. But dynamism and ambition have not been neglected. Jeffrey Koo aims to build Chinatrust into a 'global Chinese bank' ranking among the world's top banks 'in the not too distant future'. His flair for deal making over the past decade has earned him the reputation of Taiwan's best private banker, and in the process helped swell the family fortune to around US$1.5 billion. He serves on Asia-Pacific Economic Cooperation (APEC) bodies such as the Eminent Persons Group and the Pacific Basin Forum, and is chairman of Taiwan's oldest thinktank, the Taiwan Institute of Economic Research, set up by his uncle C.F. Koo in 1976. Jeffrey Koo also chairs the Chinese National Association of Industry and Commerce. Global diplomacy and the need to keep connecting with the region's powerbrokers have done wonders for his golf game – he plays off scratch.

C.F. Koo, who swapped his family's extensive landholdings for control of then state-owned Taiwan Cement Co in 1954, went on to form the Taiwan Stock Exchange in 1962 and build the Koos Group into Taiwan's fourth largest conglomerate. As part of the group's expansion into financial services, C.F. Koo established China Securities Investment Corporation in March 1966. This grew into Taiwan's largest trust company, first as China Investment and Trust Co and later renamed China Trust Co (CTC). In July 1992, CTC became the Chinatrust Commercial Bank.

Today, the Koos Group has assets of US$21.7 billion and controls more than 30 enterprises, including five listed companies: Taiwan Cement, Taiwan Polypropylene, Grand Pacific Petrochemical, China Life Insurance and Chinatrust Commercial Bank. It also holds a 70 per cent stake in Grand Pacific Trust, set up in 1992. Taiwan Cement, although it dropped sales in 1995, still ranked as the country's biggest cement producer with revenue of US$637 million and net profit of US$84 million. In the same year, Chinatrust reported a net profit of US$114 million.

Although he stepped down as chairman of China Trust Co in 1989 in favour of his nephew Jeffrey (who had been president since 1977), C.F. Koo remains active and has his own share of national responsibilities. He serves as a senior adviser to Taiwan's President Lee Teng-hui, chairs the Straits Exchange Foundation (which handles relations with China) and is a member of the ruling Kuomintang Party's central standing committee. He attended the 1996 APEC leaders' summit at Subic in the Philippines as Taiwan's representative. His eldest son Chester Koo, born in 1952, runs the group's insurance interests as head of China Life.

Jeffrey Koo, who was born in Taipei in September 1933, has three sons, Jeffrey Jr, Angelo and Andre, and a daughter, Michelle. The three boys work for Chinatrust while Michelle is a university student.

The Koos Group now has interests outside Taiwan in the United States, Thailand and the Philippines. In each country it has established links with the academic community, funding a scholarship at New York University (where Jeffrey Koo gained his MBA), the C.F. Koo Professorship at Wharton School of the University of Pennsylvania, the Thailand Institute of Technology and the De La Salle University in the Philippines, which awarded Jeffrey Koo an honorary doctorate. In 1996, the group announced its first venture into China, a stake in a US$12 million industrial plant by listed plastics maker Grand Pacific Petrochemical.

66 PRACHAI *Leophairatana and family, Thailand*

Estimated net worth: *US$1.5 billion*
Founder: *Thai Petrochemical Industries*
Educated: *The three Leophairatana brothers are engineering graduates from the United States*

THE LEOPHAIRATANA FAMILY'S THAI PETROCHEMICAL INDUSTRIES (TPI) IS Thailand's largest petrochemicals producer and second largest cement producer through its listed subsidiary, TPI Polene. TPI and TPI Polene had market capitalizations of US$1.68 billion and US$730 million respectively in late 1996.

TPI's initial public offering of 167 million shares in March 1995 raised more than US$360 million. Investors were rewarded with a 77 per cent lift in revenue in 1995 that saw sales approach US$800 million.

Prachai Leophairatana, TPI's founder and chief executive, took the family from a small agribusiness concern in the 1970s to major industrial conglomerate status through the creation of the region's first petrochemicals plant in 1982, and then into the cement industry when the government liberalized this sector in 1989. In partnership with Kuwaiti interests, it aims to have what would be Thailand's largest oil refinery operating in the southern part of the country by 1998. TPI also plans to diversify further in 1998, with a move into steel production that will put it into competition again with its perennial rival, Siam City Cement. The latter company is Thailand's biggest cement producer and a significant new player in petrochemicals.

The ethnic Chinese Leophairatana family has not put all its bets on heavy industry. It is active in insurance and financial services, and in real estate.

In March 1996, Prachai Leophairatana was one of several prominent Thai business leaders appointed to the Senate, the Thai parliament's upper house, by King Bhumipol Adulyadej.

67 T. *Ananda* KRISHNAN, *Malaysia*

Estimated net worth: *US$1.4 billion*
Chief executive: *Binariang Group; chairman, Kuala Lumpur City Centre Holdings*
Born: *1938, Kuala Lumpur*
Educated: *Melbourne University (on a Colombo Plan scholarship), and Harvard Business School*
Marital status: *Married to Supinda Chakrabhandu*

T. ANANDA KRISHNAN IS THE WELL-CONNECTED ETHNIC TAMIL BILLIONAIRE who launched Malaysia's first satellite, MEASAT-1, in January 1996, and the man behind the massive US$3 billion Kuala Lumpur City Centre (KLCC) development in the heart of the Malaysian capital.

It took Krishnan a decade to bring his KLCC concept to reality after consolidating the 39 hectare site (once the Selangor Turf Club) in the 1980s. He convinced the national oil and gas company Petronas to take a large part of the office space in the KLCC's crowning glory, the 88-storey Petronas Twin Towers. At 450 metres, the towers became Asia's tallest occupied building when the first tenants began moving in late in 1996.

KLCC provides cashflow for Krishnan's ambitious broadcasting and cable-television plans, built around his MEASAT satellite series. MEASAT-1 was launched by Binariang, the unlisted multimedia and telecoms company that Krishnan controls. One application for the MEASAT series is to provide direct-to-home television broadcasts, distance learning and remote-area telephony services. His Astro service began transmitting digital satellite television and radio programmes from MEASAT-1 in September 1996. Krishnan has plans to invest a further US$2 billion to develop satellite-based telecommunications and a digital mobile network known as Maxis GSM.

Krishnan also controls the listed lottery and racetrack operator Tanjong plc, which reported net profit of US$64 million for the year to 31 January 1996. Tanjong had a market capitalization of US$1.5 billion in early 1997.

Krishnan, who first rose to prominence as an oil trader in the late 1960s and 1970s, gradually built up an eclectic range of business holdings in the United States. Back in Malaysia, he helped set up Petronas, diversified into the gaming industry and then real estate and telecommunications. One of his main private companies is Usaha Tegas, which made an unsuccessful US$600 million bid for American Maize Products in 1995.

68 KRIT Ratanarak and family, Thailand

Estimated net worth: *US$1.4 billion*
Chairman: *Bank of Ayudhya and Siam City Cement*
Born: *1946*
Educated: *Britain, returned to Thailand in 1970s*

KRIT RATANARAK IS THE SON OF BANK OF AYUDHYA FOUNDER CHUAN Ratanarak (Chinese name Lee Mock Chuan), who arrived in Thailand from southern China in 1925 and died in August 1993, aged 73.

After labouring at the Bangkok port of Klong Toey and setting up a lighterage company as a young man, Chuan helped establish the Bank of Ayudhya, now ranked Thailand's fifth largest commercial bank, in 1945. It became the centre of the Ratanarak family's business holdings, which extend to cement (Siam City Cement), foodstuffs (Siam Flour Mill), broadcasting (Bangkok Broadcasting & TV), insurance (Ayudhya Life and Ayudhya Insurance) and financial services (Ayudhya Investment and Trust).

Krit, who is a member of parliament, became chairman of the Bank of Ayudhya on the death of his father. He is also chairman of Siam City Cement, in which the Ratanarak family is a major shareholder.

Bank of Ayudhya has more than 300 branches, including Hong Kong and Laos. It had a market capitalization in early 1997 of US$1.3 billion and a 1995 profit of US$176 million. At the same date, Siam City Cement, the nation's largest cement producer, had a market capitalization of US$650 million and turned in a profit in 1995 of US$60 million on revenue of US$540 million. Since its formation in 1969, Siam City Cement has diversified into the manufacture of bathroom fittings, ceramic tiles and asbestos and cement tiles.

69 Eugenio (Geny) LOPEZ Jr, Philippines

Estimated net worth: *US$1.4 billion*
Chairman: *Benpres Holdings, ABS-CBN Broadcasting*
Born: *1928*
Educated: *Harvard University, United States*
Marital status: *Married, son Eugenio Lopez III is president of ABS-CBN*

THE LOPEZ NAME IS SYNONYMOUS WITH BIG BUSINESS IN THE PHILIPPINES – A legacy of the empire built up in media, banking and power generation by the late Eugenio Lopez I. Lopez, regarded as the Philippines' wealthiest business figure of the 1960s, died in 1975 in the United States, a bitter and broken man after a close relationship with the late President Ferdinand Marcos turned sour in the early 1970s.

Today, his son Eugenio (Geny) Lopez Jr, who spent five years in a military jail during the Marcos era before escaping in November 1977 to the United States, guides the family's rebuilt US$1.4 billion fortune through its flagship company, Benpres Holdings. Geny Lopez Jr, who returned to the Philippines after the overthrow of Marcos in 1986, is president and chief executive of Benpres, chairman of ABS-CBN Broadcasting (where his son Eugenio Lopez III is president) and chairman of 17-per-cent-held Philippine Commercial International Bank.

While media and banking contribute the biggest profits, Geny Lopez has added interests in telecommunications, infrastructure, transport, financial services and property development. Benpres, with a market capitalization of about US$1.2 billion and a net profit in 1996 of US$69 million, is held 75 per cent by the family.

The jewel in the Benpres crown is its main media arm, 71-per-cent-held ABS-CBN Broadcasting (market capitalization US$900 million), which lifted its net profit by 33 per cent in 1995 to US$61 million. ABS-CBN is the Philippines' largest television network with a 62 per cent audience share. It produced 17 of the top 20 shows in 1995, and also distributes movies and other programmes through a network of outlets in the United States, Asia and Europe. In 1996 ABS-CBN signed a deal with ethnic Chinese tycoon Henry Sy to develop entertainment products through Sy's retail outlets, which include the nation's biggest shopping malls. As part of the deal, Sy was elected to the ABS-CBN board. ABS-CBN president Eugenio Lopez III said that the company aimed to transform itself into an international entertainment group.

The Lopez family also has strong links with another ethnic Chinese billionaire, John Gokongwei, who is vice-chairman of Philippine Commercial International Bank.

Of declining importance to the Lopez family nowadays is its small stake in power-generation firm Manila Electric Co, known as Meralco. It was his takeover of Meralco (then controlled by US interests) that propelled Eugenio Lopez I to international prominence in the 1960s. But Lopez was forced to sign away the family's holding in Meralco when Marcos turned on him in 1972.

The future for Benpres rests heavily in new growth areas such as the 20-per-cent-owned Sky Vision cable TV operation, its telecommunications joint venture with the US-based Nynex and Thailand's TelecomAsia, and its infrastructure plays, such as expanding the Manila–North Luzon expressway.

---

70 RASHID Hussain, Malaysia

Estimated net worth: *US$1.4 billion*
Founder and executive chairman: *Rashid Hussain Bhd (RHB)*
Born: *1947, Malaysia*
Marital status: *Married since 1988 to Suraya Abdullah (Sue), daughter of leading Malaysian Chinese businessman Robert Kuok*

ONE OF MALAYSIA'S PRE-EMINENT *BUMIPUTERA* (INDIGENOUS MALAY) businessmen, Abdul Rashid Hussain has built his Rashid Hussain stockbroking operation into a listed corporate group, RHB, that covers the full range of financial services: commercial banking, merchant banking, investment services, fund management, options and futures trading and, more recently, real estate.

Late 1996 saw Rashid lay the groundwork for his far-reaching plans to create Malaysia's first one-stop 'financial supermarket': a mammoth US$750 million deal to acquire 75 per cent of the Kwong Yik Bank from Malaysia's largest bank, Malayan Bank (Maybank), and inject that stake into DCB Holdings, Rashid's existing banking arm.

The merger, which brings in the retail strength of Kwong Yik Bank and its small business Chinese customers, will create Malaysia's third largest banking and financial group, but is unlikely to be the end of Rashid's ambitions.

Rashid, former deputy general manager of Bumiputra Merchant Bankers, founded Rashid Hussain Securities in 1983 with his business partner Chua Ma Yu. The pair, who split in 1992, listed the company as RHB in 1988. A major step forward came in 1990 when RHB bought a 20 per cent controlling stake in Development and Commercial Bank (since renamed DCB Bank) for about US$90 million and restructured it as part of listed DCB Holdings. In early 1997, a few weeks after Rashid's move to buy Kwong Yik Bank was announced, DCB Holdings had a market capitalization of US$2.7 billion and DCB was Malaysia's fourth largest bank with assets of US$7.4 billion.

Rashid, described by *Malaysian Business* magazine in 1995 as 'the top dealmaker in town' for successes such as lead-managing the Petronas Gas share and warrant offer, owns 17.3 per cent of RHB in his own name and another 9 per cent through nominees. The listed conglomerate Land & General has a 20 per cent stake in the company.

RHB's stockbroking arm is the biggest in Malaysia and accounts for one in twelve trades on the Kuala Lumpur stock exchange. RHB earned about US$100 million in 1995 on revenue of about US$165 million.

Rashid, who has close links to Malaysia's political leadership (he serves on the board of state-owned investment corporation Khazanah Holdings), diversified into property development and investment in the mid-1990s, with buildings such as RHB1, the RHB Centre (where DCB Bank is the major tenant) and the US$400 million Vision City project in Kuala Lumpur.

71 LEE Hon Chiu, Hong Kong

Estimated net worth: *US$1.4 billion*
Chairman: *Hysan Development*
Born: *1929, Hong Kong*
Educated: *Massachusetts Institute of Technology and Stanford University, US*

LEE HON CHIU IS CHAIRMAN OF THE LEE FAMILY'S 40-PER-CENT-HELD LISTED flagship, Hysan Development. The company makes most of its money from office rentals, primarily in the Causeway Bay area of Hong Kong, where Lee's grandfather, Lee Hysan, first bought land in the 1920s.

Lee Hon Chiu, who worked with large US corporations for more than 20 years after studying engineering in the United States, returned to Hong Kong in the mid-1970s. At the time, the Lee Gardens Hotel in Causeway Bay, built in the 1950s, was the family's premier property. In 1981, the Lees listed Hysan Development on the Hong Kong stock exchange and began developing residential property elsewhere in Hong Kong. But Causeway Bay has remained the core of the family's holdings and today Hysan Avenue is the focus of its redevelopment activity.

In 1993 Hysan financed the purchase and redevelopment of the old 660-room Lee Gardens Hotel for about US$315 million. On the site in Hysan Avenue, it is building a 50-storey tower as part of a major new office complex to be known, naturally, as the Lee Gardens. Another Causeway Bay property, the Caroline Centre, is a major profit contributor and current headquarters of the family's empire. Other properties are the Leighton Centre, the Hennessy Centre and the Lee Theatre Plaza.

Lee and fellow Hong Kong tycoon Li Ka-shing, whose flagship is Cheung Kong (Holdings), are partners with Quek Leng Chan's First Capital Corp in a residential development in Singapore. Lee has also taken the company into ventures in China, notably in Shanghai.

In early 1997, Hysan Development had a market capitalization of just under US$4 billion. It reported a net profit of US$160 million on revenue of US$255 million.

72 ANANT Asavabhokin, Thailand

Estimated net worth: *US$1.4 billion*
Chairman: *Land & House*
Born: *1950*
Educated: *University of Illinois, US*

ALTHOUGH THE ASAVABHOKIN FAMILY STARTED IN PROPERTY WITH HOTELS, IT has made its fortune from suburban detached houses. After studying in the United States, Anant Asavabhokin set up Land & House in the mid-1980s to build houses for the emerging middle-class market. He took the company public in April 1991, and it is now the largest listed housing developer in Thailand, with a market capitalization in October 1996 of US$1.14

billion. Anant's 36 per cent stake is worth more than US$400 million.

Land & House also has interests in the Philippines, where Anant is a partner with long-time Filipino friend Manuel Villar, the founder of low-cost homebuilder C&P Homes. The pair have formed a joint venture to build low-rise condominiums in Manila, with Anant's Land & House holding a 40 per cent stake. Land & House also has a 7.4 per cent share of Bonifacio Land, the consortium led by Indonesian tycoon Liem Sioe Liong's Salim Group that is developing the Fort Bonifacio military base into a major commercial centre in the heart of Manila.

In Thailand, Anant works closely with listed construction firm Christiani & Nielsen (in which L&H holds a stake) and with financial institutions such as fourth-ranked Siam Commercial Bank, and Pin Chakkaphak's ill-fated Finance One group, forced to merge with the bank Thai Danu after a shake-out in the Thai finance sector in March 1997.

73 CHEN Yu-hau, Taiwan

Estimated net worth: *US$1.4 billion*
Chairman: *Tuntex Group*

BACK IN THE LATE 1980S, CHEN YU-HAU HAD VISIONS THAT HIS 85-STOREY T & C Tower taking shape in the southern Taiwan port city of Kaohsiung would be Asia's tallest building. But Chen, whose Tuntex group is one of Taiwan's major conglomerates, with interests in property development, petrochemicals, textiles and motor-vehicle distribution, had his ambitions thwarted by the 88-storey Petronas Twin Towers in Kuala Lumpur, completed in late 1996. Still, Chen can afford to be upbeat about the group's prospects. The hotel, office and apartment tower is a 50–50 joint venture between his flagship, listed Tuntex Distinct Corp, and the group's affiliated cement company, 20-per-cent-owned Chien Tai Cement, in a city that has developed into Asia's third largest container port, behind Hong Kong and Singapore. With direct shipping links to China only a matter of time, Chen is well placed to take advantage of Kaohsiung's growth.

The Chen family's diverse interests outside Taiwan include a stake in a cement plant in the Philippines and a proposed US$3.5 billion naphtha cracker project in Thailand.

Tuntex Distinct operates in the construction and real-estate areas and is

Taiwan's fifth largest polyester fibre manufacturer, with sales in 1995 of US$760 million and a net profit of just under US$100 million. Tuntex Petrochemicals ranks 61st among industrials, with 1995 revenue of US$433 million (a massive 86 per cent gain on the previous year) and net profit of US$56 million. Other parts of the group include Tuntex Inc, Tuntex International Dynamics Corp and 55-per-cent-held The Regent Hotel, which is one of Taipei's most prestigious properties. The group also acts as the agent for Daewoo motor vehicles in Taiwan.

Market capitalization of Tuntex Distinct in late 1996 was US$1.4 billion.

74 KIM Suk-won and family, Korea

Estimated net worth: *US$1.3 billion*
Former chairman: *Ssangyong Group*
Educated: *Korea University*
Hobby: *Motor racing*

SSANGYONG (WHICH MEANS 'TWIN DRAGONS') GROUP, THE HEAVILY INDEBTED Korean conglomerate which aims to be one of the world's top 50 enterprises by 2000, underwent a change of leadership in April 1995 when Kim Suk-won, the eldest son of Ssangyong founder Kim Sung-kon, stepped down as chairman. He had guided the group for 20 years, building it into Korea's sixth largest business group with activities ranging from cement, oil refining, engineering and construction, general trading, financial services and, more recently, motor-vehicle manufacturing. He also took Ssangyong to the starting point for high-tech industries in electronics and fine ceramics.

Auto enthusiast Kim Suk-won said that he would remain an adviser to the group on its automotive business affairs, but essentially would devote himself to politics, by heading the Taegu branch of the ruling Democratic Liberal Party. Kim Suk-won's penchant for politics reflects a similar vein in his father, who died in 1975 after founding Ssangyong in 1939 as a soap-manufacturing firm. Kim's father was an influential adviser to the late President Park Chung-hee during the 1970s and a leading member of Park's Democratic Republican Party. Park, who came to power as President in December 1963 after leading a military coup in May 1961, was assassinated in October 1979. Taking Kim Suk-won's place as chairman at Ssangyong was

US-educated younger brother Kim Suk-joon, 42, who joined the family company in 1977 and had been the group's vice-president since 1990.

With US$6 billion in investment for auto plants between 1995 and 1999,
the automotive business remains the top priority for Ssangyong, fanning
speculation that it would have to bring in more foreign equity to ease its
debt load. New leader Kim Suk-joon said that cement, fine ceramics, oil and
petrochemicals were also part of his bid to reach global top 50 status.
Ssangyong Cement is already one of Asia's largest cement producers and
operator of the world's largest cement plant on the east coast of Korea.

75 HUANG Shi-hui, Taiwan

Estimated net worth: *US$1.3 billion*
Chairman: *Chinfon Group*
Born: *Taipei, 1926*
Educated: *Taipei*
Marital status: *Married, son Jing-yu*

HUANG SHI-HUI, ONCE A NEUROSURGEON AND UNIVERSITY PROFESSOR IN THE
United States, found himself with a far different horizon in the 1990s:
the economic landscape of Vietnam. But it was one he willingly embraced.
By the time he hosted a meeting in Taipei between Vietnamese and
Taiwanese business people in September 1996, his Chinfon group was
already the largest Taiwanese investor in Vietnam, with stakes in banking,
trading, motorcycle manufacture and assembly, livestock and cement.

For Huang, the journey from the Washington University Medical School
in St Louis to Hanoi and Ho Chi Minh City began in 1979, when his father
died and he returned to Taiwan to run the family business. Until then, he
had been a highly successful surgeon, hospital administrator and academic.
Huang proved just as adept with a chairman's pen as the surgeon's scalpel,
developing the Chinfon group to the point where the family's net worth is
estimated at US$1.3 billion.

The financial and industrial flagships of the group are Chinfon
Commercial Bank, ranked in the top 25 of Taiwan's banks, and Sanyang
Industry, which makes and distributes Honda motorcyles. Sanyang, with
sales of more than NT$37 billion in 1995, ranked as Taiwan's 14th largest
industrial enterprise.

Other components of the century-old group in Taiwan include general trading, construction interests, a motor-vehicle assembly joint venture with Germany's Volkswagen, high technology, and leasing, marketing and consulting services.

Sanyang, established in 1954 to produce bicycle dynamos, expanded into motorcycle production in 1962 and with more than 4300 employees is the biggest company in the Chinfon group. Another 800 staff work at the group's newest company, Ching Chung Motor, the Volkswagen joint venture headed by Huang's younger brother Arthur.

But it is Vietnam where Huang has made the most impact, with total investment of more than US$350 million since 1992. The largest venture is the Chinfon Haiphong Cement Plant, due to come on stream in 1997 with annual capacity of 1.5 million tonnes. He set up a motorcycle manufacturing and assembly operation in 1994, producing more than 800,000 units of 50cc and 150cc motorcycles a year.

Huang told his fellow Taiwanese investors in Vietnam that, compared to American and European interests there, they were small – but bold. Back home, that boldness helped Huang build Chinfon into a major conglomerate over the past two decades and justified his switch from the medical field to business.

His biggest and most dramatic decision was to acquire Cathay Investment and Trust from the government in 1988, and redevelop it as Chinfon Commercial Bank – thus setting the stage for the group's move into the high-growth financial services sector.

76 Sjamsul NURSALIM (Liem Tek Siong) and family, Indonesia

Estimated net worth: *US$1.3 billion*
Chairman: *Gajah Tunggal Group*
Born: *1943, Indonesia*
Marital status: *Married to Itjih Samsul Nursalim*

GAJAH TUNGGAL GROUP, SET UP IN 1951 AS A BICYCLE TYRE MAKER, HAS grown to become Indonesia's largest vehicle tyre, tube and rubber products manufacturer. The group, which is controlled by Sjamsul Nursalim

(Liem Tek Siong) and other family members, has diversified into chemicals and petrochemicals, and set up its own nylon and polyester yarn plants to produce tyre cord. Other business activities, spread over more than 60 companies, include telecommunications, electronics, consumer products, textiles, manufacturing, banking, financial services and trading.

The group has five listed entities: Gajah Tunggal, the cable maker Kabel Metal, 53-per-cent-owned Bank Dagang Nasional Indonesia (BDNI), which is Indonesia's ninth largest bank by assets but fifth by profits, leasing company Gajah Surya Multi Finance, and Asuransi Dayin Mitra. In Jakarta, its 60-storey BDNI Centre is Indonesia's tallest building.

In recent years the Nursalim family has sought to diversify out of Indonesia, setting up an investment company, Nuri Holdings, and a listed property company, Tuan Sing Holdings, in Singapore. Nuri Holdings is expected to become the Nursalim family's main vehicle for its investments outside Indonesia.

In September 1996, it reportedly bid US$46 million for 50-year rights to an eight-storey building on The Bund, the historic riverfront promenade in Shanghai, China.

Gajah Tunggal has head-hunted leading Singapore identities for its operations, including former minister S. Dhanabalan as a senior adviser, and former minister of state Peter Sung as chairman for listed Tuan Sing Holdings.

The Nursalim family, which arrived in Indonesia from China's Fujian province in the 1920s, is connected by marriage to Ferry Teguh Santosa's Ometraco Group, an agribusiness conglomerate based in Surabaya.

The two largest listed companies, Gajah Tunggal and BDNI, had market capitalizations of US$335 million and US$573 million in early 1997.

77 Dhirubhai AMBANI, India

Estimated net worth: *US$1.2 billion*
Chairman: *Reliance Industries Ltd*
Born: *28 December 1932 in Chorwad, Gujarat state*
Marital status: *Married Kokilaben Ambani, two sons Mukesh, 39 (vice-chairman) and Anil, 37 (managing director)*

DHIRUBHAI AMBANI, ONCE A LABOURER AND TRADER IN ADEN, TODAY HEADS India's largest private-sector company, the Bombay-based Reliance Industries Ltd, which had sales of US$1.6 billion in 1995–96 and a market capitalization of US$2.6 billion in early 1997. Ambani and his family control about 26 per cent of the company.

From humble beginnings selling fibres and textiles in 1966, Ambani built the Reliance group into a major force in textiles and petrochemicals over the ensuing 30 years. His sons Mukesh and Anil began moving into new strategic business sectors in the mid-1990s, with one of their biggest decisions being to gear up for an assault on India's deregulated telecommunications sector in concert with Nynex of the United States.

Other new ventures for Reliance include a gas and oil exploration joint venture in the Arabian Sea off the coast of Bombay, with Enron Oil & Gas of Houston and India's state-owned Oil & Natural Gas Commission. In October 1996 Reliance announced that it had completed construction of the world's largest polypropylene plant at its petrochemical complex in Surat, in western Gujarat state. The plant has a production capacity of 350,000 tonnes a year.

Dhirubhai Ambani has long been the hero of India's army of small investors, but his reputation for nimble corporate footwork was under considerable scrutiny during the mid-1990s, with one Indian newspaper dubbing Reliance 'The Evil Empire'.

A large private placement of Reliance shares led to a severe rebuke for the state-owned Unit Trust of India from the Securities and Exchange Board of India in September 1996. But despite this and a long-running share parcel scandal that dogged Reliance through much of 1995–96 – which led eventually to the company and the Ambanis being fined – Reliance remained a favourite of foreign investors. Throughout 1996 it continued to account for a large part of the Bombay stock market's volume.

78 Gordon WU Ying-sheung, Hong Kong

Estimated net worth: *US$1.2 billion*
Managing director: *Hopewell Holdings and executive chairman,*
   Consolidated Electric Power Asia Ltd (CEPA)
Born: *December 1935 in Hong Kong, seventh of nine children*
Educated: *Hong Kong Jesuits and Princeton University, US*
Marital status: *Married to Ivy Wu*

G ORDON WU IS THE HONG-KONG-BASED INFRASTRUCTURE SPECIALIST WHO
likes to take on Asia's biggest engineering projects, including toll roads
and power stations in China. But after problems over finance and govern-
ment approvals hit his mass transit scheme in Thailand and a toll road in
southern China, Wu's future looked less than rosy for much of 1995–96.
Adding to the gloom were delays to a power station in the Philippines that
Wu was counting on to generate income quickly. But then, in October 1996,
Wu had his first good news in months – the US power company Southern
Co announced that it would buy 80 per cent of Consolidated Electric Power
Asia – the region's largest private energy-production company and owned
60.4 per cent by Wu's Hopewell Holdings – for US$2.7 billion. With that
well-timed but bittersweet sale, 'Mr Infrastructure' was back in business.

After graduating from Princeton in 1958 with a BSc in civil engineering,
Wu first worked for the British government in Hong Kong, then helped his
father develop apartment complexes to meet the spiralling demand for
accommodation from the 1960s onwards. Wu formed Hopewell Holdings in
1972 and took it public in August the same year. He was one of the first businessmen to take advantage of development opportunities in China, after
Deng Xiaoping's open-door policy of 1979 loosened foreign investment
restrictions. He built the 1200-room China Hotel in Guangzhou and three
major power stations in Guangdong province. In Hong Kong, where Wu
successfully developed the slipform method of construction for high-rise
buildings, his landmark building is the 66-storey Hopewell Centre in
Wanchai.

Wu has been a member of the Chinese People's Political Consultative
Conference since 1982 and an adviser to the State Council of the PRC on

Hong Kong matters. He also serves on the World Bank's International Finance Corporation business advisory council.

In late 1995, when Hopewell stock was sliding on the Hong Kong market after profit forecasts went awry and projects in Bangkok, China and the Philippines seemed bogged down, Wu still had enough confidence to make a remarkable US$100 million bequest to his alma mater, Princeton University.

By the end of 1996 it seemed that Wu's US$3.2 billion elevated mass transit project in Bangkok, due to start in 1999, had returned to government favour, although Hopewell was likely to lose outright control of it. Then came the sale of CEPA, which Wu had spun off from Hopewell in late 1993 to consolidate it as the group's power-station builder. Wu did not particularly want to let go of his proven money-spinner in CEPA, but had no real choice if he wanted to push ahead with his big China plays. As ever, Gordon Wu remained remarkably confident about the future and urged his Hopewell shareholders to sit tight for the long haul.

In early 1997, Hopewell Holdings, held 34.6 per cent by Wu and his wife Ivy, had a market capitalization of US$2.83 billion. By then, CEPA, the Hopewell offspring, was in the hands of Southern Co.

79 TAJUDIN Ramli, Malaysia

Estimated net worth: *US$1.2 billion*
Executive chairman: *Malaysia Airlines (MAS), Technology Resources*
   Industries
Born: *13 April 1946 near Alor Setar in Kedah, Malaysia*
Educated: *University Malaya*
Marital status: *Married, two sons, twin daughters*
Hobbies: *Yachting, golf, growing durian*

TAJUDIN RAMLI IS AN IMPECCABLY CONNECTED FORMER MERCHANT BANKER who rocketed to international attention in 1994 when he took a controlling 32 per cent stake in Malaysia's national carrier, Malaysia Airlines. That highly leveraged deal through his company Malaysian Helicopter Services involved him in a US$720 million personal loan – a record for a Malaysian individual.

Tajudin thinks big in everything he does. Soon after he took control of

Malaysia Airlines he said that he would spend US$4 billion on 25 new aircraft for MAS by 2000, along with US$4 billion in aircraft purchases that were already in the pipeline.

Like most of Malaysia's most prominent entrepreneurs, Tajudin has done very well from close links with Prime Minister Mahathir and former finance minister Daim Zainuddin, now a key adviser to the government. Regarded as a protégé of Daim's, Tajudin has a controlling 38 per cent stake in listed Technology Resources Industries (TRI), which owns Malaysia's largest mobile-phone operator, Cellular Communications (Celcom). He built Celcom to its premier status after winning Malaysia's first mobile-telephone licence (which came with a competition-free guarantee period of five years) in the late 1980s. In mid-1996, Deutsche Telekom agreed to pay about US$555 million for a 21 per cent stake in TRI, with some of that likely to come from Tajudin's shareholding.

Tajudin, who grew up in a *kampung* (village) in Kedah state, got himself a good education at the University Malaya and, after working in the marketing department of Dunlop Industries, switched to merchant banking, where he rose to the post of chief executive. In 1982 he went into a manufacturing business with Daim Zainuddin which led him to take a stake in TRI in 1986.

Outside of Malaysia, TRI operates a telephone network in Cambodia and has telecommunications joint ventures in China, Iran, Tanzania and Bangladesh.

In early 1997, MAS, TRI and MHS had market capitalizations respectively of US$2.3 billion, US$1.99 billion and just over US$1 billion. Along with these three listed companies, Tajudin has stakes in several other private entities, including US satellite operator Rimsat.

80 Mohamad Bob HASAN, Indonesia

Estimated net worth: *US$1.2 billion*
Chairman: *Indonesian Wood Panel Association (Apkindo)*
Born: *1933, central Java*
Educated: *the Netherlands*
Marital status: *Married to Pertiwi*
Hobbies: *Golf, jogging, swimming*

PLYWOOD TYCOON MOHAMAD BOB HASAN IS REGARDED AS INDONESIA'S NO. 1 deal maker, the man President Suharto calls on when he needs a solution to a pressing business problem, such as how to keep the commercial peace among his competitive children. In February 1997, Hasan further cemented his Mr Fix-it reputation with his central role in two of the biggest corporate plays of 1996–97: the Busang goldmine in Kalimantan and the takeover of Indonesia's leading auto assembler, Astra International. Hasan was hailed for brokering a deal between the giant US miner Freeport McMoRan, Canada's Bre-X (which promoted Busang) and a group of Indonesian interests. Hasan's friendship with Freeport's chairman James 'Jim Bob' Moffett sealed the deal. When Busang turned out to be an elaborate fraud involving the faking of thousands of gold samples, Hasan was philosophical and relaxed. He lost nothing – except perhaps some face.

For more than three decades Hasan has been close to Indonesia's President Suharto (he plays golf regularly with the president) and, more recently, has been a business partner with the president's three sons, Sigit Harjojudanto, Bambang Trihatmodjo and 'Tommy' Hutumo Mandala Putra.

Hasan controls the Indonesian Wood Panel Association (Apkindo), a cartel-like operation which is responsible for about three-quarters of the world's plywood exports. Its annual revenue, in which prices and quotas are tightly controlled, is around US$4 billion.

Hasan, whose ethnic Chinese father was a central Java tobacco trader in *kretek* (clove) cigarettes, became friends with Suharto when the latter was a colonel in the Indonesian Army's Diponegoro Division, based in central Java. Hasan helped in the army's business affairs, and an enduring relationship was formed.

Today, along with his Apkindo role, Hasan is president of his own group, through which he has taken stakes in timber, shipping, pulp and paper, manufacturing, food processing, trading and financial services, including banking and insurance.

He holds a 20 per cent stake in Indonesia's second international carrier Sempati Air, in partnership with Tommy Suharto (58 per cent) and an Indonesian Army foundation (22 per cent). He and Tommy are also partners in Perta Oil, which has an allocation to sell oil overseas.

With Tommy's elder brother Sigit Harjojudanto, Hasan is chairman and a founding shareholder in the investment company PT Nusantara Ampera Bakti (Nusamba), set up in 1982. They each hold 10 per cent, while three foundations chaired by President Suharto hold the remaining 80 per cent. Increasingly, Nusamba is viewed as the vehicle through which Suharto's business interests are preserved. In October 1996, Hasan sparked a flurry of speculation about the future of Astra International when Nusamba bought a 10 per cent stake from Indonesian state banks. A few weeks later, Hasan emerged at the head of an informal group controlling more than 50 per cent of the company. The other ethnic Chinese businessmen in the consortium were *kretek* cigarette tycoon Putera Sampoerna with 15 per cent, Liem Sioe Liong's youngest son and Salim Group chief executive Anthony Salim with 7.4 per cent, timber tycoon Projogo Pangestu with 10.9 per cent, and Bank Danamon chairman Usman Admajaja with 7.3 per cent. Hasan, who was appointed president commissioner (chairman) of the board on 19 February 1997, foreshadowed a restructuring of Astra to make it the 'General Motors of Indonesia'.

With the president's second son, Bambang (via his listed conglomerate Bimantara), Hasan is a shareholder in PT International Timber Corp. Hasan is also a 40 per cent shareholder through the Yayasan Dakap foundation in the Ongko Group's Bank Umum Nasional (Indonesia's 14th largest bank, with assets of US$2.6 billion). He is an adviser to two Suharto foundations, Yayasan Darmais and Yayasan Supersemar.

By revenue, Bob Hasan's group ranked ninth among Indonesian conglomerates with annual sales in 1994 of about US$1.35 billion. Although of ethnic Chinese background, Hasan has converted to Islam and no longer uses his Chinese name The Kian Seng.

81 LO Ying Shek, Hong Kong

Estimated net worth: *US$1.1 billion*
Chairman: *Great Eagle Holdings*
Born: *about 1915, China*
Marital status: *Married, son Lo Ka Shui is managing director*

LO YING SHEK, PATRIARCH OF THE LO FAMILY WHICH CONTROLS PROPERTY developer Great Eagle Holdings, arrived in Hong Kong in the 1930s and began his real-estate activities in 1963. His son, Lo Ka Shui, trained as a doctor in the United States, but returned in 1980 and now runs the company. The family holds about 55 per cent of Great Eagle, which had a market capitalization in early 1997 of about US$1.9 billion.

Great Eagle listed on the Hong Kong stock exchange in 1972. It is primarily an investment holding company with interests in property development and management, finance, shipping (it owns three bulk carriers and one tanker) and hotels, including the Hong Kong Renaissance Hotel, the Eaton Hotel and the Landmark Jin Jiang Hotel in Chengdu, China. It developed one of Hong Kong's most prestigious buildings, the Citibank Plaza. Its UK assets include the Astor Theatre.

The company turned in a profit in 1996 of US$137 million on revenue of US$291 million, with Lo Ying Shek saying he was 'highly confident' of the group's future. While it has been a member of various consortia bidding for different sectors of the Hong Kong mass rapid transit and airport projects, one of its biggest ventures in the mid-1990s is a US$1 billion urban-renewal project on a site in Mongkok, Hong Kong. This is expected to generate significant earnings for the company from 1999 onwards. Great Eagle holds a 35 per cent stake in the project.

Lo Ka Shui, born in February 1947, studied medicine in Canada and the United States and practised as a cardiologist at the University of Michigan Hospital until 1980. As well as being managing director of Great Eagle, he is also a director of Hongkong and Shanghai Banking Corp, CDL Hotels International, Sun Fook Kong Holdings, the HSBC China Fund and Shanghai Industrial Holdings.

82 MONGKOL Kanjanapas and family, Thailand

Estimated net worth: *US$1.1 billion*
Chairman: *Bangkok Land, Tanayong*
Born: *1920, Hong Kong*
Marital status: *Married to Siriwan, 12 children*

DURING A 50-YEAR BUSINESS CAREER OSCILLATING BETWEEN THAILAND AND Hong Kong, Mongkol Kanjanapas (also known as Wong Chue Meng) has presided over a diversified empire that encompasses retailing, property development, watch manufacturing, media and transportation interests. Mongkol chairs the family's two listed companies in Thailand, Bangkok Land and Tanayong, and the two key Hong Kong companies, Stelux Holdings and Hwa Kay Thai Holdings.

Stelux, started by Mongkol in 1963, had 4500 employees, revenue of US$255 million and a market capitalization of US$210 million in late 1996. It draws most of its income from watch manufacturing and assembly (much of it in China), plus property development. Other Hong Kong interests include the 122-store City Chain (which also has outlets in Macau, Singapore, Taiwan and Thailand) and Optical 88 stores, which sell spectacles and provide optical services. One of Mongkol's youngest sons, Joseph Wong (whose Thai name is Chumpol), is executive director of Stelux.

Mongkol's eldest son Anant (Wong Chong Po) runs Bangkok Land, which is Thailand's largest property developer and the driving force behind Muang Thong Thani ('Golden City'), a gigantic satellite city built on the northern outskirts of Bangkok. The high-rise city, designed to house half a million people, has been a marketing disaster – only 20,000 people had moved in by mid-1997 and most of its apartments and houses, built in the early 1990s, were empty. The project reportedly represented an investment of more than US$1.2 billion by Bangkok Land, but property consultants Richard Ellis estimated that the company's land bank in 1993 was worth more than twice that figure. Anant, who is also a senator in Thailand's parliamentary upper house, remains convinced that Muang Thong Thani will eventually be a major profit earner. His younger brother Sakorn resigned as managing director of Bangkok Land in 1993.

Mongkol's third son Keeree (Wong Chang Shan) is managing director of Tanayong, which is also a Thai property developer but has become better known in the mid-1990s for its role in the US$1.5 billion Bangkok mass transit system. Keeree's major property play has been the 256 hectare Thana City project in Bangkok's eastern outskirts, and Exchange Square in the Bangkok CBD. He also runs the Tin Tin chain of restaurants in Hong Kong and Bangkok and launched Thai Sky cable television (sold in 1993).

83 UDANE Tejapaibul and family, Thailand

Estimated net worth: *US$1 billion*
Chairman: *Bangkok Metropolitan Bank*
Born: *January 1913, China*
Educated: *Srinakharinwirot University*
Marital status: *Married, nine children*
Hobbies: *Classical music, golf*

WITH INTERESTS THAT RANGE FROM MEKONG WHISKY TO KLOSTER BEER, PRIME real estate such as the Bangkok World Trade Centre, and a strong portfolio in financial services, insurance and banking, the Tejapaibul family is one of the most prominent Sino-Thai business groups in Thailand.

The family patriarch is second-generation Udane Tejapaibul, who arrived in Thailand from China's Guangdong province as a child in the early 1920s. He presides over the family's interests, which include major stakes in Bangkok Metropolitan Bank (Thailand's 10th largest bank) and two other banks, 7th-ranked First Bangkok City Bank (83 branches, market capitalization US$1.2 billion) and 11th-ranked Bank of Asia (94 branches, market capitalization US$700 million).

Bangkok Metropolitan Bank, chaired by Udane, was founded in 1950 and has more than 140 branches nationwide, with assets of around US$6.7 billion and a 1995 profit of US$60 million. The family holds a 35 per cent stake. Udane, who also heads listed Thai Financial Syndicate and a joint-venture investment house, Thai-Mitsubishi Investment, was influential in the postwar development of Thailand's banking system.

Despite inter-family tensions over the years, other senior members of the clan serve in board positions. Vichien Tejapaibul is managing director of Bangkok Metropolitan Bank, which had a market capitalization in early 1997 of about US$400 million. In July 1996 the bank was forced to close its operations in the United States and fined US$3.5 million after it admitted falsifying bank records. The Tejapaibul family agreed to lend money to the bank to ensure that there was no disruption to its normal activities.

84 Ratan N. TATA, India

Estimated net worth: *US$1 billion*
Chairman: *Tata Group, director of the Reserve Bank of India*
Born: *1937, Bombay*
Educated: *Cornell University (engineering) and Harvard University (business)*

THE TATA BUSINESS EMPIRE, INDIA'S LARGEST AND MOST RESPECTED, WAS established by Jamshetji Tata in Bombay in 1868. He was a Parsi, the followers of the Zoroastrian religion which entered India from Persia. The trading firm that he set up became Tata Sons, which today is the chief holding company, with Tata Industries, of the Tata business group. Ratan Tata inherited the leadership of Tata in 1991 from his uncle, the late Jehangir Ratanji Dadabhoy Tata, who died in November 1993 aged 89. J.R.D. Tata was India's pioneer civil aviator and presided over the forerunner of Air India until its nationalization in the 1960s. More importantly, he built Tata Sons into the nation's largest corporate empire and ran it for more than 50 years.

With group revenue of US$8 billion, the house of Tata is highly diversified. Tata Sons has investments in about 27 listed companies and 19 private companies, covering activities such as steel, engineering, motor vehicles, telecommunications, chemicals, tea, household goods, cosmetics, computer software and financial services.

In September 1996 Ratan Tata lamented to the *Far Eastern Economic Review* that the group's greatest missed opportunity was not having established 'substantial enterprises overseas in our core competence areas'. Yet, domestically, there was much to be proud of. Flagships Tata Iron & Steel Co (TISCO) and Tata Engineering & Locomotive (TELCO) ranked among the top five private-sector companies in India, and accounted for about half the group's total revenue in 1996.

But as India's economy opened up in the 1990s, Tata faced powerful new competitors from abroad and questions were raised about the viability of the empire and whether it was too diverse. Could Ratan Tata maintain control and prevent a split? To head off that possibility, Ratan Tata announced in late 1996 that the two unlisted firms which manage the Tata empire, Tata Sons and Tata Industries, would strengthen their strategic cross-holdings through a private rights issue. Tata Sons substantially lifted its shareholding in Tata Iron & Steel and in Tata Chemicals. Earlier in the year, Tata sold a 20 per cent stake in Tata Industries to the British trading house Jardine Matheson for about US$35 million.

In late 1996, the integrated steel producer Tata Iron & Steel had a market capitalization of about US$1.8 billion, annual sales of US$1.65 billion and a net profit of US$146 million. The figures for motor-vehicle manufacturer and distributor Tata Engineering and Locomotive were market capitalization of US$3.1 billion, annual sales of US$2.21 billion and net profit of US$142 million.

85 John GOKONGWEI, Philippines

Estimated net worth: *US$1 billion*
Chairman: *JG Summit*
Born: *1927, Cebu City, the Philippines*
Educated: *De La Salle University, Manila (MBA) and Harvard Business
    School (advanced management program)*
Marital status: *Married, four children*

JOHN GOKONGWEI WAS BORN INTO A WEALTHY CEBU-BASED TRADING FAMILY originally from China's Fujian province. His grandfather, Pedro Gotiaoco, set up Gotiaoco Hermanos in the nineteenth century and built it into one of the biggest enterprises in Cebu. But the family fortune was lost during the Second World War and it was Gokongwei's responsibility to put food on the table during the difficult years of the Japanese occupation.

He started his business career during the war, buying and selling rice, cloth and scrap metal. After the war, he set up a cornstarch factory called Universal Corn Products with his brothers. From there he ventured into textile production, property development, retailing and, later, banking, aviation, petrochemicals, infrastructure and telecommunications.

Gokongwei made a tilt at the nation's biggest corporation, San Miguel, in the 1970s, but was rebuffed by the controlling Soriano family after building – and later selling – a 4 per cent stake.

In the turbulent days after the fall of President Ferdinand Marcos in 1986, real estate in the Philippines was cheap. Gokongwei saw the potential and bought land in the now-booming Ortigas business district, where he built his Robinson's Galleria mall in 1987.

His 73-per-cent-owned holding company for a host of subsidiaries and affiliates is the listed JG Summit, which had a market capitalization in early 1997 of US$1.2 billion.

Other major companies are listed food company Universal Robina Corp (market capitalization US$750 million), property company Robinson's Land Corp (market capitalization US$370 million), PCI Bank (fifth largest bank in the Philippines, with assets of US$3.6 billion) and in financial services through PCI Insurance Brokers, PCI Capital Corp and Philippine Commercial Credit Card Inc.

Gokongwei is president and holds a controlling 57 per cent stake in the new phone company Digitel Telecom, which he aims to make the nation's second largest carrier after Philippine Long Distance Telephone (PLDT). When Digitel listed in November 1996, Gokongwei announced plans to list two more of his companies, JG Summit Petrochemical Corp and Apo Cement Corp, before the end of 1997.

His power and oil interests are through 20 per cent stakes respectively in First Philippine Power Corp (with old partner Eugenio Lopez) and Oriental Petroleum and Minerals Corp.

Gokongwei's latest property developments include Robinsons Tower, a 30,000 square metre block in Makati, and the 81,000 square metre PCIB Tower in Ortigas. His ambitions have also taken wing with Cebu Pacific Air, an airline he set up in March 1996 to compete with Lucio Tan's Philippine Airlines on the busy Manila–Cebu route.

Gokongwei's brothers Henry, Ignacio, Johnson and James (who have kept the Chinese family name Go) and sister Lily work in the business with him in Manila and at home base in Cebu, as do his children, including daughter Robina, after whom his food company Universal Robina Corp is named. His son, Lance, born in 1966 and a graduate of the University of Pennsylvania's Wharton School of Finance in the United States, is senior vice-president of JG Summit and heir apparent.

86 *Alfonso* T. YUCHENGCO, Philippines

Estimated net worth: *US$1 billion*
Founder and former chairman: *House of Investments, former chairman of Philippine Long Distance Telephone*
Born: *1923, Manila*
Educated: *Columbia University, US*
Marital status: *Married to Paz SyCip, eight children. Eldest daughter Helen is heir apparent*

BOARD CHAIRMAN, INDUSTRIALIST, DIPLOMAT AND CHIEF *TAIPAN* OF THE Filipino-Chinese, Alfonso T. Yuchengco is one of the five most important leaders of the international Chinese business community in Asia. An MBA graduate from Columbia University, a former ambassador to China and current ambassador to Japan, Yuchengco's influence is extraordinarily broad. When the Philippines President, Fidel Ramos, wanted to bring the nation's six big ethnic Chinese tycoons together on an infrastructure project, it was Alfonso Yuchengco whom he tapped for the chairman's role. The result was Asia Emerging Dragon Corp, set up in 1994 with equal shareholdings from Yuchengco, John Gokongwei, George Ty, Henry Sy, Andrew Gotianun and Lucio Tan.

Unlike most of his fellow tycoons, Alfonso Yuchengco was born into a wealthy family. His father, Enrique, was the son of an immigrant from China's Fujian province; the family traded in timber, rice, tobacco and wine, before diversifying into construction and insurance. His father set up Malayan Insurance, which became the foundation of the Yuchengco fortune. Alfonso Yuchengco joined his father in business in 1950 and today chairs 15 companies, with 42-per-cent-owned listed House of Investments (established in 1959) and 16-per-cent-owned Rizal Commercial Banking Corp (established 1960) as the flagship vehicles. Rizal Commercial Bank is the Philippines' eighth largest bank, with assets of US$2.5 billion.

Yuchengco's business partners include major Japanese business groups such as Mitsui Bank, Sanwa Bank and Nomura International. He holds a stake in the country's largest telecommunications carrier, Philippine Long Distance Telephone Co (PLDT), and was its chairman until his appointment as ambassador to Japan late in 1995.

Yuchengco married Paz SyCip of the well-connected SyCip family. Their eldest child and heir apparent, Helen, is president of Pan Malayan Insurance and married to Peter Dee, president of Manila's China Bank. Youngest son, 35-year-old Alfonso S. Yuchengco III, is president of House of Investments and is seen as a rising star. In October 1995 he replaced his father as chairman of 55-per-cent-owned BA Savings Bank, a joint venture between House of Investments and US-based Bank of America. Another daughter, Suzanne Yuchengco Santos, is a board member and director of several companies.

Through its many subsidiaries, House of Investments is involved in banking, consumer finance, construction, power, infrastructure, agribusiness, real estate, pharmaceuticals, manufacturing and services.

87 Sukanto TANOTO and family, Indonesia

Estimated net worth: *US$1 billion*
Founder and chairman: *Raja Garuda Mas Group and Asia Pacific Resources International*
Born: *1950, Medan, Sumatra*

SUKANTO TANOTO (LIM SUI HONG) AND HIS BROTHERS RUN INDONESIA'S 19TH largest conglomerate, Raja Garuda Mas, which had revenue in 1995 of about US$700 million. Although the group started in the timber industry in Sumatra in the 1970s, it later moved into pulp and paper, palm oil, textiles, banking and financial services. It owns palm-oil plantations, the small Indonesian bank Unibank (38 branches, assets US$500 million) and an insurance company.

The group's two listed companies are Inti Indorayon Utama, which had a market capitalization on the Jakarta stock exchange in late 1996 of US$360 million, and Asia Pacific Resources International Holdings Ltd (APRIL), listed in Singapore and New York.

To raise funds for his international expansion plans, Tanoto took APRIL public in April 1995, raising US$150 million on the New York market, but lower pulp prices in 1996 saw the company dip into red ink and its New York price skidded. APRIL, still 60 per cent held by Raja Garuda Mas, also faces tough competition in the regional pulp and paper market from home-grown rival Asia Pulp & Paper, which is owned by Eka Tjipta Widjaja's Sinar Mas Group. APRIL (1995 revenue US$1.2 billion) expects to produce 900,000 tonnes of fine paper a year from its Sumatra and Sarawak plants when they come onstream in mid-1997. Its major target markets are expected to be Indonesia, China and India.

88 R. Budi HARTONO and family, Indonesia

Estimated net worth: *US$1 billion*
Chief executive: *Djarum Group*
Born: *1943, central Java*

ROBERT BUDI HARTONO AND HIS ELDER BROTHER MICHAEL BAMBANG Hartono (born 1941) jointly run the Djarum Group, which is the second-ranked *kretek* (clove) cigarette manufacturer in Indonesia, behind the Wonowidjojo family's Gudang Garam Group and just ahead of Putera Sampoerna's HM Sampoerna Group. The company, based in central Java, was established by the Hartonos' ethnic Chinese parents in the 1960s.

Djarum is well behind Gudang Garam's 45 per cent share of the Indonesian cigarette market, which is estimated to be worth more than US$5 billion and growing at 20 per cent a year. Even so, Djarum still has a substantial stake of around 20 per cent that translates into revenues of at least US$1 billion a year. Djarum's premium hand-rolled *kretek* brand Classic and its Super brand are the mainstays of its market push.

In addition to *kretek* cigarettes, the Djarum Group has interests in food processing, textiles, timber and furniture, electronics, building materials and other consumer goods. In 1994 the group's total revenues were just over US$1.3 billion, ranking it the eighth largest conglomerate in Indonesia by revenue. In comparison, Gudang Garam had revenue of more than US$2.2 billion and ranked fourth.

89 Mochtar RIADY and family, Indonesia

Estimated net worth: *US$1 billion*
Chairman: *Lippo Group*
Born: *1929, East Java*
Educated: *Indonesia and China*
Marital status: *Married, six children. Son James (born 1957) is heir apparent; Stephen (born 1959) runs Hong Kong operations*

LIPPO GROUP FOUNDER MOCHTAR RIADY SUDDENLY BECAME INDONESIA'S BEST known businessman in the United States in 1996 when his name figured prominently in the US presidential election campaign as a foreign friend of Bill Clinton. Riady, through his former US representative John Huang (a Commerce Department official in 1994–95), was said to have arranged large donations to the Democratic Party, a claim seized on by the Dole campaigners. While the Lippo name was new to much of America, in truth the Riadys had known the Clintons for almost 20 years and Mochtar Riady had built a reputation as one of the most astute financiers and bankers in Asia.

Riady, whose Chinese name is Lie Wen Chen, is the son of immigrants from China's Fujian province who settled near the port city of Surabaya in East Java. His early life was eventful – first deported from Indonesia to China for anti-Dutch activities, then forced to flee to Hong Kong after the Chinese Communist takeover in 1949. He found himself back in Indonesia in the early 1950s, initially in Surabaya and then in Jakarta, where he worked in a bicycle shop. Riady, who had always wanted to be in banking, got his start in 1960 when he was offered a role with Bank Kemakmuran. That led to a stint with Bank Buana from 1963, and from 1971–75 with the Gunawan family's Panin Bank. In 1975 he took a management role and a 20 per cent stake in Liem Sioe Liong's Bank Central Asia, and built it into Indonesia's leading private bank. Today, Bank Central Asia is Indonesia's fourth largest bank, with assets of more than US$11.5 billion. The Riady family's own Lippo Bank, formed in 1989 from the merger of two other banks, ranks 11th with assets of US$3.3 billion.

Riady's Lippo Group, founded in the mid-1970s, has expanded from banking and financial services into property investment and development in

Indonesia, and infrastructure in China. Son James, who is group vice-chairman and heir apparent in charge of the Jakarta operation, spent some time in Arkansas after Riady bought control of the Worthen Bank there. That was the start of the Riadys' Clinton connection. James also developed the family's banking interests on the US West Coast, expanding from a base in San Francisco south to take in the large Asian customer base in California. Younger brother Stephen runs the Hong Kong and China interests, and a daughter, Minny, has also joined the family business. In Hong Kong, the family has a stake in the landmark Lippo Centre in the Central business district. Total group assets are estimated at US$8 billion.

One of the group's biggest developments is Lippo Karawaci, a 2360 hectare mix of upmarket residential, office and retail space 30km west of Jakarta. Hong Kong tycoon Li Ka-shing has taken a 5 per cent stake. East of Jakarta is Lippo Cikarang, a similar urban development on a 5500 hectare site.

In September 1996 a complex restructuring of the Lippo Group was approved by shareholders by which the Riady family will sell its stake in Lippo Bank. Lippo Securities will acquire 27 per cent of Lippo Life, which in turn will lift its stake in Lippo Bank to just over 40 per cent. The Riady family pledged to put proceeds from the deal (around US$390 million) into increasing its stake in Lippo Securities.

90 KHOO Kay Peng, Malaysia

Estimated net worth: *US$1 billion*
Chairman: *Malayan United Industries*
Born: *1920s, Malaysia*

AFTER YEARS OUT OF THE SPOTLIGHT, THE 1990S HAVE SEEN THE RETURN WITH A vengeance of reclusive Malaysian businessman, Khoo Kay Peng. Khoo, a former banker, was one of the commercial stars of the 1970s and early 1980s, when his close friend Tengku Razaleigh Hamzah was Malaysia's finance minister. But Razaleigh's failed bid for power against Malaysian Prime Minister Dr Mahathir Mohamad in 1986 saw Khoo's star wane and his Malayan United Industries group seemed to lose direction in the late 1980s.

Another long-time friend and business ally has been fellow Malaysian tycoon Robert Kuok, with whom Khoo shares Hokkien ancestry. Over the years, they have helped each other out with strategic investments and in warding off unwelcome takeover bids, such as that faced by Khoo in 1991 when Malaysian Chinese businessman Vincent Tan Chee Yioun's Berjaya Group bought more than 20 per cent of Khoo's Malayan United Industries. Frustrated at not being able to control MUI, Tan eventually sold out in 1993.

Since Kuok first helped Khoo win control of MUI in 1980, the hardworking banker turned entrepreneur has built the diversified group into a formidable empire in Malaysia, Hong Kong, the United States and Australia, with interests in insurance, hotels, cement, retailing, education services, leisure and the media.

Khoo also holds a 25 per cent stake in the Kuok-controlled *South China Morning Post* newspaper in Hong Kong, and in other Kuok vehicles such as Manila-based Shangri-la Properties and Kerry Financial Services. In early 1996, Khoo backed Kuok's move to seize control of Hong Kong media group TVE Holdings from its other major shareholder, movie mogul Sir Run Run Shaw. Khoo also has a large stake in CETV, a company set up to broadcast family entertainment programmes by satellite into China.

Elsewhere, MUI has taken a stake in a Spanish-language media group based in the United States, and bought five hotels there, including the 760-room four-star Radisson Twin Towers in Orlando, Florida. Khoo also has two hotels in Malaysia and acquired a slice of the Australian three-star hotel market, with properties in Sydney, two in Melbourne, and others in Adelaide, Hobart and Alice Springs.

In 1993 MUI raised about US$400 million from the sale of its Malaysian banking and finance company interests to Quek Leng Chan's Hong Leong Group and used the funds for its overseas media forays. Then in 1996 Khoo ventured back into the domestic market when MUI took control of listed Malaysian stockbroking, manufacturing and property-development company Pengkalen Holdings through a hostile takeover that began in April 1996.

In early 1997 MUI had a market capitalization of US$1 billion.

91 Eduardo COJUANGCO Jr and family, Philippines

Estimated net worth: *US$1 billion*
Co-founder: *United Coconut Planters Bank; former chairman and stockholder, San Miguel Corporation*

ONE PART OF THE COJUANGCO NAME IS SYNONYMOUS WITH THE POWERFUL business elite who supported the late President Ferdinand Marcos in the Philippines during the 1970s and 1980s. When Marcos fell in the April 1986 'People power' revolt, Eduardo Cojuangco Jr fled Manila and spent 1986–89 in exile in the United States. But Cojuangco, who is godfather to Marcos's son Bong Bong, returned in 1989, regained three seats on the board of the United Coconut Planters Bank that he co-founded in 1975, and made an unsuccessful run for the vice-presidency in 1992.

For Eduardo Cojuangco, the most enduring legacy of the Marcos years has been a stockholders' battle with the government that is still unresolved. For a decade, the Cojuangco group led by Eduardo Jr has been seeking to reclaim ownership of companies that hold more than 50 per cent of the food and beverage conglomerate, San Miguel Corporation (SMC). With 33,000 employees and a market capitalization, including A and B shares, of around US$5.7 billion in early 1997, San Miguel Corporation is the Philippines' leading company. Its annual revenue is around US$2.6 billion.

Every year Cojuangco, who was chairman of SMC until 1986, and his allies seek to vote their contested SMC stock, which would give them eight seats on the 15-member board. And every year, the SMC's government-controlled board, led by Cojuangco's arch rival Andres Soriano III, rejects their claim on the basis that the shares have been sequestered by the Philippines government, through the Presidential Commission on Good Government set up by former president Cory Aquino. The nation's Supreme Court upheld the sequestration order in 1993, meaning that 869 million shares worth around US$2 billion were considered 'ill-gotten wealth'. Eduardo Cojuangco's personally held stake of 108 million shares, or about 18 per cent, is valued at US$220 million. The government has said that it will sell about 26 per cent of the shares, but Eduardo Cojuangco is contesting its right in the courts, claiming that the sequestration sends the wrong signal to foreign investors.

Before the downfall of Marcos, Cojuangco had monopoly control of the Philippines' coconut industry. In addition to SMC and the United Coconut Planters Bank, his business interests today include agribusiness, mining, shipping, plantations, beverage distribution and a stake in the Mudgee wine-growing district of Australia, where he also runs a horse stud.

Another family faction is led by 45-year-old Antonio 'Tony Boy' Cojuangco, who is chief executive of Philippine Long Distance Telephone (PLDT). His younger brother, Ramon, is president of the mobile-phone company Piltel, one-third held by PLDT.

The third Cojuangco faction is led by Pedro 'Pete' Cojuangco and includes former president Corazon 'Cory' Aquino.

92 Andres SORIANO III, Philippines

Estimated net worth: *US$1 billion*
Chairman and chief executive: *San Miguel Corporation*
Born: *Manila*
Educated: *Wharton School, Pennsylvania, US*

US-EDUCATED ANDRES SORIANO III IS CHAIRMAN AND CHIEF EXECUTIVE OF THE largest non-oil company in the Philippines, San Miguel Corporation, which had 1995 revenue of US$2.6 billion and profits of US$456 million.

The Soriano family, who have been major shareholders in SMC for decades, have been long-time business rivals of the Cojuangco clan which rose to prominence in SMC during the Marcos era (see previous entry). Eduardo Cojuangco Jr was chairman of SMC until the downfall of Marcos in 1986, when Cojuangco fled into exile in the United States. Since he returned in 1989 he has been trying unsuccessfully to reclaim about 51 per cent of the stock in SMC which was sequestered as 'ill-gotten wealth' by former president Cory Aquino's Presidental Commission on Good Government.

For Soriano, eldest son of Don Andres Soriano Jr, the ritual clash with Eduardo Cojuangco's supporters at the SMC annual general meeting is a byplay to the big issue: getting SMC's overseas expansion into profit, particularly the push into breweries in China. SMC opened its third brewery in China in October 1996, giving it total production capacity of 5 million hectolitres a year. China's beer market, around 150 million hectolitres in 1996, is growing at 10 to 12 per cent a year.

Back in the Philippines, SMC's principal businesses are beverages, food, agribusiness and packaging. With its five breweries, San Miguel holds 85 per cent of the domestic beer market and the company, which started out in 1890 as a small brewery, today generates about 4 per cent of the Philippines' gross domestic product. In April 1997 SMC said it would take a 25 per cent stake in Australia's Coca-Cola Amatil in a US$2.5 billion stock and asset swap. CCA takes over SMC's 70 per cent stake in Coca-Cola Bottlers Philippines Inc.

With 33,000 employees, SMC is the Philippines' largest private employer. It had a market capitalization, including A and B shares, of around US$5.7 billion in early 1997.

Apart from their stake in SMC, the Sorianos have their own listed business group, A. Soriano Corporation, which acts as an investment and management company. They also have a stake in Atlas Consolidated Mining and Development Corp.

93 William SOERYADJAYA and family, Indonesia

Estimated net worth: *US$1 billion*
Founder and former chairman: *Astra Group*
Born: *1922, West Java*
Educated: *Dutch secondary school*
Marital status: *Married, eldest son Edward, second son Edwin*

THE SOERYADJAYA CLAN HELD THE MANTLE OF ONE OF INDONESIA'S HALF- dozen richest families, but the fortune came crashing down in the early 1990s when founder William Soeryadjaya's eldest son Edward over-extended with his Bank Summa finance subsidiary. That in turn led to the family losing control of Astra International, flagship of its Astra Group and Indonesia's largest assembler and distributor of motor vehicles and motorcycles.

Astra International's ownership was split up between various powerful business groups in Indonesia, led by the timber tycoon and Suharto family associate, Prajogo Pangestu. Prajogo became chairman of Astra and held a 10.7 per cent stake; other key stakeholders were Toyota Motor Corp with 8.3 per cent and the World Bank affiliate International Finance Corp with 7.7 per cent. Four years later, control of Astra International was again the subject of intense speculation when *kretek* (clove) cigarette tycoon Putera Sampoerna built a 15 per cent stake. In November 1996, another Suharto family associate, Mohamad Bob Hasan, eventually emerged at the head of an informal group (including Putera and Prajogo), controlling 51 per cent of Astra.

To further muddy the waters, the Soeryadjaya clan themselves were said to be quietly reacquiring shares in Astra International in a bid to see William Soeryadjaya returned as chairman. After a spell in the import–export business in the 1950s, William (whose Chinese name is Tjia Kian-liong) founded the Astra Group in 1957 with his younger brother Tjia Kian-tie and by 1991 had built it into the second largest conglomerate in the country, with interests in the motor industry, agribusiness and finance. But when part of the group's financial arm, Bank Summa, set up by eldest son Edward in 1979, almost collapsed in 1991, the US$1 billion bailout cost the family control of its flagship Astra International the following year. William had to sell off the family's 75 per cent stake, Edward resigned from the group and his younger brother, US-educated Edwin, was made responsible for managing the rest of the family's business interests.

Since then, the family has regrouped and begun rebuilding its Astra Group fortune, which stood at an estimated US$1 billion in 1996. In September 1996 the Soeryadjya family emerged as shareholders in a US$600 million telephone project in West Java, designed to install 500,000 telephone lines in the Indonesian province by 1999. The family held a share in PT Artimas Kencana, a partner with US West in the project operator Ariawest International.

94 Hashim DJOJOHADIKUSUMO, Indonesia

Estimated net worth: *US$1 billion*
Chairman: *Semen Cibinong*
Born: *1955*
Educated: *United States (public administration)*

THE INTERESTS OF HASHIM DJOJOHADIKUSUMO, ONE OF THE BEST-CONNECTED *pribumi* (indigenous) businessmen in Indonesia, extend to cement, banking, trading and energy. His flagship is the listed Semen Cibinong, which is the third largest cement and concrete producer in Indonesia behind Liem Sioe Liong's Indocement and the partly state-owned Semen Gresik. His banking interests include stakes in four small banks: Bank Industri, Bank Universal, Bank Pelita and Bank Papan Sejahtera.

Hashim Djojohadikusumo's father, Professor Sumitro Djojohadikusumo, is a noted economist, an adviser to President Suharto, and a former minister in the Sukarno era.

Hashim Djojohadikusumo is in business with Suharto's second daughter, Siti Hedijanti Harijadi, known as Titiek. Together they control Batu Hitam Perkasa, which has 15 per cent of the US$2 billion Paiton power project with Mitsui and General Electric. They are also partners in a Jakarta shopping mall project. Titiek is married to Hashim's younger brother, Major-General Prabowo Subianto, who is tipped for high office – possibly even as Suharto's successor.

Another partner in supplying coal on long-term contract to Paiton is Australian Graeme Robertson, through PT Adaro, which has large deposits in East Kalimantan, South Kalimantan and Queensland. Hashim Djojohadikusumo put together US$1.8 billion in financing for the Paiton project, which involves twin 600 megawatt plants in East Java due to come on stream in 1998.

While global trading in Central Asia, Russia and Africa are part of his operations, along with plans for a US$2 billion plastics plant in Indonesia, it is cement which has been the basis of Hashim Djojohadikusumo's emerging fortune.

In 1988 he took control of Semen Cibinong, the first publicly listed company on the Jakarta stock exchange (1977), and is now chairman and chief executive. Semen Cibinong has 25 per cent of the cement market in Java, which is the fastest-growing region of Indonesia and has a population of more than 100 million. Announcing a 22 per cent profit rise in the first half of 1996, Hashim Djojohadikusumo said that the result reflected the company's strengths in West and Central Java.

95 William CHENG Teng-jem, Malaysia

Estimated net worth: *US$1 billion*
Founder and chairman: *Lion Group*
Born: *1945, Kuala Lumpur*
Marital status: *Married, three daughters*

MALAYSIA'S WILLIAM CHENG HAS SET HIS DIVERSIFIED LION GROUP A HIGHLY ambitious goal: revenue of US$23 billion by 2000. By early 1996 he had concluded that he would not achieve that from his home market in Malaysia, and announced that China and Hong Kong were the logical places for expansion.

In Malaysia, the Lion Group manufactures steel products, including steel furniture and safes, and also has interests in logging, pulp and paper production (through Sabah Forest Industries), construction, property development, hospital management, financial services, retailing (the Parkson chain), tyre manufacturing, and the assembly and marketing of Isuzu motor vehicles in Malaysia. Its major listed concerns are investment holding company Lion Corp, Lion Land, Amsteel Corp and Angkasa Marketing.

Cheng, whose father, Cheng Chwee-huat, arrived in Singapore from China in 1930, began expanding the family's steel-fabrication business in the 1970s. He was awarded a licence by the Malaysian government in the mid-1970s which allowed him to set up Amalgamated Steel Mills (Amsteel). Today, Amsteel is Malaysia's main steel producer with products such as cargo containers, fasteners and motors. Amsteel had revenue in 1995 of US$1.65 billion and a market capitalization in late 1996 of US$920 million.

In China the Lion Group has invested about US$600 million in ventures that include tyre manufacturing, motorcycle assembly and pharmaceuticals.

96 Sir Run Run SHAW, Hong Kong

Estimated net worth: *US$1 billion*
Executive chairman: *TVB, Shaw Brothers*
Born: *October 1907, Shanghai*
Marital status: *Widowed in 1987, two sons, two daughters. Remarried May 1997to Mona Fong*

THE ELDER STATESMAN OF ASIA'S MOVIE INDUSTRY, SIR RUN RUN SHAW, WAS barely out of his teens when he moved from Shanghai to Singapore in 1927. The moving film was still a marvellous novelty, but one with magnificent potential in the eyes of Sir Run Run and his elder brother, the late Sir Runme Shaw. Together, they set up cinemas to show American films, and later started to distribute Chinese-language movies to eager audiences.

That set in train the two brothers' journey on a path that brought them to Hong Kong in 1959, where they set up Shaw Brothers Studios. With Shaw Brothers as the production base, Sir Run Run saw how the new technology of television could combine to create a fresh world of entertainment. The Hong Kong broadcaster Television Broadcasts Limited (TVB) was the result. TVB operates two free-to-air television stations in Hong Kong, Jade and Pearl, plus TVB Super Channel (launched in 1993 as a Mandarin-language channel), TVBS Golden (movies and specials), TVBS Newsnet and TVB Zongyi.

Sir Run Run Shaw is executive chairman of TVB, which today has one of the most valuable commodities in Asia – the world's biggest library of Chinese-language films and television programmes. TVB produces around

4000 hours of Chinese-language programming a year. The family's main listed company, Shaw Brothers (Hong Kong), and the Shaw Foundation hold around 34 per cent of TVB, which had a market capitalization of US$1.66 billion in early 1997 and recorded a net profit of US$63 million in 1995–96 on revenue of US$354 million.

Sir Run Run Shaw had been chairman of the Hong Kong property and media investment company TVE Holdings, with his Shaw Brothers holding 30 per cent. But Robert Kuok's South China Morning Post (Holdings) began a bidding war which ended with Kuok taking control in June 1996 at a cost of about $150 million and Shaw Brothers realizing about US$45 million for its stake.

97 Estate of YAHAYA Ahmad, Malaysia

Estimated net worth: *US$1 billion*
Chairman: *DRB-Hicom Group*
Born: *1946, Terengganu State, Malaysia; died 3 March 1997*
Educated: *Malay College, Kuala Kangsar, Perak, and as an automotive engineer in Britain*
Marital status: *Married to Rohana Othman, four children (daughters Yatina and Nadiya, sons Othman and Faez)*
Hobby: *Cars*

MALAYSIAN AUTOMOTIVE KING YAHAYA AHMAD AND HIS WIFE ROHANA WERE killed in a helicopter crash in Malaysia on 3 March 1997, dealing a tragic blow to their four children and the nation at large. Yahaya, the man who bought the quintessentially British sports carmaker Lotus in 1996, drove a red Ferrari 355 for fun. But his real fame and fortune came from a much more prosaic motor vehicle – the Proton, which accounts for about 60 per cent of the Malaysian domestic market. Yahaya, whose Diversified Resources Bhd (DRB) was an auto assembler with the Citroën and Isuzu truck franchises, took the leap of his short life in late 1995 when he masterminded a massive US$680 million acquisition of 32 per cent of state-owned conglomerate Hicom Holdings in November 1995. That move not only expanded his range into the Proton, Mazda and Mercedes-Benz marques, but lifted the market capitalization of 12 listed companies under his control to more than US$8 billion.

Cars, trucks and buses had always been part of Yahaya's life; after study-ing as an automotive engineer in Britain, he sold cars for a living back in Malaysia, then set up his own company, Master Carriage, in 1982 to deal in auto accessories. Then came the Citroën franchise and later a deal to assem-ble Isuzu trucks. In 1995, after a discussion with Daim Zainuddin – former finance minister and mentor to many of Malaysia's leading *bumiputera* (indigenous Malay) business figures – Yahaya made his bid to acquire 32 per cent of Hicom through a complex restructuring involving DRB and another conglomerate, Gadek, with interests in rubber, finance and motor vehicles. Yahaya said that the core activities of his DRB-Hicom group would be motor vehicles, financial services, and construction and property development.

The Proton uses run-of-the-mill technology from Japan's Mitsubishi Motors, but Yahaya was keen to diversify his R&D sources. In October 1996 he paid about US$80 million for 80 per cent of the British engineering and sports carmaker, Lotus Cars. The deal gave him access to the suspension, engine-making and engineering capability of Lotus's research and develop-ment unit, opening the way for a future technology leap by the humble Proton past its more established automotive rivals in the region.

Yahaya's key listed companies, DRB and Hicom, had market capitaliza-tions of US$863 million and US$2.89 billion respectively in early 1997. His long-time business partner Mohamed Saleh Sulong took Yahaya's place as chairman. Saleh said that Yahaya's children would be appointed to the DRB-Hicom group companies' boards 'when they are ready'.

98 ONG *Beng Seng, Singapore*

Estimated net worth: *US$1 billion*
Chairman: *Hotel Properties Ltd, Kuo International*
Born: *1946 in Perak State, Malaysia*
Educated: *Anglo-Chinese School, Singapore*
Marital status: *Married to Christina Fu, one daughter, one son*

SINGAPORE'S 'BUSINESSMAN OF THE YEAR' IN 1991, ONG BENG SENG CONTROLS a string of landmark properties around the world through his listed company Hotel Properties Ltd (HPL), but the big dollars flow through Kuo International, the private oil-trading company of his father-in-law, Peter Fu Yun Siak.

In Britain, Ong's HPL is in a US$500 million joint venture with Canary Wharf to develop residential, hotel and retail space on the Docklands site, while on Australia's Gold Coast he plans to build Australia's largest hotel of 1570 rooms in a US$250 million redevelopment of the Chevron Hotel site.

Ong, who started out in insurance and underwriting in the late 1960s, moved into commodities trading in Singapore when he joined Kuo International after marrying Christina, daughter of Kuo's owner, Peter Fu. They set up HPL in 1980 and took it public in 1982 to buy and develop hotels, condominiums and office space. Ong also had an eye for leisure trends and what people were spending their disposable income on. Today, he controls the Hard Rock Café, Planet Hollywood and Häagen-Dazs franchises in parts of Asia, and, with wife Christina, is in joint ventures with fashion names like Giorgio Armani, Bulgari, Donna Karan/DKNY and Christina's own Club 21 line.

Along with a motor-vehicle franchise in Australia and interests in tourism through hotels like the Hilton, the Four Seasons in Singapore and Bali and the Perth Parkroyal and Travelodge, Ong's HPL has developed condominiums in Singapore.

But Ong found himself in hot water in mid-1996 when he gave unsolicited discounts on condominium purchases to two key political figures in Singapore: Senior Minister and former Prime Minister Lee Kuan Yew, and Deputy Prime Minister (and Lee's son) Lee Hsien Loong. The ministers said that they would turn the discounts over to the government, and the Stock Exchange of Singapore rebuked Ong's HPL for withholding or delaying information.

Ong seemed unperturbed by the fuss over the Lee condominiums and nor did the market seem to mind. His Hotel Properties Ltd entered 1997 with its market capitalization sitting at around US$650 million, while privately held Kuo International turned over an estimated US$2 billion for 1996.

99 Mu'min Ali GUNAWAN and family, Indonesia

Estimated net worth: *US$1 billion*
Founder: *Panin Group*
Born: *1939 in Jember, near Surabaya, East Java*

MU'MIN ALI GUNAWAN (LIE MO MING) HEADS THE PANIN GROUP, WHICH has assets of about US$2 billion and concentrates on banking and financial services, including insurance, stockbroking, leasing and venture capital. It also has some property interests. The Panin Group ranks as the 12th largest conglomerate in Indonesia, and several members of the Gunawan family rank among the top 100 individual taxpayers.

The group's flagship is PT Pan Indonesia (Panin) Bank, which is regarded as one of the most conservative banks in Indonesia. Mu'min Ali Gunawan, who started his business career in shipping, founded Pan Indonesia Bank in 1964 and merged it with two other small banks in 1971. It listed on the Jakarta stock exchange in 1982, the first bank to do so. Mochtar Riady, founder of the Lippo Group and a prominent Indonesian banker and businessman, was involved in its early growth, and a family connection exists between the Riady and Gunawan clans.

Although relatively small with assets of US$1.8 billion (ranking it 15th among Indonesia's banks) and a market capitalization of about US$200 million, Panin Bank, under its president H. Rostian Sjamsudin, is regarded as one of the best-managed banks in Indonesia – primarily because it is not involved in intra-group lending. Panin Bank controls Panin Life (the largest life-insurance operation in Indonesia, measured by assets) and Panin Insurance. In turn, these two are the main shareholders in the bank with stakes of 21.4 per cent and 13.7 per cent respectively.

Mu'min Ali Gunawan, his brother Gunadi and other family interests hold about 44 per cent of Panin Bank. Gunawan's eldest son Chandra, who holds an MBA from the United States, is deputy president.

In the mid-1990s, the Panin Group entered into two joint ventures with Australian groups. Panin Bank owns 15 per cent of a joint venture with Australia's ANZ Bank called PT ANZ Panin, while in 1994 Australia's largest insurance and investment group, AMP, bought a 40 per cent stake in Panin Life and established a joint venture, PT AMP Pan Indonesia Life.

---

100 TUNG Chee-hwa and family, Hong Kong

Estimated net worth: *US$1 billion*
Public office: *Hong Kong Chief Executive (from July 1997)*
Former chairman: *Orient Overseas International Line*
Born: *May 1937, Shanghai*
Educated: *University of Liverpool, UK*
Marital status: *Married to Betty Chiu Hung-ping*
Hobby: *Morning tai chi exercises*

TUNG CHEE-HWA, CHIEF EXECUTIVE DESIGNATE OF THE HONG KONG SPECIAL Administrative Region following its return to Chinese sovereignty from 1 July 1997, is the eldest son of the late shipping magnate C.Y. Tung (Chao Yung), founder of the Orient Overseas Container Line. In the early 1980s the shipping line, then run by the younger Tung, almost went broke, but was saved by a group of pro-China businessmen led by the influential Hong Kong tycoon Henry Fok Ying-tung. Fok helped raise a US$120 million syndicated loan that included Chinese money – a fact finally confirmed by Tung in October 1996 after he declared himself a contender for the chief executive's job.

Tung was born in Shanghai where the family had strong commercial interests. But the Tungs fled to Hong Kong in 1950 after the Communist takeover of China in 1949. In Hong Kong and Taiwan, C.Y. Tung, who was a supporter of Chiang Kai-shek's Kuomintang government, began building up a fleet of tankers and cargo ships that at one point numbered 150 vessels. Meanwhile, his son C.H. Tung went to the UK to study at the University of Liverpool, and later spent time in the United States. By the 1970s, he was back in Hong Kong, working in his father's company; he eventually took over as chairman in 1979 when his father fell ill (and subsequently died in 1982). In the first half of the 1980s, a global downturn in the shipping industry and some ambitious over-ordering of new vessels had the company in trouble; by August 1985 it looked as if a US$2.6 billion debt load would send

Orient Overseas Line to the bottom.

But Tung was able to convince his creditors to agree to a restructuring that involved the Bank of China and the Hongkong and Shanghai Bank, along with a US$120 million investment from Henry Fok's group that turned the tide. There was a widely held view at the time – now confirmed by Tung – that Fok's 8 per cent interest included some mainland Chinese players. But Fok, through his partnership with Stanley Ho in the Macau casino business and his links with other wealthy businessmen such as Li Ka-shing, was also thought to have had more than enough cash to fund the rescue of Tung's group in his own right.

Fok and Li were again in Tung's camp in the mid-1990s, when the choice for the mid-1997 job of Hong Kong's first Chief Executive started to concentrate the minds of the rich and powerful. Throughout 1996, although an undeclared candidate until October, Tung was the business community's front runner, with his main opponents being fellow business tycoon Peter Woo Kwong-ching (former chairman of Wharf Holdings and Wheelock) and former Hong Kong chief justice (Sir) Yang Ti Liang. In the final runoff of a stage-managed poll on 11 December 1996, Tung won easily, picking up 320 of the 400 votes from the selection committee, while Yang and Woo received 42 and 36 votes respectively. Tung's early promise to Hong Kong's citizens was that he would be a 'hands-on administrator', ready to 'deal resolutely' with Chinese city and provincial officials seeking 'special favours' in the territory.

Tung's standing with the Beijing leadership had been given its first boost one year earlier, when he was chosen in December 1995 as one of five Hong Kong vice-chairmen of the Preparatory Committee charged with overseeing the changeover. In June 1996 he took another step towards the top job when he resigned as a member of Hong Kong's Executive Council, which gave advice to the British Governor, Chris Patten. Then, with a decision on the Hong Kong Chief Executive's job less than two months away, in October 1996 Tung stepped down as chairman of Orient Overseas Container Line (OOCL) and of Orient Overseas International Line (OOIL) to run for office. His younger brother, Tung Chee-chen, vice-chairman of the Hong Kong General Chamber of Commerce, became chairman of Orient Overseas Container Line.

The Tung family's expansion plans for Orient Overseas include putting into service by the end of 1997 six new vessels that are the world's largest container ships, each capable of holding 4690 20ft containers.

Notes and References

Chapter 1: The Nature of Guanxi

1   G. Hiscock, 'Technology breaches China wall', *The Australian*, March 26, 1996.
2   East Asia Analytical Unit (1996) *Asia's Global Powers: China-Japan Relations in the 21st Century*, Australian Department of Foreign Affairs and Trade, Canberra, p25.
3   G. Hiscock, 'Technology breaches China wall', *The Australian*, March 26, 1996.
4   G. Hiscock, 'Saving the future', *The Australian*, April 1, 1996.
5   D. Clayton, 'Cultural traits hit promotion of brand names', *South China Morning Post*, December 7, 1996.
6   W. McGurn, 'Prophet of profit', *Far Eastern Economic Review*, November 28, 1996.

Chapter 2: Starting with Food – From Seeds to Satellites

1   'Asia and the world in the 21st century', address by Lee Kuan Yew at the 21st Century Forum in Beijing, September 4, 1996, in *The China Post*, September 6, 1996.
2   Charoen Pokphand Group company profile, November 1995.
3   C.P. Fitzgerald and M. Roper (1972) *China: A World So Changed*, Thomas Nelson, Australia, pp46–7.
4   Interview, Charoen Pokphand Group, Korat, Thailand, November 1995.
5   'Shaping the nation's banking system, 50 Thais who Helped Shape Thailand', *Bangkok Post*, August 1, 1996
6   S. Seagrave (1995) *Lords of the Rim*, Bantam Press, London, pp167–78.
7   Bangkok Bank statement, August 1996.

Chapter 3: The Fujian Connection

1   'China in 2046', *Far Eastern Economic Review* 50th anniversary issue, 1996, pp188–9.
2   G. Hiscock, 'Kuok brings Asia synergies to Coca-Cola deal', *The Australian*, August 9, 1996.
3   East Asia Analytical Unit (1995) *Overseas Chinese Business Networks in Asia*,

Australian Department of Foreign Affairs and Trade, Canberra, p31.

4 Material supplied by Robert Kuok's office, July 1996.

5 Account adapted from a report on the death of Sir Henry Gurney in *Keesing's Contemporary Archives*, 1951.

6 D. Ch'ng (1993) *Overseas Chinese Entrepreneurs*, CEDA, Sydney, pp85–7.

7 G. Hiscock, 'Kuok poised for $4bn HK property float', *The Australian*, July 1996.

8 'Kerry posts profit surge as revenue grows steadily', *Asian Wall Street Journal*, August 21, 1996.

9 Better Hong Kong Foundation profile, May 1996.

10 G. Hiscock, 'There is money in Chinese muck', *The Australian*, September 20, 1995.

11 G. Hiscock, 'Salim shuffle cements tycoon's spot at the top', *The Australian*, February 17, 1995.

12 D. Ch'ng (1993) *Overseas Chinese Entrepreneurs*, CEDA, Sydney, pp96–7.

13 S. Seagrave (1995) *Lords of the Rim*, Bantam Press, London, p191.

14 Jardine Fleming, *Regional Earnings Guide*, September 1996.

15 G. Hiscock, 'Salim shuffle cements tycoon's spot at the top', *The Australian*, February 17, 1995.

16 East Asia Analytical Unit (1995) *Overseas Chinese Business Networks in Asia*, Australian Department of Foreign Affairs and Trade, Canberra, pp163–75.

17 'Asia's banking families', *Asiamoney*, October 1995, p45.

18 R. Borsuk, 'Salim moves into basics: water and rice', *Asian Wall Street Journal*, February 28, 1996.

19 Statement by First Pacific, March 1997.

20 'A multi-faceted conglomerate', Metro Pacific company statement, *Asiamoney*, March 1996, and East Asia Analytical Unit (1995) *Overseas Chinese Business Networks in Asia*, Australian Department of Foreign Affairs and Trade, Canberra, pp163–75.

21 Ibid.

Chapter 4: Filipino Money-Go-Round

1 'Mr Billion', *Asiaweek*, August 18, 1995.

2 N. Ghosh, 'Sarah Balabagan smiles and sobs with relief', *Straits Times Weekly*, August 3, 1996.

3 G. Hiscock, 'Low-cost villas make Villar's stock and trade', *The Australian*, April 11, 1996.

4 W. Paras, 'Getting rich by really trying', *Asiaweek*, August 18, 1995.

5 Ibid, p47.

6 R. Tiglao, 'Mall mogul', *Far Eastern Economic Review*, August 31, 1995 and A. Lopez, 'Discount billionaire', *Asiaweek*, June 28, 1996.

7   A. Labita, 'From down at heel to boots and all taipan', *The Australian*, June 11, 1996.

8   Ibid.

9   'SM Prime to open 4 malls by 1998', *Asian Wall Street Journal*, May 8, 1996.

10 D. Ch'ng (1993) *The Overseas Chinese*, CEDA, Sydney, p78.

11 A. Labita, 'Mall tycoon pins his faith on the Philippines', *The Australian*, April 2, 1996.

12 'Digitel's profit advances sharply', *Asian Wall Street Journal*, August 2, 1996.

13 'Building on strengths', Filinvest Development company statement, *Asiamoney*, March 1996.

14 'Gotianun quits as Filinvest Land president', *Asian Wall Street Journal*, May 24, 1996.

15 A. Labita, 'Ayala's smooth transition', *The Australian*, September 1995.

16 'Faith in the Filipino', statement by Jaime Zobel de Ayala, *Philippine Business*, September 1994, p38.

Chapter 5: Hong Kong's Land Barons

1   Sir David Ford, 'A rare alchemy', in Government Information Services (1994) *Hong Kong 1994*, Hong Kong, p15.

2   C.P. Fitzgerald and M. Roper (1972) *China: A World So Changed*, Thomas Nelson, Australia; and A. Toynbee (1973) *Half the World*, Thames and Hudson, London.

3   History section, Government Information Services (1994) *Hong Kong 1994*, Hong Kong, p420.

4   Ibid, p423.

5   G. Hiscock interview with Vincent Cheng in Hong Kong, May 1996.

6   The account of Li's early life is drawn principally from D. Ch'ng (1993) *The Overseas Chinese*, CEDA, Sydney; J. Dikkenberg, 'Superman's Midas touch', *The Australian Business Asia*, December 1, 1993; and E. Huang and L. Jeffery (1995) *Hong Kong: Portraits of Power*, Orion, London.

7   E. Huang and L. Jeffery (1995) *Hong Kong: Portraits of Power*, Orion, London, p38–43.

8   G. Hiscock interview in Hong Kong, May 1996.

9   New World Development Co annual report, 1995.

10 G. Hiscock interview with Henry Cheng in Hong Kong, May 1996.

11 The account of Cheng Yu-tung's early life draws on material in E. Huang and L. Jeffery (1995) *Hong Kong: Portraits of Power*, Orion, London; and New World Development Co's annual report and company profile 1995.

12 P. Sito, 'Mega-tower plan for Central', *South China Morning Post*, May 18, 1996.

13 E. Huang and L. Jeffery (1995) *Hong Kong: Portraits of Power*, Orion, London, p96–101.

14 B. Porter, 'The making of HK's top tycoon', *South China Morning Post*, July 30, 1994 and C. Smith,'Lee Shau-kee builds success on confidence', *Asian Wall Street Journal*, August 15, 1996.

Chapter 6: Star Wars – the Thirst for Water and Information

1 Visit to Hong Kong, May 1996.
2 G. Hiscock, 'There is money in Chinese muck', *The Australian*, September 20, 1995.
3 G. Hiscock, 'Flushing out opportunities in Asia', *The Australian*, October 30, 1995.
4 Telecommunications survey, *Asiamoney*, July 1996; and 'The Next Wave', *Far Eastern Economic Review*, August 22, 1996.
5 'A different future on the line', profile of Thaksin Shinawatra in '50 Thais Who Helped Shape Thailand', *Bangkok Post*, August 1, 1996.
6 G. Hiscock, 'Throw Thailand a line and the new rich get richer', *The Australian*, April 15, 1996.
7 B. Head, 'Systems go for Iridium's first satellites', *Australian Financial Review*, December 18, 1996.

Chapter 7: Malaysia's Power Plays

1 'Malaysia lobbies for its 2020 vision', *The Australian*, January 28, 1997.
2 I. Stewart, 'Mahathir acts to restore confidence in Tenaga', *The Australian*, August 13, 1996.
3 J. Studwell, 'Reach for the sky', *Asia Inc*, March 1996, pp32–9; and T. King, 'Tenants will soon reach for the stars', *The Weekend Australian*, September 14, 1996.
4 *Asia Inc*, op cit.
5 G. Hiscock, 'Malaysia Airlines soars with billionaire at the helm', *The Australian*, February 3, 1995.
6 'MAS considers super jumbo', *The Australian*, September 17, 1996.
7 J. Studwell, 'What next for Vincent Tan?', *Asia Inc*, July 1995, pp42–9.
8 I. Stewart, 'World's longest building to straddle river', *The Australian*, September 17, 1996.
9 'Mutiara Telecom to invest $480m by 1998', *AFP*, October 20, 1996.
10 'Bridging Malaysia to the future, to the world', Renong company statement, *Asiamoney*, October 1996.
11 R. Pura, 'A Malaysian morality tale for the 1990s', *Asian Wall Street Journal*, July 30, 1996.
12 Telecommunications survey, *Asiamoney*, July 1996, p42.
13 G. Klintworth (ed.) (1994)*Taiwan in the Asia-Pacific in the 1990s*, Allen and Unwin, Sydney.

14 G. Hiscock, 'Visa buys hope for the future', *The Australian*, October 10, 1996.

15 Interview with Chiang Ping-kun, chairman, Council for Economic Planning and Development, Taipei, September 1996.

Chapter 8: Korean Car Wars

1   Quoted in Chung Ju Yung's autobiography*There Are Difficulties, But No Failures.*

2   Ministry of Culture and Information (1982) *A Handbook of Korea*, p93.

3   'Tripitaka Koreana now on CD-ROM', *Samsung Newsletter*, June 1996, p25.

4   G. Hiscock, 'Samsung dividend balloons Lee fortune',*The Australian*, April 23, 1996.

5   'Learning from the best', *Samsung Newsletter*, April 1996, p24.

6   Ibid.

7   S. Glain, 'Speaking freely can prove costly for Korean firms', *Asian Wall Street Journal*, August 21, 1995.

8   Reported in 'Hollywood on the Han?', *Far Eastern Economic Review*, May 11, 1995.

9   'Learning from the best', *Samsung Newsletter*, April 1996, p24.

10 'Cheil Foods becomes independent from Samsung to start as Cheiljedang Group', *Korea Economic Weekly*, May 13, 1996.

11 'Daewoo Group. Working hard to become a truly global enterprise', statement by Kim Woo-choong, *Forbes*, August 14, 1995.

12 W. Webster, 'Shooting for the stars', *Sunday Telegraph*, June 30, 1996.

13 Ibid.

14 Hyundai company statement, January 1996.

15 'Hyundai Group unveils $2.3 bn investment into China for three years', *Korea Economic Weekly*, June 17, 1996.

16 'Big 3 automakers expanding overseas production plants', *Korea Newsreview*, April 13, 1996.

17 Shim Jae Hoon, 'Adversity knocks', *Far Eastern Economic Review*, May 18, 1995.

18 B. Cheesman, 'Self-made tycoon spreads a billion-dollar message', *Australian Financial Review*, July 22, 1994.

19 Statement by Kim Woo-choong, 'Daewoo Motor intensifies its globalisation drive', *Korea Economic Weekly*, August 19, 1996.

20 Biography of Kim Woo-choong, *Korean Business Review*, November 1995, p7.

21 'Conservative Ssangyong turns progressive under new chairman', Ssangyong company statement, *Forbes*, August 14, 1995.

22 Ibid.

Chapter 9: Singapore Laps up the Luxury

1   'Luxury operator suspends Vietnam link', *Bangkok Post*, October 26, 1996.

2   Chairman's statement, Genting International annual report, 1995.

3   Ibid.

4   'Singapore to be world's richest nation by 2020, says report', *Straits Times Weekly*, September 21, 1996.

5   D. Brady, 'CDL, luxury hotel chains discuss strategic alliance', *The Asian Wall Street Journal*, September 17, 1996.

6   K. Rashiwala, 'HPL to develop London site with Canary Wharf', *Straits Times Weekly*, July 27, 1996.

7   'Ong Beng Seng tells how HPL condos were sold', *Straits Times Weekly*, May 25, 1996.

8   Company structure, as shown in M. Weidenbaum and S. Hughes (1996) *The Bamboo Network*, Free Press, New York, p38.

9   New World Development annual report, 1995; and J. Kohut, 'Invasion of the hotel snatchers', *Asia Inc*, September 1996, pp42–7.

10 G. Graham, 'Now there are more rich to get richer', *Financial Times*, August 15, 1996.

11 'Beri ranks Singapore No 2 for investments', *Straits Times Weekly*, September 21, 1996.

12 L. Lopez, 'Proton to buy Lotus car firm', *The Asian Wall Street Journal*, October 22, 1996.

Chapter 10: 'First Family' Fortune – the Suharto Children

1   'Help the poor or be forced to, Suharto warns the rich', *Straits Times Weekly*, October 5, 1996.

2   G. Hiscock, 'Wealth sprouts on Suharto family tree', *The Australian*, October 10, 1996.

3   The material on Suharto's early life has been sourced mainly from J.D. Legge's *Sukarno*, B. Grant's *Indonesia*, H. Hill (ed.), *Indonesia's New Order*, S. Seagrave's *Lords of the Rim*, and articles by P. Walters, I. Stewart, G. Sheridan and G. Hiscock in *The Australian*, 1995–96.

4   I. Stewart, 'President loses his spouse of perfection', *The Australian*, April 29, 1996 and Dr Ong Hok Ham, 'A pillar of Indonesia's New Order', *The Australian*, May 1, 1996.

5   Material on the 1965 coup is mainly from Legge's *Sukarno* and Grant's *Indonesia*.

6   B. Grant (1964) *Indonesia*, Melbourne University Press, Melbourne, p99.

7   P Walters, 'Death raises the Suharto succession question', *The Australian*, April 29, 1996.

8   General Soemitro, 'Suharto should pave the road to transition', *Asian Wall Street Journal*, November 16, 1996.

9   L. Williams, 'Time you stepped aside, Soeharto told', *Sydney Morning Herald*, November 7, 1996.

10 R. Borsuk, 'Astra's informal group unveils its plans', *Asian Wall Street Journal*, November 27, 1996.

11 G. Hiscock, 'A good deal lies ahead', *The Australian*, February 10, 1997.

12 S. Berfield and K. Loveard, 'Marked for the top', *Asiaweek*, July 12, 1996.

13 R. Borsuk, 'Sempati Air makes a change at the top', *Asian Wall Street Journal*, December 11, 1996.

14 M. Backman, 'The economics of corruption', *Asian Wall Street Journal*, September 3, 1996.

Chapter 11: A Sultan's Wealth Beyond Measure

1 Brunei Government handbook, 1994.

2 I. Stephen, 'Brunei will reduce dependence on oil, gas', *Straits Times Weekly*, July 20, 1996.

3 The best account of the attempted rebellion in Brunei is in A. Chalfont (1989) *By God's Will*, Weidenfeld & Nicolson, London, pp68–77

4 *Brunei Investment Guide*, Ministry of Industry & Primary Resources, January 1996.

5 Company statement on Scott Creek–Willeroo stations, November 1996.

6 Brunei Government handbook, 1994.

7 'Airborne cars crash and burn', *The Australian*, November 7, 1996.

Chapter 12: India's New Money, Old Tensions

1 'Top gun', *Business India*, December 20, 1993.

2 'Whither the Indian diaspora in the 21st century', Dr Mukul G. Asher, *The Business Times* (Singapore), July 27–28, 1996.

3 *Asiaweek*, August 23, 1996.

4 'Mitsubishi weighs key problems in India', *Asian Wall Street Journal*, February 11, 1997.

5 G. Piramal (1996) *Business Maharajas*, Viking Penguin India, New Delhi, p83.

6 Ibid, pp165–8.

7 Ibid, p153.

8 *Financial Express*, 7 September 1996.

9 'Living in today's world', *Business India*, June 19, 1995, p54.

10 Ibid, p56.

11 *Far Eastern Economic Review*, September 12, 1996, p48.

12 *Business India*, June 19, 1995, p56.

13 *Forbes*, July 17, 1995, p128.

Chapter 13: Billion-Dollar Babies – the Next Generation

1 'I am fully in control', *Asiaweek*, January 31, 1997, p20.

2 A. Labita, 'SM Prime goes on the road', *The Australian*, September 1996.

3   A. Aw, 'Ms Ho's small screen gamble', *South China Morning Post*, September 14, 1996.

4   Material on Stanley Ho is based on a visit to Macau in May 1996, plus an extensive profile by J. Leung, 'South China's merchant prince', in *Asian Business*, September 1996, pp18–26 and in E. Huang and L. Jeffery (1995) *Hong Kong: Portraits of Power*, Orion, London, pp138–43.

5   G. Hiscock, 'From rags to riches: the power of Wang', *The Australian*, October 1, 1996.

6   Formosa Plastics Group annual report and company profile, 1995.

7   S. Moffett, 'Softbank's Masayoshi Son builds an unconventional empire', *Far Eastern Economic Review*, 50 years anniversary issue, November 1996, p206.

8   'Japan Sky Broadcasting Co Ltd established', statement by News Corporation, December 17, 1996.

9   Tokyo press conference by Masayoshi Son, *Bloomberg*, June 25, 1996.

10 Statement by News Corporation, December 17, 1996.

11 'Softbank buys US giant for $1.5bn', *South China Morning Post*, August 24, 1996.

12 'Industry sows seeds in expensive real estate', *The Australian*, November 26, 1996.

13 W. Purcell, 'Resort pioneer whose only hobby was work', *The Australian*, January 12, 1994.

14 E. Johnston, 'Bombing won't stop Yeppoon project', *The Australian*, December 6, 1980.

15 K. Takeda, 'Resort founded on friendship breaks even at last', *The Australian*, February 1, 1996.

Bibliography

1996 Companies Handbook, Part Four, Stock Exchange of Singapore, Singapore

Asia-Pacific Economic Literature (Vol 10, No 1, May 1996), Research School of Pacific and Asian Studies, Australian National University, Canberra

Bartholomew, James (1989) *The Richest Man in the World*, Viking, London

Bourchier, David and Legge, John (eds) (1994) *Democracy in Indonesia, 1950s and 1990s*, Centre of Southeast Asian Studies, Monash University, Melbourne

Brown, Colin (ed.) (1996) *Indonesia: Dealing with a Neighbour*, Allen & Unwin, Sydney

Calder, Kent (1996) *Asia's Deadly Triangle*, Nicholas Brealey Publishing, London

Chalfont (Lord), Alun (1989) *By God's Will*, Weidenfeld & Nicolson, London

Chen Li-chu (ed.) (1994) 'Trademarks of the Chinese (II)', *Sinorama Magazine*, Taipei

Cheong, Sally (1996) *Bumiputera Entrepreneurs in the KLSE*, Volume One, Corporate Research Services, Kuala Lumpur

Chu, Chin-Ning (1995) *The Asian Mind Game: A Westerner's Survival Manual*, Stealth Productions, Sydney

Ch'ng, David (1993) *The Overseas Chinese Entrepreneurs in East Asia: Background Business Practices and International Networks*, CEDA Monograph M100, Sydney

Cragg, Claudia (1995) *The New Taipans*, Century, London

Crouch, Harold (1996) *Government & Society in Malaysia*, Allen & Unwin, Sydney

East Asia Analytical Unit (1994) *India's Economy at the Midnight Hour*, Australian Department of Foreign Affairs and Trade, Canberra

East Asia Analytical Unit (1995) *Overseas Chinese Business Networks in Asia*, Australian Department of Foreign Affairs and Trade, Canberra

East Asia Analytical Unit (1995) *Growth Triangles in South East Asia*, Australian Department of Foreign Affairs and Trade, Canberra

East Asia Analytical Unit (1996) *Asia's Global Powers: China-Japan Relations in the 21st Century*, Australian Department of Foreign Affairs and Trade, Canberra

Edwards, Ron and Skully, Michael (eds) (1996) *ASEAN Business, Trade and Development*, Butterworth Heinemann, Melbourne

Faulkner, George (1995) *Business in Indonesia*, Business and Professional Publishing, Sydney

Financial and Investment Yearbook ROC 1996 (1996) China Economic News Service, Taipei

Fitzgerald, C.P. and Roper, Myra (1972) *China: A World so Changed*, Thomas Nelson, Australia

Forbes, Dean (1996) *Asian Metropolis: Urbanisation and the Southeast Asian City*, Oxford University Press, Australia

Garnaut, Ross (1990) *Australia and the North East Asian Ascendancy*, Australian Government Publishing Services, Canberra

Garrett, Jemima (1996) *Island Exiles*, ABC Books, Sydney

Grant, Bruce (1964) *Indonesia*, Melbourne University Press, Melbourne

Hill, Hal (ed.) (1994) *Indonesia's New Order*, Allen & Unwin, Sydney

Hill, Hal (1996) *The Indonesian Economy Since 1966*, Cambridge University Press, Cambridge

Hodder, Rupert (1996) *Merchant Princes of the East: Cultural Delusions, Economic Success and the Overseas Chinese in Southeast Asia*, John Wiley, Chichester

Hong Kong 1994 (1994) Government Information Services, Hong Kong

Huang, Evelyn and Jeffery, Lawrence (1995) *Hong Kong: Portraits of Power*, Orion, London

Klintworth, Gary (ed.) (1994) *Taiwan in the Asia-Pacific in the 1990s*, Allen & Unwin, Sydney

Korea Handbook (1982) Korean Overseas Information Service, Seoul

Kristof, Nicholas D. and Wudunn, Sheryl (1995) *China Wakes*, Nicholas Brealey Publishing, London

Legge, J.D. (1972) *Sukarno*, Praeger Publishers, New York

Liu, Philip (ed.) (1994) *Taiwan 2000: The Outlook for Taiwan's Economy*, China Economic News Service, Taipei

McGregor, Richard (1996) *Japan Swings*, Allen & Unwin, Sydney

MeesPierson Guide to Hong Kong Companies (1994) David Tait/Edinburgh Financial Publishing (Asia) Ltd, Hong Kong

Nailer, C. and Martin, R. (1996) *Finding the Right Market in Asia*, International Market Assessment, Melbourne

Naisbitt, John (1995) *Megatrends Asia*, Nicholas Brealey Publishing, London

Phongpaichit, Pasuk and Baker, Chris (1996) *Thailand's Boom*, Silkworm Books, Chiang Mai, Thailand

Piramil, Gita (1996) *Business Maharajas*, Viking Penguin India, New Delhi

Rafferty, Kevin (1995) *Inside Japan's Power Houses*, Weidenfeld & Nicolson, London

Reid, Anthony (1996) *Sojourners and Settlers: Histories of Southeast Asia and the Chinese*, Allen & Unwin, Sydney

Republic of China Yearbook (1995) Taipei Government Information Office

Robison, Richard (1996) *Pathways to Asia: The Politics of Engagement*, Allen & Unwin, Sydney

Salisbury, Harrison E. (1989) *Tiananmen Diary*, Little, Brown, US

Seagrave, Sterling (1989) *The Marcos Dynasty*, Macmillan, London

Seagrave, Sterling (1995) *Lords of the Rim*, Bantam Press, London

Tee, Ming San (1995) *The Singapore Successful Business Elites*, Cross Century Creative City, Singapore

The Estimate Directory, Pacific Basin, September 1996 (1996) Edinburgh Financial Publishing, Edinburgh

Toynbee, Arnold (ed.) (1973) *Half the World*, Thames and Hudson, London/Holt, Rinehart and Winston, New York

Weidenbaum, Murray and Hughes, Samuel (1996) *The Bamboo Network*, Free Press, New York

Index